Where
We Stand

Where We Stand

Jewish Consciousness on Campus

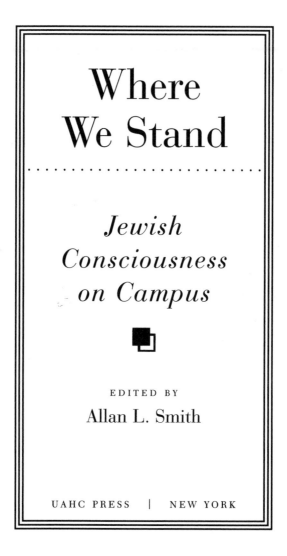

EDITED BY

Allan L. Smith

UAHC PRESS | NEW YORK

Library of Congress Cataloging-in-Publication Data

Where we stand : Jewish consciousness on campus /
    edited by Allan L. Smith
        p.   cm.
    Includes bibliographical references.
    ISBN 0-8074-0539-6 (pbk.)
    1. Reform Judaism—United States. 2. Ethics, Jewish
3. Judaism and social problems. 4. Jewish college students—
United States—Religious life.   I. Smith, Allan L.
BM197.W48   1997
296.8'341—dc21
                                      96-47902
                                         CIP

This book is printed on acid-free paper.
Copyright © 1997 by the UAHC Press
Manufactured in the United States of America
10 9 8 7 6 5 4 3 2

Contents

Foreword

What does it mean to be a Jew?

While your rabbis and religious school teachers probably asked you this often when you were in grade and high school, the question takes on a whole new meaning in college.

In your dorm and classrooms, during late-night pizza sessions and over coffee in the student lounge, you will find yourself searching for answers. You will be challenged on points of fact and tenets of belief. The challenges will come from your peers, but, undoubtedly, you will be asking yourself questions as well. You may also be questioned by other Jews—those who did not grow up in the Reform tradition and feel a need to challenge your authenticity as a Jew.

You may also be confronted by a new challenge: the challenge of being Jewish in a non-Jewish world; of being identified as a Jew by those who out of ignorance or narrow-mindedness speak of us in negative terms. It may not be obvious, but you will come to recognize anti-Semitism just as your parents, grandparents, and great-grandparents experienced it. How you respond to these questions and challenges depends in part on your sense of Jewish identity and, in part, on your knowledge of your religion and heritage.

This text has, in short form, the facts to help you answer questions about Judaism from a Reform perspective. It provides resources if you want to look further into a particular area, and it also may be helpful in your course work or research in your field of interest.

I hope that this guide is useful and that you will keep it throughout your college years. We would also like to know how you use this text and what your suggestions are for future editions.

Rabbi Eric Yoffie
President
Union of American Hebrew Congregations

Acknowledgments

College students are an important portion of the Reform Jewish constituency. The College Education Department hopes that this book will aid students during their years on campus. We hope to see this book become an important and useful resource on critical issues and identity from a Reform perspective. We appreciate all of the people who have been vital in the production of this book. It has taken a long time for this book to travel from the creative stages to the bookshelves, and we have many people to thank for their hard work during the various stages of this process.

First, thank you to all of the authors who contributed articles—who have taken the time to write pieces for this book or who have graciously allowed us to reprint their pieces. It was your work that truly allowed this volume to be published.

In addition, we would like to thank all of the professionals and laypeople who have been instrumental in the process. The efforts of John Stern and Jan Epstein, along with the other members of the College Committee, have been invaluable.

The professionals at the UAHC Press have greatly assisted and been patient and helpful throughout the process. We would especially like to thank Seymour Rossel, David Kasakove, Rabbi Ellen Nemhauser, Elyn Wollensky, Rabbi Sharon Forman, Judith Goldman, Bennett Lovett-Graff, Peter Ephross, Kathy Parnass, and Cara Schlesinger for their help.

Within the Youth Division, many individuals have contributed to this volume. Thank you to David Frank, who in many ways began the long process. Thank you also to Paul Reichenbach and David Terdiman, each of whom served as College Director during different portions of the process.

Finally, we are especially indebted to Rabbi Glynis Conyer Reiss, Jill Strassler, James Gelsey, and Elisa Koppel, all of whom served as assistant editors at various points in the production of this volume. Without their hard work and devotion, this book would never have come into being.

We are finally grateful to everyone who had a hand in this book. Thank you for all you have done. We hope this book is deserving of your efforts.

Introduction

For most of your life, you have been told that you are a Jew. Grandparents, parents, or other family members might have told you this in order to instill a sense of pride in this accident of birth or familial choice we call Jewish identity. At other times your sense of Jewishness may have been stirred by friends curious about the different things your family does at certain times of the year. Sometimes your feelings about your Jewishness may have arisen in response to the narrow-mindedness of those with nothing nice to say about Jews.

Whatever the source, you are going to be repeatedly confronted during your college years by the fact of your Jewishness. The pressures will come from both on-and off-campus. They will be present in your academic program, in your dorm, and in your recreational and social environment. It may not be obvious at first, but you will come to know it, just like the rest of us. It is just beneath the surface. You are Jewish, and that poses many questions and challenges. There is no time like the present, while you are establishing your identity and your future direction, to begin to resolve this part of your character.

We have compiled this text to answer, in short form, a range of questions about what Reform Judaism is. It maps a direction for those of you who wish to look further into the matter. It may give you an idea for a term paper or research in a specific field. For those of you interested in a more active Jewish life, the topics covered can provide you with a range of program ideas. We would like to hear how you have used this text and whether you have found it to be useful.

In conclusion, it is our privilege to thank the many rabbis and scholars whose research has made this effort possible. Turn its pages; there is so much to be learned.

Rabbi Allan L. Smith
Director, UAHC Youth Division

Editor's Note

How Best to Use This Book

Where We Stand is a series of articles by Reform scholars and other experts who discuss, from a Reform perspective, critical issues you will most likely confront during your college years. Ideally, you would read straight through; however, we realize that, sometimes, this is neither possible nor helpful.

You will notice that chapters in the table of contents are arranged by topics and that each chapter contains several articles. So look in the table of contents to find the articles that best suit your purpose. Feel free to use this book as an educational resource in activities on your college campus, campus Hillel, and local synagogue.

We hope that this resource will be helpful in shaping your Jewish identity and enriching your college experience.

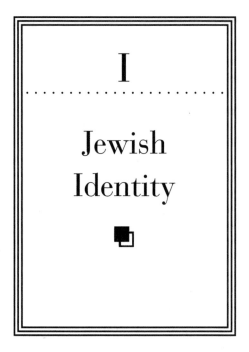

I

Jewish
Identity

A Reform View of Jewish Law

ARON HIRT-MANHEIMER

The first type of defense made on behalf of Reform was a halachic one.[1] The greatest Orthodox rabbis of the time had published a book of responsa which set out to prove that the changes in the worship made by the Reform temple in Hamburg were in willful violation of Jewish law. Since the indictment was halachic, the defense had to be halachic also; and so, the first writings of the Reformers were intended to show that it is quite permissible under certain circumstances to change Jewish laws and customs.

This defense, though, was soon abandoned, as it became immediately evident to the Reformers that no adjustment in Jewish services or ceremonies could be made as long as the authority of the Orthodox rabbinate remained unchallenged. If there was to be Reform, there was no other way than to renounce the authority of the old rabbinate. The Reform movement was, therefore, from its beginning, adverse to the rabbinical literature, the Talmud, and the codes which were the sources of rabbinical authority. The early Reform movement became essentially biblical. Its leaders held proudly to the inspiration of Scriptures—or at least to the Ten Commandments revealed at Sinai—and of the inspired prophets.

The Reform movement was well served by this emphasis on the prophetic tradition, which also enabled it to exert a strong influence on the Jewish community. In an era of fading tradition, where multitudes were abandoning their faith, Reform saved thousands of deserters by giving them an acceptable ideal and proclaiming it Jewish.

The Reform movement is no longer certain, though, that it has found in prophetism a sure foundation for its Judaism. There is now a search in Reform national meetings for a revived relationship with the postbiblical legal literature.

The self-description of Reform as being solely biblical was simply not true. All of Reform Jewish life in all its observances was actually postbiblical in origin. None of the arrangements of worship, the hours of service, the text of the prayers, no matter how written, was primarily biblical. The whole of Jewish liturgy is an achievement of postbiblical times. The religious calendar, though based on Scripture, was elaborated and defined in postbiblical times. Marriage ceremonies and burial rites were all postbiblical. The Bible, of course, was the source of ethical ideas, but the actual religious life was rabbinic. Whatever percentage of the total traditional legislation Reform Jews observe, it is mainly postbiblical in origin. Our life is inspired by the Bible, but organized by the Talmud.

Soon after the founding of the Reform movement, the Bible itself began to be viewed by scholars as a human book, depriving it of its special uniqueness. It was now not necessarily different in status from the confessedly human, argumentative talmudic literature. However, since God speaks in "the language of human beings," God may be speaking through both literatures. If hitherto God was revealed to the writers of the Bible by the flame of the human conscience, then afterward God was revealed to the debating scholars of the Talmud by the light of human intellect; and it may well be that the intelligence is as worthy a vehicle of revelation as the conscience.

Also, perhaps the facts of our own progress as a Reform movement have affected our relationship to the older legal literature. In the early days of Reform we were fighting against an overmastering Jewish legal authority. We could not attain our independence without denying and defying that authority. But now we are strong and can afford to be much more tolerant of the authoritative past.

We find it easier to honor the learning and wisdom of the rabbis of the past than to imagine our bowing to the pronouncements of the Orthodox rabbis of the present. Our pioneers freed us from Orthodox control, and we will do nothing now that might restore any authority to it. Having been freed from older customs, we have had an opportunity to become creative, to transform old ceremonies, to invent new ones. In the totality of Jewish religious life, this inventive creativity of Jewish ceremonial observance may well be our true and specific function.

It is difficult to make even a simple practical decision without having an attitude on the question of the authority of the *halachah*. Of this much we are sure: that whatever authority the *halachah* has for us, it is certainly only a selective authority. There are vast sections of law about which we are never questioned and on which we do not volunteer decisions. No question among the Reform responsa concerns the mixing of meat and milk, the selling of leaven to a Gentile before Passover, or the construction of the ritual bath. These observances have ceased among Reform Jews and among large numbers of other Jews. Nor do Reform rabbis feel the obligation to restore them. These observances are in the Talmud, but they have no legal status for us.

We obey many rabbinic customs and neglect many more. As long as we are thus selective, we cannot believe that rabbinic law is God's mandate. It is, of course, possible that by some future date our part of the tradition will grow first habitual, then legal, then authoritative. But it is not authoritative now and cannot and perhaps should not be. The law is to us a human product. That does not mean that God is not somehow revealed in the "language of human beings." To us the law is human, but nobly human, developed by devoted minds who dedicated their best efforts to answering the question, "What doth the Lord require of thee?" Therefore, we respect it and seek its guidance. Some of its provisions have faded from our lives. We do not regret that fact. But as to those laws that we do follow, we wish them to be in harmony with tradition.

The law is authoritative enough to influence us, but not so completely as to control us. The rabbinic law is our guidance, but not our governance. Our concern is more with the people than with the legal system. Whenever possible, interpretations are developed which are feasible and conform to the needs of life.

If we were to list those observances that we adopt and then contrast them with those we do not, it would be noticed that we do not adopt, or are not likely to adopt, the ceremonial prohibitions, the restrictive negatives in the law, except, of course, those of direct moral impact. We increasingly accept folk commandments, *minhagim* —customs—that have emerged from the life of the people and are dear to the people. It may well be that behind our readoption of such observances there is not so much theology as sociology. We are strengthening our folk feeling. Some of the greatest changes in Jewish ceremonial life did not come from some decision of a legal scholar, but arose spontaneously, almost mysteriously, out of the mood of the Jewish people. No rabbi and no group of rabbis ever ordained the use of the *chupah*—marriage canopy—or the yearly practice of *yahrzeit*—marking a close relative's death—or the synagogue ceremony of bar mitzvah. These observances which carry such strong emotional appeal arose anonymously among the people of Israel.

Above all, our objections to much of the law are protests of conscience. The laws which will never be acceptable to us are those which concern chiefly the status of the Jewish woman. Aside from all the special tragedies in the life of Jewish women with regard to marriage and divorce, the very concept of her inferior legal status tends to turn us against the legal tradition. Perhaps the grandest achievement of Reform Judaism is its liberation of the Jewish woman.

As for the creation of a Reform *halachah*, worthy actions may grow into religious duties, and so our Reform code will develop *mitzvah* by *mitzvah*, as each action achieves its sanctity. Some of these may be new *mitzvot*, but most of them will be rediscoveries of actions which our tradition has cherished. We will have to find out which elements in the Jewish traditional life style we can truly accept as a mandate and which will remain merely custom and therefore changeable.

The Reforming of
Reform Judaism

MALCOLM H. STERN

Origins

Most historians trace the origins of Reform Judaism to Moses Mendelssohn's translation of the Pentateuch from Hebrew into German, published in 1783; this may certainly be considered the movement's intellectual start. David Philipson, the pioneer historian of Reform, traces reforms in Judaism to the Bible itself; and, indeed, a case can be made that Judaism through the ages has constantly reformed itself. The Jewish Reformation did not touch the Jewish masses in Germany and France until Napoleon's time. Napoleon, recognizing that the Jews under their own legalistic system might prove an underground of opposition to his government, in 1806 convened an Assembly of 110 Jewish notables—rabbis and laymen—and put before them a series of searching questions: on marriage and divorce laws, on the authority of rabbinic law versus the authority of civil laws, and on the loyalty of Jews to the country of their birth. To the Jewish communities, this Assembly spelled recognition by the government, and Napoleon was hailed as a liberating hero. The Emperor, upon receiving the replies to his questions, ordered the Assembly of Notables to create a Grand Sanhedrin, convened in February 1807, which promulgated into law civil marriage. They thereby made the law of the land supersede Jewish religious law, and made possible the recognition of Jewish-Gentile marriages. The Sanhedrin also released Jewish soldiers from Jewish observances.

Such events as these had a dramatic assimilative effect on many of the Jews in the French Empire, but it was undoubtedly, although few histories mention it, the edict of July 20, 1808 which was to Westernize every Jewish home under Napoleon's control. The edict required every Jewish family, within three months, to adopt a permanent family name. A similar edict had been promulgated with less effect by Holy Roman Emperor Joseph II in 1787, and the concept gradually penetrated Eastern Europe as well.

Reform in America

In America, the successful completion of the War of 1812 ended British domination for all time. Democracy became established, and the decade of the 1820s could properly be called "the era of the common man." Every American, it seemed to the popular mind, could potentially achieve his desired goal in life. The 1824 nomination and 1828 election of Andrew Jackson, a "Tennessee hillbilly," brought to the presidency of the United States not a Virginia or New England aristocrat like his predecessors but a man of the people. It was an age of utopian schemes in all walks of American life, and the Jews were affected. Mordecai Noah's plan to establish a Zion for Europe's oppressed Jews on an island in the Niagara River is probably the best-known example. More rational was the effort by a group of Jews in Charleston, South Carolina, at that time the largest and most cultivated Jewish community in the United States, to reform the worship in Congregation Beth Elohim. Meeting with rigid opposition, a dozen of them established The Reformed Society of Israelites on November 21, 1824. The Society grew to a membership of fifty and even collected funds for a synagogue, but the death and removal of a number of its members from the community led to an abandonment of the project. The spirit of Reform had been breathed into the soil of America, and it was here that Reform Judaism was to have its most abundant flowering. The Charleston Reformers were ahead of their time.

Within a generation, associations of young German immigrants became such Reform congregations as Har Sinai of Baltimore (founded 1842), Emanu-el of New York (1845), and Keneseth Israel of Philadelphia (1855). The East coast, for decades to come, was to be strongly divided between those rabbis who were radically Reform, like David Einhorn, and arch-conservatives, some Orthodox, like Isaac Leeser, and some moderate Reformers, like Benjamin Szold. It was the heyday of the flaming editorial, which did not refrain from character assassination. Isaac M. Wise, who moved from reactionary Albany in 1854 to more liberal-minded Cincinnati, began his German *Die Deborah* and English *Israelite* to break down the Orthodoxy of Leeser's *Occident*. When Einhorn's far more radical paper, *Sinai*, began to appear, Wise became the champion of the middle of the road.

It was Wise who tried to bring the American rabbinate together. He recognized the growing need for American-trained rabbis for the new American-born generation. Through the 1850s and 1860s, his efforts were frustrated. The Civil War, like most wars in

American history, had an Americanizing effect on the immigrants who participated in it. By 1873, the laity of the assimilated communities in the South and Midwest were ready to heed a call from Wise to gather in Cincinnati for the purpose of creating a Union of American Hebrew Congregations and a Hebrew Union College. By 1878, the Board of Delegates of American Israelites, a civil rights organization of some Eastern congregations, was prevailed upon to join the Union, and along with them came such important New York congregations as Emanu-el and Beth El.

The Pittsburgh Platform

In 1883 the Hebrew Union College graduated its first class—all but one of whose four members was American-born. Significantly, it was the German-born member of the class, twenty-seven-year-old Joseph Krauskopf, who suggested to the intellectual leader of Reform Judaism, Rabbi Kaufmann Kohler of New York, that the time had come to enunciate a platform for American Reform Judaism. In November of 1885, Kohler brought together in Pittsburgh fifteen of the most liberal-minded rabbis of the day, and together they created a platform which divorced Reform from Orthodoxy and is still exerting a powerful influence on all the older congregations of the Reform movement. In their attempt to be as American as possible, the authors of the Pittsburgh Platform eliminated most ceremonies, *kashrut*, and the influence of rabbinic law. They denied the need for any Jewish nation and identified Judaism as purely a religion. They also affirmed the hope that the Messianic Era was about to dawn—without a Messiah.

With such a platform the Jews of German birth and extraction were just beginning to feel established as Americans when the persecution of the Jews of Czarist Russia started inundating America with the largest Jewish population it was to receive from Europe. Yet these immigrants, fresh from the ghettos of Eastern Europe, brought with them the customs and traditions, the ways of dress and behavior, which the Pittsburgh Platform and its followers were vigorously denying as Jewish. Was it any wonder that for the next generation and more, the Reform congregations remained the citadels of German Jewry?

World War I had its own Americanizing influence on the Russian-Jewish immigrants. The Balfour Declaration of 1917 brought the Zionist dream closer to reality. The elitism of the German-dominated American Jewish Committee as the champion of Jewish rights was challenged by the more democratic American Jewish Congress, which numbered among its leaders many of Russian-Jewish origin. In the decades following World War I, the American-born children of Russian immigrants, as well as the immigrants themselves, became the majority of rabbis ordained by the Hebrew Union College and swelled the rolls of Reform congregations.

The Columbus Platform

Hitler's Nuremburg Laws of September 1935, coming as they did on top of America's economic depression and rising anti-Semitism, brought to America's Jews a renewed sense of their separateness. In 1937, meeting in Columbus, Ohio, the Central Conference of American Rabbis adopted its "Guiding Principles of Reform

Judaism," which had been prepared by a committee headed by Russian-born Rabbi and Professor Samuel S. Cohon. The two most far-reaching principles enunciated were the idea of "peoplehood" and the fact that Zionism and Reform Judaism are not incompatible.

The closing years of World War II, with their revelations of the Nazi atrocities, brought to American Jewry the realization that we, the survivors, could not escape our destiny as Jews. We emerged as the most powerful and prosperous Jews of the world—more prayerful and more concerned for our self-identity. The twenty years following World War II doubled the number of Reform congregations in America.

The birth of Israel and its subsequent military victories have evoked new self-pride among America's Jews and a new interest in Hebrew and in Jewish education among Reform Jews.

Update: The Centenary Perspective and Beyond

As successor to the Pittsburgh Platform and the Columbus Guiding Principles of Reform Judaism, came the movement's A Centenary Perspective. Its authors found themselves trying to define a movement so diverse in its views and practices that they produced a picture of a newly dynamic Reform Judaism whose future could not be readily described.

Greater Hebrew literacy among our congregants created *chavurot*—prayer and study circles. A growing enthusiasm for ceremonial is not, as the classic (Pittsburgh Platform) Reform Jews claim, a return to

Orthodoxy, but rather a response to Reform's almost-total support for Israel, and a desire to display one's Judaism through Jewishness. These directions have produced an outpouring of new materials from the Central Conference of American Rabbis and the Union of American Hebrew Congregations. In the intellectual sphere, no work has had a more profound influence than the UAHC's *The Torah: A Modern Commentary;* while the CCAR has introduced books for family observance and study, such as *Gates of the House, Gates of Mitzvah, Gates of the Seasons, Gates of Understanding,* and, for small children, *Gates of Wonder* and *Gates of Awe,* among many others.

While most Reform rabbis had long accepted as Jews the children of Jewish fathers who were given a Jewish education, when Rabbi Alexander Schindler, as President of the UAHC, institutionalized patrilineal descent, it set off a barrage of criticism from non-Reform groups. The acceptance of patrilineal descent has been consistent with Reform's effort to find a place for those Jews who intermarry. In recent years, this effort has been expanded to outreach to "Jews-by-choice," the title given those who convert to Judaism and to those who marry Jews. These efforts are having a strong impact on helping intermarried families integrate into synagogue life. Intermarriage will always be a threat to Jewish survival, but Reform Judaism has been staunch in accepting it as a fact of contemporary Jewish life. Although a considerable percentage of Reform rabbis feel conscience-bound to perform Jewish ceremonies for Jews only, none will deny a couple the right to counseling when a mixed marriage is contemplated.

Reform has also taken the lead in not only recognizing the equality of women, but in electing women to every office in the synagogue, ordaining women rabbis, and investing women cantors.

Reform, with its special genius for reacting to the pulse of every generation, will continue to reform itself.

"A Vote, Not a Veto"
A Reconstructionist Approach to Halachah

LESTER BRONSTEIN

If *halachah* means the adherence to talmudic law as filtered through our medieval codes and as presently interpreted by rabbinic authorities, then Reconstructionism, like Reform, is not a halachic movement. Some even describe it as "posthalachic," that is, as a movement which argues that the entry of Jews into the mainstream of modern Western (secular) society has forever erased the authority of rabbinic law. In this view, even Orthodox Jews *voluntarily* choose to submit to halachic authority, since the Jewish community is no longer a closed system with the power to sanction those who violate its precepts. Furthermore, while the Reform movement is non-halachic and only makes recommendations about how its followers should practice Judaism, the Conservative movement strongly urges the following of *halachah*.

We live in a time that, in Jewish terms, is postlegal, when the edicts of the past have necessarily become the wisdom of history. We can still look to *halachah* for guidance, but we cannot be required to submit to it unquestioningly.

Reconstructionists follow the famous phrase of the movement's founder, Rabbi Mordecai Kaplan: "The past has a vote, not a veto." Essentially, this means that *halachah* possesses a definite historical authority for us, though not a legal one. Reconstructionists see *halachah* as the repository of our people's historical wisdom in applying the genius of Judaism to diverse circumstances through the ages. The law is halachic not because any God made it so, but because it reflects the social history of the Jewish people. Our reading of history assumes that in previous centuries our local and regional rabbinical authorities constantly adapted Jewish law to meet the needs of their constituents, with whom they were intimately familiar, although this evolutionary process was never explicitly discussed. As a result, their codes and responsa reflect a sensitivity to the Jewish conditions of their time. Thus, much of our present Jewish custom and practice, including an evolving ethical wisdom, began with the will of the Jewish people and filtered upward to the rabbinic authorities, where it has been standardized in halachic writings.

Today, much of the thinking and practice of the past remains relevant. Indeed, if we were to divest ourselves of so much of what is seen as official halachic practice, we would essentially abandon the great ritual and moral framework that makes us Jewish. To this extent, then, *halachah* exercises a strong "vote" with regard to the decision-making process of the Reconstructionist Jew;

this is to say, we choose to observe much of the *halachah* not because it is "law" per se, but because it is the reservoir of custom and belief which we Jews created and which distinguishes us as the Jewish people.

To our way of thinking, however, much of our inherited *halachah* does not reflect our present situation. In an age of democratic societies and critical scholarship, the authority of the rabbis past or present simply cannot go unchallenged. Just as lay people exercised unofficial influence on *halachah* in ages past (mostly unconsciously), so modern Jews want to exert a conscious and deliberate influence on Jewish life today. Acknowledging this need, Reconstructionists ideally follow a decision-making process that is both communal and individual, both rabbinic and popular, both historical (giving the past a "vote") and contemporary (not letting the voice of the past "veto" decisions which we ourselves necessarily make from our own experience). Our movement asks Jews to approach any given issue, whether an ethical dilemma like abortion or a ritual matter like *kashrut*, by going through a three-step process in the company of one's rabbi and Jewish community (e.g., synagogue board or *chavurah*). These steps comprise the following:

1. We examine our own intellectual and emotional preconceptions before looking up the halachic opinion. This way we know what we actually think and feel. To begin with "official" halachic positions without knowing our own independent beliefs is to fall into the potential trap of re-reading the tradition to say what we want it to say in order to justify our own position.

2. We examine the breadth of *halachah* on this issue (including the opinions of Conservative, Reform,

Reconstructionist, and other contemporary respondents). This is best done under the guidance of an able teacher of Judaism. Here is one of the key roles of Reconstructionist rabbis. They are expert guides to the tradition rather than its enforcers. Important in this process is the possibility of discovering a range of halachic opinions from different periods, from eighth-century Baghdad to nineteenth-century Vilna.

3. We compare the two sets of conclusions. To the extent that they are dissonant, we must push further. We ask ourselves whether our own values are historically Jewish or derived from other sources. We must look at the *halachah* in light of what we take to be inherently Jewish values to see whether the *halachah* indeed follows those values. (In some cases we may conclude that, for whatever reasons, *halachah* clashes with deeper Jewish values.) This questioning continues until we come to some satisfactory conclusions for our Jewish community. We may also wish to consult the opinions of like-minded communities.

Ultimately, each individual may decide on his or her own course of action. But more often than not, individual Jews working through an issue as a community decide as a group what is proper. This decision is often traditional in tone, even if it is not the fully halachic position. Moreover, it is a decision which directly reflects the influences of rabbi and laity working together to formulate a Jewish practice that is wedded to both the value of tradition and the demands of contemporary belief. This method is the halachic process *reconstructed* by and for committed Jews. It is neither authoritarian nor totally autonomous. It is communal, covenantal, and, one hopes, workable. It is exactly this sort of "living *halachah*" that is the heart of the Reconstructionist approach to Jewish life.

Halachah in Conservative Judaism

SEYMOUR SIEGEL

Conservative Judaism is committed to *halachah*. It teaches that the ancient rules of the Jewish faith, which regulate everything from what you eat to how you pray, are an essential part of a Jew's obligations. This does not mean, of course, that all or most Conservative Jews observe these laws today, but for some they remain a guiding light for life in a constantly changing world.

Legal decisions in the Conservative movement are based on precedent and interpretation. There is a long history in Judaism of discussions concerning Jewish law. It begins with the Bible, continues through the Talmud, and is carried forward in the codes of Maimonides, Joseph Karo, and others. In addition there are collections of legal decisions known as *she'elot*—questions— and *teshuvot*—responsa.

In the Conservative movement, legal questions are submitted to the Committee on Jewish Law and Standards. Whenever Conservative *poskim*—decisors—

are faced with a halachic question, they first search out the relevant precedents. The next step is to analyze the roots and basic assumptions of the precedents. The *poskim* then consider whether or not these assumptions can be accepted under present conditions. Sometimes the conclusions drawn by the decisors conflict with those of the traditional authorities. This may be because many of the assumptions of the past cannot, in good conscience, be accepted today. Though the conclusions may differ, the process is the same one that has always characterized the interpretation of Jewish law.

When do new conditions and developments require modifications of Jewish law according to the interpretation of Conservative Judaism?

Ethical Considerations

When the outcome of the precedent is immoral—as in the case of the *agunah*—the precedent may be changed. An *agunah* is a woman who is unable to obtain a divorce from her husband, either because his whereabouts are not known or because he refuses to grant her one. (In Jewish law, only the husband can initiate a *get*, a divorce.) To remedy this problem, the Conservative movement grants powers of annulment to rabbinical courts in cases when a husband refuses to give his wife a *get* after a civil divorce has taken place. Orthodox rabbis are still wrestling with the *agunah* problem. Reform rabbis solve such problems by recognizing the jurisdiction of civil courts to terminate a Jewish marriage.

Technological Advances

A precedent may be changed if it is based on outdated scientific knowledge. Technological advances in medicine, for example, make it possible to transplant organs from a dead body into a living person. But are these transplants permissible by Jewish law? On the one hand, any mutilation of the dead body is considered a desecration. On the other hand, it can be argued that the principle of *pikuach nefesh*—the saving of a life—permits the transplant. But is a person dead when the heart continues to beat artificially (a condition necessary for a successful transplant) after the brain has died? A controversy arose among the Conservative *poskim* concerning the definition of death. The majority decided that death occurs when the brain stops functioning. Other questions affected by or resulting from technological advances include those concerning test-tube fertilization, abortion, and euthanasia.

Sociological Change

Conservative Judaism holds that precedents based on outmoded sociological attitudes may be changed. In recent years, the issue of women's rights in the synagogue has been a major agenda item for the Committee on Jewish Law and Standards. Ancient practice ordained that men and women worship separately in synagogues because it was believed that men could not pray with full concentration when sitting near women. Apparently, in past eras, a woman's dignity was not diminished by sitting behind a *mechitzah*—partition. But in light of our modern belief that women are equal participants in society, this kind of separation now offends many. Thus, the Conservative movement holds that synagogues may have family pews instead of segregated seating. Orthodox synagogues do not normally accept this interpretation and generally continue the tradition of separate seating. In Reform synagogues, seating is mixed.

Several years ago, the Committee on Jewish Law decided that women should be included in the *minyan*—the prayer quorum—and that they should be given *aliyot* to the Torah. Local congregations, however, have the right to accept or reject these practices.

Needs of the Times

Sometimes the needs of the times require modifications in Jewish practice. The prohibition of driving a vehicle on the Sabbath and festivals is a case in point. This prohibition is based on the idea that a Jew should not kindle a fire or travel far from home on a rest day. Such rules are fine for Jews who live in urban areas with easy access to a synagogue, but they create hardships for those who live in suburban areas, where distances between home and synagogue are much greater. The Law Committee decided that a congregant who is unable to walk to synagogue on the Sabbath or festivals can drive, but only to and from the synagogue.

Orthodox rabbis, believing that Jewish law cannot be altered even if there seems to be good reason, generally regard Conservative interpretations as too liberal. Conservative rabbis, in turn, regard Reform Judaism as too liberal. One could say that the Orthodox Jews are strict constructionists (of Jewish law), Reform (and Reconstructionist) Jews are loose constructionists, and Conservative Jews fall somewhere between the two.

The Conservative movement has tried to remove the embarrassments and barriers that have made observance of Jewish law difficult for many modern Jews. However, to be effective interpreters of the law, our people's interest and commitment to Jewish law must be strengthened. For, in the end, it is the Jewish people, striving for a relationship with God and speaking through their spiritual leaders, who determine Jewish law.

Halachah in Orthodox Judaism

BERNARD M. ZLOTOWITZ

Orthodox Judaism—a name first coined by the nineteenth-century rabbi Samson Raphael Hirsch, of Frankfort-Am-Main—may also be termed halachic Judaism. *Halachah*, translated literally, means law, and Orthodox Judaism defines itself by its strict adherence to the laws given in the Torah (the first five books of Moses, also known as the written law) and the Talmud (oral law).

Orthodox Judaism bases its strict adherence to all laws on the belief that God appeared at Mount Sinai and dictated the Torah and Talmud to Moses. Moses, in turn, transmitted the written and oral law to Joshua, who, in turn, transmitted them to the elders, the elders to the prophets, and the prophets to the men of the great synagogue (*Pirke Avot* 1:1).

Because its practitioners believe that the Bible is the

literal word of God, Orthodox Judaism holds that all the laws are immutable and applicable for all time, and while there are instances when changes in laws do occur, any changes made to existing laws are never complete departures from the originals. Instead they function as interpretations of a meaning already inherent in the law. In other words, changes made by rabbis in the interpretation of a law are really just expansions or extensions of that law's original meaning.

In Orthodox Judaism, there are three categories of laws: *chukim* (statutes), *mishpatim* (ordinances), and *mitzvot* (commandments).

Chukim are laws in the Torah for which there is no explanation of why they should be observed beyond the fact that they are to be obeyed on faith alone. An example of a *chok* (singular form of *chukim*) is any law of *kashrut* (a law concerning the cleanliness and uncleanliness of animals for consumption). The word *kasher* never actually appears in the Torah and was introduced at a much later date in Jewish history. Instead, the Torah simply states, "So you shall set apart the clean beast from the unclean, the unclean bird from the clean. You shall not draw abomination upon yourselves through beast or bird or anything with which the ground is alive, which I have set apart for you to treat as unclean" (Leviticus 20:25). Meanwhile, in an earlier passage (Leviticus 11:3–8), the reader is given a detailed list of which animals are prohibited and which are permitted for consumption. For example, those beasts that chew their cud and have a split hoof and fish that have fins and scales may be eaten, but there is no explanation why animals with these characteristics are singled out. If any reason is offered, it is that of individual holiness (Leviticus 20:26).

The connection between food and health was an alien concept to the biblical mind. The idea that pigs were prohibited because consumers might contract trichinosis is an erroneous attempt to give a modern rationale for an ancient practice. As another example, one of the more mysterious *chukim* is that of the ritual of the red heifer. According to this *chok,* a ritually unclean person sprinkled with the ashes of a red heifer is made clean while the ritually clean individual who sprinkles the ashes becomes unclean from having handled the ashes. Again, there is no explanation for this particular and unusual *chok.*

The second category of laws is *mishpatim,* oral laws that the talmudic rabbis expanded through a complex system of rules and regulations of interpretation called hermeneutic principles. *Mishpatim* have the same weight and validity as written laws in Orthodox Judaism. These laws are believed to have been given simultaneously with the written law at Sinai. The laws of Shabbat, for example, are *mishpatim.* For while the Ten Commandments include a commandment that Jews observe the Sabbath (Exodus 20:8–11; Deuteronomy 5:12–15), the only rules concerning the observance of Shabbat that appear in the Bible are those that forbid one and one's family and servants from working, kindling a fire (Exodus 35:3), and gathering wood (Numbers 15:32). According to the rabbis, however, because this list of restrictions left too much room for personal interpretation of what might or might not be considered work, they developed a primary list of 39 *av melachot* (the genus of labor). This list clearly defines the rules that one must obey to be in agreement with the laws banning work on Shabbat. They include, among others, prohibitions on sowing, plowing, reaping, sewing two or more stitches, writing two or more letters, erasing in order to write two letters, striking with a hammer, and carrying from one domain to another (*Mishnah Shabbat* 7:2).

The third set of laws is *mitzvot*. Literally translated, *mitzvot* means commandments, but the word is generally interpreted to mean good deeds. When *mitzvot* are mentioned in the Torah, the reason for their observance is given. The wearing of *tzitzit* (fringes representing the 613 *mitzvot* in the Torah) on the four corners of one's garments is a *mitzvah*, and the Torah gives a clear reason for the law: "Speak to the Israelite people and instruct them to make for themselves fringes on the corners of their garments throughout the ages; let them attach a cord of blue to the fringe at each corner. That shall be your fringe; look at it and recall all the commandments of the Lord and observe them, so that you do not follow your heart and eyes in your lustful urge" (Numbers 15:38–39).

In addition to these three groups of halachic laws, there are several other groups of laws that were enacted in response to dangers confronting the Jewish community, laws enacted either to strengthen the waning Jewish identity or secure the welfare of the Jewish community. *Takanot* (improvements), for example, are laws enacted to secure the welfare of the Jewish community. Some of the most important *takanot* come from Rabbi Gershom, who issued rulings in 1000 C.E. prohibiting polygamy and anyone from opening another person's correspondence. He was also responsible for the requirement that both parties agree to a divorce before its issue, a ruling that prevented a husband from unilaterally and arbitrarily divorcing his wife.

Over the centuries other laws centered on enhancing Jewish life and enriching Jewish existence have found their way into the codes of Orthodox Jewish law. Some of these laws include the requirement that no male walk four cubits (about three and a half feet) without a head covering; that parents hug their children and express their love for them; that worshipers dignify the Sabbath by dressing immaculately, enjoying three meals, praying in the synagogue, blessing their children, lighting Sabbath candles, and reciting *Kiddush*. Among the most illuminating is the requirement that one respect the rights of others, a law so important that it even takes precedence over the study of Torah.

In summary, Orthodox Judaism observes laws directly from the Torah (and, in some instances, those moderately modified by rabbinical interpretation) because it believes that these laws are derived from God. To abide by the laws, with or without explanation, is to fulfill the will of God and continue the covenant between God and the children of Israel at Mount Sinai.

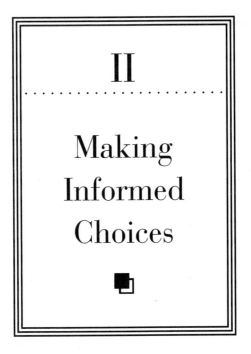

II

Making Informed Choices

Why Patrilineal Descent?

ALEXANDER M. SCHINDLER

The best spirit of Reform Judaism has, since its founding, been one of preservation through interpretation. Ours is a progressive and dynamic approach to Judaism, rooted in the belief that the vibrancy and spiritual depth of Jewish life depend upon the interaction between God and human beings. *Halachah*—Jewish law—must, therefore, be measured with a knowledge of Jewish history, custom, and law—carefully and soberly, with a conservatism bred naturally of our respect for tradition.

Reform Judaism, in other words, believes that if we are to continue to harvest tradition's fruits of wisdom and survival, we have to prune the tree of *halachah*. Halachic innovation (the concept itself is an oxymoron for certain hidebound forces in the Jewish community) thus becomes our grave responsibility and opportunity.

This spirit motivated Reform Judaism's 1983 resolution that made the patrilineal principle coequal with the matrilineal principle in determining Jewish status. There was and is a demographic imperative confronting American Jews: an interfaith marriage rate over 30 percent, yielding at least 100,000 souls annually who are threatened with exile or alienation from our community, in no small measure, by the exclusively matrilineal rule of descent. This can mean a swing of 2 million, more or less, Jews in a decade, of 4 million by the year 2000—out of our present population of just under 6 million in the United States.

Such demographic statistics are shocking yet abstract. But each number also represents a human being, a child of intermarriage who has suffered damage from our past lack of a forthright declaration that that child is fully Jewish. Thus, some two years ago, I received the following letter from a young woman named Adrianne Gorman:

> When I read your speech, I realize how deeply the subject of Jewish identity has wounded me…and how successfully I had covered over the wound through the years. I was raised to be aware that some part of me was Jewish, and that with that birthright came the responsibility to remember the six million victims of the Holocaust—to remember them not as a detached humanitarian who, on principle, abhors extermination, but on a far more fundamental level, where the soul of the witness resides. I can't recall when I first came to understand that my sort of allegiance was to be considered nothing more than a sympathizer's, or when I tried to answer for myself the question of what choice I would make if Hitler came again, this time using the halachic definition of a Jew in rounding up his candidates for the ovens and the camps. But at some point over the years, I did decide that where my father's faith—or more precisely, his heritage—was an issue, I would, without reservation, take my stand as a Jew. Thus, I effectively bestowed on myself all of the deficits of an oppressed group with none of the benefits of that community. Jews consider me a non-Jew, non-Jews consider me a Jew…and, with a despair

tinged with as much humor as I could muster, I
began to think of myself as nothing at all.

How could we fail to respond to such people? Why
should we have continued to demand that they undergo
a formal conversion when their Jewish identities are
already secured by far more than a symbolic act? Why
should we not say to the Adriannes of this world:
By God, you are a Jew! You are the daughter of Jewish
parents. You have resolved to share our fate. You are,
therefore, flesh of our flesh, bone of our bone. You are,
in all truth, what you consider yourself to be—a Jew.

Should we have continued to enforce our opposition
to intermarriage itself by punishing and rejecting those
who intermarry? Can we afford, in numbers or in spirit,
to alienate them and their—our—children? On the
contrary, we are resolved to reach out to them, to
embrace them, to do everything we humanly can to
make them a part of Jewish life.

The hallmark of Reform Judaism has been honesty—
never to pretend to be what we are not, always to
proclaim proudly what we practice. No one in our midst
truly believes that Nikita Khrushchev's grandchild is
Jewish, while Ben-Gurion's is not and had to be converted. Yet, this is the Jewish reality, by light of Orthodox
halachic tradition, in which blood can run thicker than
faith and feeling. Therefore, in our real-world practice of
Judaism, we have struck a real-world definition of "who
is a Jew" that is at times more stringent than that of
Orthodox Jewry. For us, Jewish identity is established
by "acts of identification," as our patrilineal resolution
stated, "with the Jewish people" and by "the per-

formance of *mitzvot.*" Jewishness cannot only be pre-
sumed; it must be expressed in concrete ways through an
active involvement in Jewish life and the willingness to
share the fate of the Jewish people. Our numbers reflect
real people with active Jewish identities.

There is, moreover, another positive reality of Jewish
life to which the Reform decision on patrilineal descent
is an affirmative response, and that is the deepened
involvement of Jewish fathers in raising their children.
The impact of the women's liberation movement upon
the general American culture, particularly upon the
more educated, has resulted, for many Jewish couples,
in a more equal sharing of the burdens, chores, decision-
making, and joys of childrearing. Are we to ignore this
social reality, assuming that only the mother's religious
and ethnic identity will be transmitted to the children
of intermarriage—an assumption that statistics clearly
disprove?

We undertook our halachic reform not out of ignorance or contempt for the past, but in dialogue with
tradition. We affirmed patrilineal descent with the
awareness that the genealogical tables of the Torah are
overwhelmingly patrilineal. In matters of inheritance,
the paternal line alone was followed. Solomon married
many foreign wives, and the child of one of them,
Rehoboam, succeeded him to the throne. Moses married Zipporah, the daughter of a Midianite priest, yet her
children by him were considered Jews. Joseph married
Asenati, the daughter of a priest of On, and the children
of their union were considered Jews. Indeed, even today,
all male children of Israel receive the blessing that they
be like Ephraim and Manasseh—even though their

natural grandfather was a priest who worshipped the sun in the heathen shrine at Heliopolis near Cairo.

Evidence of the patrilineal tradition is manifest in rabbinic literature as well. We invoke the God of our fathers in prayer. We are summoned to the Torah by our father's name. We are reminded that we live by *zekhut avot,* the merit of our fathers.

Perhaps most significantly, both the Torah and rabbinic law hold the male line absolutely dominant in matters affecting the priesthood. Whether one is a *cohen* or a *levi* depends upon the father's priestly claim. If the father is good enough to bequeath priestly status, why isn't he good enough to bequeath Jewishness?

Will Reform Judaism's decision somehow shatter the unity of the Jewish people? That argument could have been made, and doubtlessly was made, at every step in our development as a distinctive movement within Judaism. Certainly, the halachic principle of *taharat hamishpachah* ("family purity") was not held inviolate when we, as a religious community, determined to accept a civil divorce without *gittin.* From the Orthodox perspective, we reared a generation of *mamzerim* (illegitimate offspring)—an irremedial step halachically, while the acceptance of the paternal line is, at least theoretically, subject to remedy by means of *halachic* conversion for the "patrilineal Jew" who becomes Orthodox. Still, our spiritual progenitors did not wilt, the imprecations were forgotten, and the Jewish world is still whole.

Our resolution concerning patrilineal descent was born of necessity and conviction—a combination of motivations that is worthy of our essential character. Our spiritual forebears did not create Reform Judaism in order to have us turn into a tinsel imitation of Orthodox Judaism: Let us not be afraid of our differences. Judaism is, for us, a flowering plant. It is not merely a tangle of roots but a plant that draws nourishment from those roots. It is not only a bare stem but a firm and growing stem. It is not simply a cut flower, fast to fade, but one that blooms anew in each generation. Our community is committed to cultivating that plant, fertilizing it with new passions and new ideas, and trimming its tangled excess so that it can grow in the harsh conditions of today's world.

Evolution and the Bible

ALLAN L. SMITH

That what is written in the Bible is literally true is a key doctrine for many religious people. Until the twentieth century, the question of whether the Bible was literally true did not seem all that significant. With the challenge of modern science, however, the significance of that question has grown dramatically. There are those who believe that if the literal truth of the Bible is challenged, then all religious authority loses its validity. This belief is especially prevalent among those in America whom we call the religious right. Because there is so much at stake in this question, opponents to and proponents of the literal truth of the Bible are prone to lose perspective in the heat of argument.

One of the greatest debates has circled around the apparent conflict between the creation stories in the Bible (belief in the literal truth of these stories is called *creationism*) and the theories of evolution and the big bang. The debate is not new. In fact, it has been going on for over 100 years. The question is where do we, as liberal modernists, stand in this debate.

To begin with, it is our view that the Bible and today's scientific theories are not in conflict. The Bible expresses views about life in a particular time period. The science expressed in the Bible is the science of that period and meant only for that period. There is no reason to attempt to reinterpret the text in order to bring its science into focus with modern life. There are individuals who try to rationalize biblical science by teaching things like the following: "A day in the Bible may not be twenty-four hours. It could have been thousands of years." From the liberal perspective arguments such as these are at best naive. They beg the question. They do justice neither to the biblical text nor to the people who read the text.

For the nonfundamentalist, there should be no problem at all with the issue of modern science versus biblical science. The modern view is scientific truth for our time. When the times change, science sometimes changes, too. Then that new science becomes the new scientific truth. From our perspective, it is that simple. Do we have a problem with the biblical text or with the truth of the Bible? Absolutely not! We believe the Bible is true. We believe the Bible makes a contribution to our time. It just needs to be understood within its context.

So what do we believe?

We believe that the Bible was written down by

individuals at a particular time; that the stories in it were compiled over a long period of time from differing sources and traditions; and that the compilers or editors, as they are called, interwove the stories and traditions so that the appearance is of one whole. With a range of tools at their disposal, from archaeology to other literature from the biblical era, and a better understanding of the meaning of particular words and expressions, modern scholars have the capacity to unweave the tapestry and study its individual strands. Each of those strands gives us a rather complete picture of the life and values of the Hebrews and Israelites of particular periods ranging from 1400 to 400 B.C.E. The Bible is about as accurate in describing the life and events of those times as we can expect it to be. So the Bible is true.

Therefore, the science question becomes quite irrelevant and meaningless. Individuals who believe that religious law and authority is based in Divine revelation at Mount Sinai cannot accept modern biblical scholarship. The conflict is irresolvable for them. They are correct in their view that acceptance of modern biblical criticism undercuts the basis of religious authority. Modern biblical scholarship does, however, provide the academic basis for a non-Orthodox approach to religion. It gives movements such as Reform Judaism a basic legitimacy.

Conversion

MAYER SELEKMAN

Judaism and the Jewish people have always welcomed those who wished to join the faith and family of
Judaism. Circumstances throughout our history made
access to Judaism sometimes easy, sometimes nearly
impossible. But whatever the circumstances, wherever
the location, there was at least a trickle of those who
bonded to our faith. The traditional term for one who
becomes Jewish is "convert." Today, however, "Jew-by-
choice" is preferred, especially within Reform Judaism.

It is now thought that the term *ger* referred in
biblical times to a convert because such a person was
granted the same rights as a person who was born a Jew.
According to Isaiah 56:6–7, *gerim* were entitled to full
Jewish Temple rites, such as celebrating in God's house
of prayer and having their offerings and sacrifices
accepted on God's altar. They were accepted as full
members of the Jewish community without qualification.

With the emergence of the Hasmoneans and the
Pharisees (circa mid-second century B.C.E.), conversion
to Judaism was vigorously pursued. During the
Hasmonean period, for example, captured peoples, like
the Idumeans, were forcibly converted (130–125 B.C.E.).
The Pharisees also engaged in active proselytizing,
employing passionate persuasion instead of physical
force. Evidence of this bold proselytizing, in fact,
appears in the Gospel of Matthew 23:15: "Woe unto you,
scribes and Pharisees, hypocrites! for ye compass sea and

land to make one proselyte...." The hostile rhetoric aside, the pharisaic fervor to seek converts is clear.

Even where avid proselytizing was minimal or absent, scores of conversions to Judaism occurred. Judaism's appeal to all segments of Roman citizenry was compelling. It affirmed (and still does) a single unique God, Creator, Organizer, and Sustainer of life. This belief was in stark contrast to polytheism, which depended on a fragmented view of reality in order to host its many deities. Whereas the God of Israel was a single entity, concerned with the preciousness and uniqueness of each individual made in God's image, the gods of polytheism were capricious and whimsical. As a result, their worshipers were always ill at ease and insecure, forever striving to placate too many deities in an effort to maintain some sort of stability.

The God of Judaism affirmed a loving, compassionate, and just partnership with each person committed to God. This love and mutual devotion would be rewarded at the end of time, when those who chose Judaism would have their immortal souls rejoined to their resurrected bodies to live eternally in God's dominion. (This belief system, so closely identified with Christianity, was created by the Pharisees and was transformed by Paul [Saul], who was also a Pharisee.) Polytheism could not withstand the power of Christian and Jewish monotheism and it eventually withered away.

As the Roman Empire disintegrated, the Emperor Constantine (327–337) made Christianity the empire's religion. From then on, Judaism lost its legal status, and proselytizing on behalf of Judaism was prohibited. A host of laws were enacted that extinguished Judaism's conversionary flame; at the same time the proselytizing energy of Christianity was unleashed.

During the medieval period, although Judaism remained open to those who wished to become Jewish, circumstances made it extremely difficult. Those who did become Jewish were few in number, although often significant in stature; for example, some highly placed, well-respected Christian clergy and members of the nobility became Jewish. Moreover, while Islamic countries explicitly prohibited Jews from seeking converts, records indicate that conversions nonetheless occurred.

Beginning with the period of Emancipation (eighteenth century), Jews began to be welcomed as citizens of the countries in which they lived; they became citizens who openly practiced Judaism. This new-found political freedom was warmly embraced by many but not all Jews. Some, believing that they really could not succeed without embracing Christianity, did so. Although some Christians did convert to Judaism, more Jews converted to Christianity. This imbalance eventually ended, in part because of the rise of Reform Judaism with its religious embrace of the gift of freedom and the importance of the individual.

A contemporary perusal of all modern branches of Judaism indicates a willingness and openness to accept Jews-by-choice. Both the Orthodox and Conservative movements require a lengthy period of study; Reform Judaism, although making intensive study a strong recommendation, leaves the decision to the individual rabbi. Both the Orthodox and Conservative movements also require actual circumcision—*berit milah*—or symbolic circumcision, plus *mikveh*—ritual immersion. The Reconstructionist and Reform movements encourage, but do not demand, circumcision and immersion.

In 1978 Rabbi Alexander Schindler, President of the Union of American Hebrew Congregations, proposed the creation of a Reform Outreach program with three goals. First, it would provide Introduction to Judaism classes across the country. These courses would be open to any person who wants to learn more about Judaism; these courses are primarily filled with couples who are considering intermarriage or who have already intermarried. The second goal would be to encourage Christian spouses who, with their partners, belong to Reform congregations and want to become Jewish. Finally, the Outreach program called for a renewed proselytizing effort to the unaffiliated in America. Rabbi Schindler boldly challenged the Reform movement to let all who hunger and thirst for a faith and family know about Judaism.

We live in a world that is rapidly becoming a village. We live in a country where all ghetto walls—physical, educational, and psychosocial—are crumbling, if they have not already collapsed. We live on the edge of a new religious age. We already see more and more people searching for a faith and family to call their own. The faith and family into which they were born may not be the ones in which they will remain. A recent survey indicates that today there are as many Jews leaving Judaism as there are non-Jews entering.

If we as Jewish people are convinced of Judaism's preciousness and uniqueness, then each of us must become an emissary of our faith and people. We can never know when we, as the living embodiment of our faith and family, may strike a resonant chord in an acquaintance, a good friend, a family member, a son- or daughter-in-law. Suddenly, another may discover the beauty and power of Judaism, and that person's search will be over.

Judaism's future will indeed depend on living our faith for all to see and opening our arms to all of God's people, welcoming and embracing all who choose to join.

Are You What You Eat?

ROBERT H. LOEWY

There you are, trying to decide what to have for lunch at the snack bar, and the thought of a bacon cheeseburger has become quite tempting. Suddenly a silent alarm goes off inside your head, and it is more than an alternative craving for a cheese pizza. For many people today, selecting what to eat is more than a matter of deciding what appeals to one's taste. There are many issues that affect what one eats. Some of these issues revolve around questions of health, some concern themselves with the ethics of animal slaughter, and some even take into account the treatment of the workers who work in the farms, fields, and slaughterhouses that provide us with most of our food.

Jewish Dietary Laws

For Jews, eating has long been much more than a way to meet bodily needs and cravings. A careful reading of the story of creation reveals that in the beginning it was intended that we all be vegetarians; only after Noah and the flood was humankind permitted to eat meat. And even then, there were restrictions on how meat could be eaten, with a special emphasis on avoiding the consumption of blood.

Over time, the Jewish people developed the system of *kashrut*, laws which regulate what a Jew can and cannot eat. Permitted and prohibited foods are delineated in the Book of Leviticus (11:1–23) and repeated in the Book of Deuteronomy (14:3–20). In Jewish tradition foods which can be eaten are called *kosher*. The word *kosher* also has a broader meaning of being ritually fit or proper. Forbidden foods are known as *tref*.

The verse, "You shall not boil a kid in its mother's milk," which occurs three times in the Torah (Exodus 23:19 and 34:26, and Deuteronomy 14:21), has been interpreted in the rabbinic tradition to refer to the separation of all foods considered meat products, called *fleishig* or *fleishdig*, from all milk products, known as *milchig* or *milchdig*.

The combination of the Torah laws along with their rabbinic interpretations has resulted in the following basic rules of *kashrut*:

1. All animals (mammals) that have both a split hoof and chew their cud may be eaten, such as beef cattle or sheep; while all others, like pigs, are expressly prohibited (e.g., ham sandwiches, BLTs, or pepperoni pizza).

2. Domestic birds, such as chicken, turkey, duck, or goose, may also be eaten, while birds of prey are banned.

3. Permitted animals and birds are both categorized as "meat" and must be slaughtered according to the Jewish laws, which have historically stressed kindness toward animals.

4. Any fish that has fins or scales may be eaten; those without both fins and scales, such as shellfish or catfish, are forbidden.

5. Meat, or meat products, and milk, or milk products, may not be eaten together, and the utensils used to prepare and serve each must be kept separate. A designated amount of time must elapse before eating a milk product after having consumed a meat product, and vice versa.

6. Fish, fruit, and vegetables are considered *pareve*, which means they are neither milk nor meat. They can be eaten with either category of food.

Searching for Reasons

Many theories have been promulgated to explain the laws of *kashrut*, but there is no universally accepted opinion. The Torah simply says that the laws are designed to make us holy, without giving a specific purpose for their observance. Even the term "holy" is subject to interpretation. It has one component that connects us with God, but it is also understood to mean separate and apart. The Book of Leviticus does speak about observing the dietary laws in one verse and, in the next, refers to Israel as a separate people from the others who inhabited the land of Canaan. Still, the Bible provides no single, definite explanation for the laws.

Nonetheless, scholars and sages have sought a rationale, such as the belief that if we control our bodily appetites we are better able to control our passions and emotions. Perhaps the most popular explanation for why Jews keep kosher, however, comes from Maimonides, who wrote that the system was created for reasons of hygiene. However, though medical science would consider *kashrut* to be healthy, this does not mean that it was the intent of the original legislation. There is also much in the legislation which makes no sense from a health perspective. Others claim that the laws of *kashrut* prompt a greater awareness of our consumption of meat, which was a concession to the human appetite following the flood. The mere fact that the laws are found in the Torah is enough of an incentive for some people to comply. Regardless of the reason, Jews have observed the dietary laws for centuries.

Kashrut and Reform Judaism

As Reform Judaism developed in America, the observance of *kashrut* was generally abandoned for both practical and philosophical reasons. The Pittsburgh Platform of 1885, an influential statement of Reform Jewish belief, declared, "We hold that such Mosaic and rabbinical laws as regulate diet, priestly purity, and dress originated in ages and under the influence of ideals altogether foreign to our present mental and spiritual state. They fail to impress the modern Jews with a spirit of priestly holiness; their observance in our day is apt rather to obstruct than to further modern spiritual elevation." From a philosophical perspective, the early Reformers did not find meaning in observing the laws of *kashrut* and clearly viewed them as an obstacle to becoming part of the new, open American society. The fact that it was difficult in America to find proper kosher food contributed to the willingness to discard what was seen as an anachronistic practice.

Even today one finds Reform Jews who and Reform Jewish institutions that observe all or some Jewish dietary laws. They do so for a variety of reasons. Aware of how pork has been used to taunt and torture Jews throughout history, some Jews refrain from eating pork products because they regard pork as not only *tref* but as anti-Semitic. Others seek the sense of discipline that kashrut requires and enjoy the awareness that eating is changed from a simple biological function to a religious act. Some Jews observe a form of *kashrut* in order to identify with the worldwide Jewish community, while others do so in order to make their homes a place where all Jews can eat comfortably. Finally, others simply observe *kashrut* out of a desire to grant Jewish law a certain amount of authority in their lives.

It's Your Choice

Keeping kosher need not be an all-or-nothing proposition. Some people observe what they call "biblical *kashrut*," refusing to eat any of the foods strictly forbidden by the Torah. Others abstain from mixing milk and meat, though they do not separate their dishes or purchase strictly kosher products. Some choose to become vegetarians, combining their opposition to animal cruelty with their understanding of Jewish tradition.

The Possibilities and Combinations Are Endless

Consistent with the fundamental principles of Reform Judaism, a Reform Jew can be anywhere on the spectrum of observance, from fully "keeping kosher" to being totally nonobservant of any Jewish dietary laws. However, it is incumbent upon a Reform Jew at least to be knowledgeable about the practice of and reasons for *kashrut*. Then, when that bacon cheeseburger appears on the menu, you can make a Reform Jewish decision, which will be the right one for you.

Bibliography

Dresner, Samuel H., and Seymour Siegel. *The Jewish Dietary Laws*. New York: Burning Bush, 1959.

Maslin, Simeon, J. *Gate of Mitzvah*. New York: Central Conference of American Rabbis, 1979.

Plaut, W. Gunther, ed. *The Torah: A Modern Commentary*. New York: UAHC Press, 1981.

Siegel, Richard, Michael Strassfeld, and Sharon Strassfeld. *The Jewish Catalogue*. Philadelphia: Jewish Publication Society, 1973.

The Messianic Age

EUGENE B. BOROWITZ

Thorleif Boman, in a provocative book, has argued that the Hebrews had a radically different sense of time than did the Greeks. Biblical thought, he contended, was linear. It moved from a beginning to an end, from creation, through history, to the coming of the Messiah. Greek thinkers, he alleged, had a cyclical view of time. For them, history repeated itself endlessly after long intervals. Subsequent scholarship has disparaged Boman's thesis. Many Greek writers did not think of time as repetitive, but refer to the mythological notion that a Golden Age awaits humankind in some distant future. What remains of Boman's study is his insight that Hebrew messianism, and not merely its monotheism, distinguishes its faith from even its most enlightened Mediterranean neighbors.

With some exaggeration, we may say that Judaism's messianic belief makes it unique among world religions. Believing Jews look forward devoutly to an end to history as we know it. In that "world-to-come," all the ills of contemporary existence will be remedied and human life will be perfected in the full acceptance of God's rule.

Internally, Jewish messianism animated Jewish piety and empowered Jewish survival over many difficult centuries. In their extremity, the believing martyrs of the Holocaust sang *Ani Ma'amin,* a song about the coming of the Messiah. Its text is an abridgement of the twelfth of Maimonides' thirteen principles of Jewish belief. "I believe with perfect faith in the coming of the Messiah and even though he tarries, with all that, I daily await his coming." How can one hope to understand Judaism without insight into so stubborn a faith?

Objectivity about Messianism

A major difficulty prevents our gaining an undistorted view of this central Jewish aspiration. Christian belief developed out of the Jewish messianic hope and in the process transformed that faith in terms of its particular religious experience. Today, despite decades of secularization, one can hardly discuss messianism without hearing the Christian overtones which surround that doctrine. For example, consider the English words "salvation" and "redemption." When we use them to translate the Hebrew *yeshuah* and *geulah*, we bring words heavily laden with christology into whatever is said. One needs to be on guard, then, against reading back into Judaism notions which are inauthentic to it. The topic is also complicated by the long history of polemics between Jews and Christians. For a while, as the American appreciation of religious pluralism grew, the antipathy which animated the discussions seemed to have been largely overcome. More recently, as evangelical Christian groups have pressed their claim that Jesus fulfilled the Hebrew Bible's messianic texts, passionate arguments have become more common.

We cannot circumvent that problem by appealing to academic historians for an objective view. Scholars have not reached any well-accepted consensus in this area. The origin and earliest development of the people of Israel's messianic faith remains obscure. Such data as we have is scanty and difficult to interpret. Much of what later Jewish (or Christian) generations saw as messianic prophecies seems to critical-minded academics today the backward projection of a later belief. The interpretations testify more to the personal commitments of those who made them than to a commonly available standard of judgment. Prudence therefore demands that we not try to reconstruct the beginnings of the Jewish faith in the Messiah. We shall have to content ourselves with an overview of the messianic traditions of Judaism.

A Messianic King and/or a Messianic Era

Some prophecies in the Bible look forward to the coming of an ideal king. Thus, Isaiah, allowing for poetic exaggeration, seems to look beyond political ideals to a qualitatively unique age. Here are some pertinent excerpts from that vision:

A sprout will come forth from the trunk of Jesse
   [King David's father]
And a shoot will rise up from his roots.
The spirit of *Adonai* will fill him,
A spirit of wisdom and understanding,
A spirit of counsel and might,
A spirit of knowledge and faith in *Adonai*....
With righteousness he will judge the poor
And bring justice to the little people of the land....
The wolf will live with the lamb,
The leopard lie down with the kid....
No one will hurt or destroy
In all My holy mountain,
For the earth shall be full of knowledge of *Adonai*
As the sea is full of water.

(Isaiah 11:1–9)

This passage is richly symbolic. We would like to know what to expect and how it will come about. Instead, the poet speaks of plants, animals, and water. The symbols being "alive," we have little problem understanding what he is driving at: justice, peace, and general well-being. But we cannot tell whether Isaiah meant it as a practical, soon-to-come expectation or an abstract, distant dream. Did he look forward to a reasonably benevolent king or did he anticipate God's wondrous transformation of the natural order through a specially inspired king? Simply put, we do not know how "messianic" this passage was to the prophet.

In the biblical references to the coming ideal king, he is never called the Messiah, *mashiach* in Hebrew. (True to its cultural context, the monarchical Messiah tradition is masculine, awaiting a king, not a queen.) The word *mashiach* derives from a common Hebrew root meaning "to anoint with oil." When priests and kings were installed in office, the Bible calls for them to be touched with oil. Hence anyone serving in such a special role, such as the priest accompanying the Israelite army, can be called "an anointed one," a *mashiach*. In the old English transliteration system (by way of the Latin), this became "messiah." By rabbinic times, the general term, *mashiach*, had also acquired a specific meaning. It referred to the perfect king who, with God's help, would bring history to its fulfillment.

Some passages in the Bible which envision the ideal future do not mention a king. They refer only to what God will do in those extraordinary days. Perhaps the most famous of all the messianic passages is of this sort. Oddly enough it appears in almost identical form in

Micah 4 and Isaiah 2, with the Micah version continuing
a bit further:

> This is what will happen at "the end of days"
>   [the future? some day?]
> The mountain of *Adonai's* House will be
>   raised up.
> It will be higher than any hill.
> Peoples will come to it in streams.
> Nations will go around saying,
> "Come, let's go up to *Adonai's* mountain,
> To the House of the God of Jacob.
> He will teach us of His ways
> And we will walk in His paths...."
> They will beat their swords into plow blades,
> Their spears into tree pruners.
> No nation will raise a sword against another
>   nation.
> They won't even study war any more.
> People will sit under their vines and fig trees
> And no one will make them afraid.

(Micah 4:1–4)

Here, the encompassing well-being is associated with
the coming of one religion for all humankind. "For Torah
will go forth from Zion and *Adonai's* word from
Jerusalem" (Micah 4:2). All people will see the truth of
Judaism and live it. The result is messianic peace.
Though a King Messiah is not mentioned here, the
passage contains, characteristically, both national and
religious elements.

Judgment and Resurrection

Two other major motifs need to be considered. Various prophets warn the people of a coming day of judgment:

> [In those days]
> I will show wonders in the heaven and on
>   the earth,
> Blood and fire and pillars of smoke.
> The sun shall be turned into darkness
> And the moon into blood
> Before the coming of the great and terrible day
>   of *Adonai.*
> But it will come to pass
> That whoever calls on *Adonai's* name
>   will be saved,
> For in Mount Zion and in Jerusalem
> There will be those that escape....

(Joel 3:3–5)

On the Judgment Day those who have been faithful to God will be rewarded and evildoers will be punished.

By the time of the Book of Daniel, "the end of days" is associated with a great cosmic transformation. In Daniel, too, we can see the other significant idea associated with the coming of the Messiah. Judgment will be passed not only on the living but on the revived dead as well. The righteous among them will be rewarded with everlasting, ideal life (Daniel 12:2–3). For the rabbis this meant the bodily resurrection of the dead, and this teaching became a major feature of Jewish messianism.

How God finally gets the recalcitrant human to accept freely God's sovereignty is never made fully clear.

Some biblical and rabbinic authors emphasize the Messiah's wisdom and piety. Others cherish the possibility that all Israel might one day become observant. A number daringly assert that the Messiah will come only to a thoroughly impious generation, their faithlessness provoking a loving God to action. Some envision God beneficially filling all humankind with knowledge of the Lord. Whatever the method, it seems "logical" to me that if God is the supreme ruler of the universe then one day God's kingdom must be realized on earth among people.

Rabbinic Views on the Messianic Times

In rabbinic literature, a full-scale messianic belief is evident, but opinions concerning it are imprecise, variegated, and occasionally inconsistent. However, much of it can be brought together in a scheme depicting the end of days as a drama with a prelude and four acts.

The time preceding the coming of the Messiah is the worst of times. It abounds with natural catastrophes and extreme social upheaval, "the [birth] pangs of the Messiah." In every period of Jewish disaster this doctrine has given rise to the hope that God might soon send deliverance. On the basis of Malachi 3:23 it is also commonly believed that Elijah will first come to announce the Messiah's advent.

As the first act begins, the Messiah's immediate task is military, to defeat the enemies who have been attacking the people of Israel—symbolically, the kings of Gog and Magog (based on Ezekiel 38:2). He restores in Jerusalem the rule of the Davidic dynasty, of which he is a descendant. He brings back Jewish exiles from all over the world to his Jewish kingdom, where they will live in peace and happiness. And he institutes a universal, ideal social order. This period, "the days of the Messiah," seems so this-worldly and historical that the rabbis can speculate just how many years this period of messianic rule will last.

In line with the naturalism of this stage of the messianic era, the rabbis do not consider the Messiah an angelic or divine being. Though he succeeds because of God's special help, he is only another inspired human being like a biblical judge or king.

In the second act—some time after the messianic rule begins—the dead are resurrected. The graves open and the corpses, healed, purified, and perfected, receive their souls back, thereby coming to life.

The third act, the judgment day, is distinguished by its corporate aspect, the judgment of the nations. Though each individual soul has received evaluation and subsequent atoning punishment immediately after death, a climactic judgment now also decides each person's eternal fate. The rabbis generally affirm that "each Jew has a share in the life of the world-to-come." Some rabbis except notorious sinners, and the wholesale acceptance usually involves some additional punishment being imposed at this stage.

With act four, the stage, which has been growing dimmer and more indistinct, reaches the point of bare visibility. After the judgment and purifying punishment comes the great reward of existence, entrance into the *atid lavo*—the "future-to-come" (also called the *olam ha-ba*—the "world-to-come"—a term which likewise refers to the state of the individual after death).

The rabbis do not discuss what this afterlife consists of, what one does then, or why it is so blissful. Except for stray speculation, they tell us little about it. God, having graciously given the Torah to the people of Israel, the proper human concern is studying and living by its guidance, not fantasizing about life in the future-to-come. Because of that emphasis, traditional Judaism may properly be called a this-worldly religion. It has, as we have seen, a strong other-worldly commitment and a rich doctrine of "last things." But it bids its adherents devote their lives to the spiritual challenges of everyday existence rather than concentrate on what is likely to happen to us in the world-to-come.

Modern Reinterpretation of Messianism

The Emancipation of the Jews in the nineteenth century persuaded the early Reformers that the Jewish hope for the Messiah needed reconsideration. Some German Reform Jews decisively changed Jewish belief. In 1841, in a prayer book created for use in the Hamburg Temple, all the traditional prayers for the coming of the Messiah were replaced with aspirations for a messianic age.

The religious liberals had three arguments for their innovation. First, they felt that praying for a King Messiah would hurt their chances of gaining full citizenship. The anticipated Son of David was to reestablish political rule and bring the exiles of his people back to their homeland. If they prayed for such national restoration, could the Jews be genuinely loyal to the countries in which they lived? Should citizenship be granted to people of such divided loyalties? The traditional Messiah-idea, by blocking the full emancipation of the Jews, seemed an impediment to Jewish survival.

Second, messianism had become highly miraculous. The modern temper, increasingly impressed with science's accomplishments, found such an attitude toward history utterly unacceptable. Who could believe that one person, by some special powers of leadership, would reestablish a Jewish state, bring back all the Jews, establish an ideal social order, revolutionize international relations, and inaugurate a time leading to a resurrection of the dead and God's judgement day? Moreover, over the ages, the Jewish imagination had attached a host of legends to the coming of the Messiah. In the Talmud we hear that in the messianic time each grape would yield thirty kegs of wine! (*Ketubot* 111b)

Third, the liberals felt they had a much more realistic theory of messianism: democracy. Here they followed their principle that traditional Judaism had given too great an emphasis to God's acts and that modern religiosity ought to focus on humanity's powers. Instead of God sending an ideal king, they foresaw all humankind working together and by social reconstruction producing a perfected world. In place of people being relatively passive, performing their religious duties by relying on God to redeem history, they would become activists, applying their reason and conscience to effect their salvation.

Most Reform Jews found these arguments convincing. They therefore gave up the belief in a Messiah and substituted for it a belief in the coming of a Messianic Age. Though no other Jewish groups openly adopted this stance, the traditional personal language for the Messiah soon became highly symbolic for almost all modernized Jews.

Much chasidic teaching stresses human change as the key to bringing the Messiah. However, chasidic activism, unlike that of the liberal Jews, was directed inward, to personal spiritual transformation. The liberals' messianism was oriented to society and its improvement through politics and education. They had a substantially different sense of human power than did the unemancipated pietists of Eastern Europe. Their optimistic view of human nature forms the foundation of their concept of the Messianic Age. It motivated Jews to unparalleled involvement and accomplishment in humanitarian affairs wherever they received equal rights.

Revitalizing the image of the Messiah makes it easier in liberal belief to acknowledge God's role in transforming history. In the older, liberal rhetoric of "our partnership with God" in bringing the Messianic Age, God was often little more than a euphemism for human self-reliance and social action. Being more modest in our self-estimate today, we are ready to acknowledge our need for God's help in finally redeeming this sinful world. Accepting God as a true partner does not require us to surrender the sense of healthy self-reliance we identify with personal maturity. Rather, an able but not omnipotent humankind, acting as co-creator with God of the ideal society, reflects the classic covenantal relationship between God and the people of Israel. The accents may be modern and the tone is surely more activist. But with this understanding we are entitled to say, as previous generations did, that we too are working and waiting for the coming of the Messiah.

Are Jews the Chosen People?

GARY ZOLA

The concept of chosenness is central to the identity of the Jewish people and is deeply rooted in its intellectual history. The people of Israel have long conceived of themselves as the Chosen People; it is a designation which first appears in the Bible and is later developed in talmudic, philosophic, mystical, and contemporary Jewish literature.

Biblical and Rabbinic Sources

The theme of Israel's chosenness—as expressed in the covenantal relationship between God and the Children of Israel—resonates throughout the Torah. The Book of Deuteronomy introduced the technical phraseology that communicates the idea that the people of Israel occupy a special and unique relationship with the God of all humanity: "For you are a people consecrated to the Lord your God: Of all the peoples on the earth, the Lord your God chose you to be His treasured people" (Deuteronomy 7:6). According to the Book of Deuteronomy, God was motivated by love to select Israel as God's own: "It was not because you are the most numerous of peoples that the Lord set His heart on you and chose you— indeed, you are the smallest of peoples; but it was because God loved you" (Deuteronomy 7:7–8).

As God's Chosen People, Israel is responsible for carrying out special duties and tasks. Just as God chose Israel, so, too, must Israel choose God, which it does when it keeps God's statutes and ordinances. When the people of Israel live in accordance with these divine laws, they become God's agent among the nations of the world by bringing happiness and light to humankind. In this way, their status as the Chosen People provides Israel with the unique opportunity to be a "prophet to the nations," spreading the word of God's salvation.

The ancient rabbis stressed that the notion of Israel's unique relationship with God stems from its willingness to accept the Torah at Mount Sinai. This rabbinic theme is amplified in the frequently quoted talmudic teaching that the Torah was first offered to the other nations of the world but was rejected because it would have required them to alter their way of life. Only Israel accepted it (*Avodah Zarah* 2b, 3a; *Numbers Rabbah* 14:10; *Sifre Deuteronomy, Piska* 343). Ever since Mount Sinai, Israel has carried out its primary obligation as God's Chosen People by serving as the guardian of the Torah for all time. This is why the blessing recited prior to the reading of Torah proclaims, "Blessed are you, O Lord our God, King of the Universe, who has chosen us from all peoples, and has given us Your Torah."

In rabbinic literature, there is an attempt to downplay the arbitrary nature of Israel's chosenness as described in the Bible. The rabbinic sages maintained that Israel's elevated status derives, in part, from the merit of the patriarchs and matriarchs, who were extraordinarily compassionate, obedient, humble, loyal, and merciful human beings (cf. *Betzah* 32b, *Yevamot* 79a).

The Rise of Christianity

In response to Christianity's claim that the Church was the "true Israel" and that Christians were, therefore, God's Chosen People, the Jews took greater pride in their sense of chosenness. The belief in their special relationship with God served as a source of tremendous strength and loyalty to tradition during periods of stress and forced conversions. In fact, some have observed that many Jews adopted the most extreme and exclusive interpretation of the doctrine of election in response to the intense oppression from the outside world during the Middle Ages. Confined to the ghetto and ostracized from the outside world, Jews took refuge in their chosen status in order to rationalize and cope with their suffering.

The Modern Period

As Jews gained access to the outside world, the more extreme and elite interpretations of Israel's election seemed less and less relevant. This conflict—which has been characterized as a contest between "exclusiveness and tolerance"—prompted intellectual efforts to reconcile the exclusivity of Israel's chosen status with the modern ideals of equality and fraternity of all peoples. How was it possible for modern Jews to maintain that all people were created equal and claim simultaneously that they were God's elect?

Some modern Jewish thinkers, in an attempt to resolve this ideological tension, have denounced the doctrine of Israel's election. Mordecai Kaplan, for example, argued that modern-minded Jews can no longer believe that the Jews constitute a divinely Chosen People.[1] In keeping with this position, the prayer book of the Reconstructionist movement eliminated all references to the concept of chosenness.

The conflict between universalism and particularism was not the only source of tension prompting modern Jews to reinterpret the concept of Israel's election. The anti-Semite pointed to the Jewish doctrine of chosenness as proof that Jews believed themselves to be superior to all other peoples. Ultimately, it was this type of bigotry that fueled belief in a secret plan possessed by the Jews to achieve world domination. The most notorious version of this anti-Jewish canard came in the form of that pernicious forgery, *The Protocols of the Elders of Zion*.

The Concept of Chosenness in Reform Judaism

Reform Jewish thinkers have also struggled to redefine the traditional notion of chosenness in a way which highlighted Judaism's universalistic values without diminishing the concept's spiritual and historical significance. These thinkers increasingly emphasized chosenness as a state of "uniqueness," downplaying notions of Jewish theological superiority. Leo Baeck, for example, wrote in his book *This People Israel*, "Every people can be chosen for a history, for a share in the history of humanity.... But more history has been assigned to this people than other people." [2]

Perhaps the best-known reinterpretation of the Chosen People concept may be seen in the Reform idea of "The Mission of Israel," which stressed the role of the Jews as teachers of God's message to the world. Thus, chosenness was expressed in their role as messengers of God's teaching to the nations of the world.

The Contemporary Scene

The doctrine of election continues to affect contemporary Jewish life. The founding of the State of Israel leads to the question of what chosenness means today. Does Israel have an obligation to serve as "a light unto the nations"? Has Israel been selected to play a special role in God's plan for humankind? Are we entitled to hold Israel's actions to a higher ethical standard than the one we apply to the other nations of the globe?

On a more personal basis, individual Jews continue to experience the dialectic between covenant and chosenness. What does it mean to be a part of the Chosen People today? How do we explain this concept to ourselves and to others?

Bibliography

Borowitz, Eugene. "The Chosen People Concept, as it Affects Life in the Diaspora." *Journal of Ecumenical Studies* 12, no. 4 (Fall 1975): 553–568.

Borowitz, Eugene. *Reform Judaism* Today. New York: Behrman House, 1983.

Eisen, Arnold. *The Chosen People in America*. Bloomington: Indiana University Press, 1983.

Kaplan, Mordecai. *Judaism as Civilization: Toward a Reconstruction of American Jewish Life*. Rev. ed. Philadelphia: Jewish Publication Society, 1981.

Korn, Bertram W. "The Evolution of the Concept of the Chosen People in the Bible." Rabbinic thesis, Hebrew Union College-Jewish Institute of Religion, Cincinnati, Ohio, n. d.

Plaut, W. Gunther. *The Case for the Chosen People*. Garden City, NY: Doubleday, 1966.

Klal Yisrael and Reform Judaism

ALLAN L. SMITH

Klal Yisrael, loosely translated as "the community of Israel," is clearly an important concept in our time. Indeed, many in the Jewish community still take the idea of *klal Yisrael* into consideration when they make decisions about Jewish issues. Yet, despite its importance, there are many who now feel that the diversity of twentieth-century Jewish religious belief and practice has rendered the idea of *klal Yisrael* impotent. In light of such doubts, perhaps it is time, as the twentieth century comes to a close, to take a second look at the unconditional, unlimited concept of *klal Yisrael*. What is the price of *klal Yisrael*? What are the demands made upon one's own movement and practice for the sake of it? At what point does one compromise in order to maintain it?

Perhaps we should recognize and accept the idea that *klal Yisrael* means that while the community of Israel is one and united, Judaism, the religious community of Israel, is not a united, monolithic entity. Nor can it be.

Perhaps it is time to recognize that there are differences between Jews which cannot be addressed to anyone's satisfaction, and that the costs of compromise to bridge those differences are just too great a price to pay in this new age. A number of significant religious questions focus the issue for us.

A child has a Jewish father and a non-Jewish mother. The child has been raised as a Reform Jew for all of his or her life. Will Orthodox parents allow their child to marry this individual? No. Is this child Jewish? Yes, according to Reform Judaism. Should we compromise for the sake of *klal?* That is not so easy to answer

A couple has just divorced. The wife wishes to marry again, but she has no *get*—religious divorce. Will an Orthodox person marry this woman? Would her children by a second marriage be considered legitimate Jews by Orthodox Jewry and accepted in all matters? Should there be some middle position to prevent this confrontation? Again, should we compromise?

In both situations, there is little room to do so according to Orthodox *halachah*. For Orthodox Jews, questions of religious status and divorce are serious matters. For Reform Jews, however, they are no less serious since to compromise in these circumstances would deny the very legitimacy of Reform Judaism and its institutions.

Should we serve non-kosher food at a party where there are Orthodox Jews? Should we wear a head-covering and use the traditional prayer book at joint religious services? Should we refrain from halachic violations of Shabbat during community activities? We are tempted to say that since it is so serious a violation of traditional practice, and we do not want to insult the Orthodox, and it really does not cost nontraditional Jews anything, why not compromise? But is this really an appropriate response to the conflict at hand? Is compromise here any less insulting to the sensitivities of Reform Jews or to the legitimacy of Reform Judaism? We cannot allow others to define our Jewish identity and experience. Reform Judaism is, unequivocally, a legitimate articulation of our commitment and vision for a bright Jewish future and for our spiritual fulfillment.

And yet, lest one conclude that the idea of *klal Yisrael* can be so easily disregarded, we ought not forget just how central the unity of Israel has been to Jewish survival. Throughout Jewish history, there is clear evidence that Jewish unity allowed the Jewish community to thrive and prosper. When one Jewish community was threatened, a second came to its rescue. The unity of the Jewish people gave the community a strength far beyond its numbers. Benefits and advantages were distributed effectively because of *klal Yisrael*. The disadvantaged had a place to which they could turn. Clearly, the concept of *klal Yisrael* is one of the essential ingredients of Israel's uniqueness. It cannot be treated lightly or discarded at will.

The questions and challenges for the American Jewish community in the twenty-first century will not be easy. The greatest challenges to *klal Yisrael* are yet to come as we search for the proper balance between compromise and mutual respect. How do we find it? That is the question we must address.

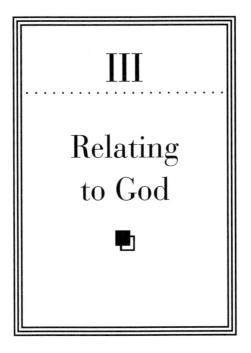

III

Relating to God

Belief in God

SHELDON ZIMMERMAN

To be Jewish is to be part of an ancient people and community and, at the same time, a member of a community in covenant with God. Today many people claim to be secular Jews, humanistic Jews, or ethnic Jews. Some want tradition without God, food without faith, a feeling of belonging without "supernatural" involvement. Yet to be a Jew involves both sides: sacred community and culture, ethnicity and holiness, food and faith.

A real part of the dilemma is that for most of us being Jewish is something that has been true since birth. According to Jewish tradition, if my mother is Jewish, I am as well. Even in cases of mixed marriages, Reform Judaism recognizes that the child of a Jewish father or mother has a presumptive claim on the child's religious status. Aside from those who are Jews-by-choice, we are born Jewish. How can we then require belief as part of our religious self-understanding and definition?

Religious self-understanding and definition—that's the point. We are who we are because of that ancient covenant with God, which has bound our people and the Eternal ever since Sinai. We are born Jewish, but we need to become good Jews. Even if we choose to become Jewish, we still strive to become good Jews, which one achieves, according to our tradition, through a blend of belief and *mitzvot*.

The biblical authors understood that there were those who rejected God or a belief in God. Yet the Bible was so suffused with God-belief that its authors saw the non-believer as a *nabal*—a simpleton—someone who saw neither the world nor its wonders with open eyes, someone who was unwilling to encounter the living God in human experience and sacred community. Anyone with open eyes, heart, and spirit surely would believe, or so the Bible assumes. No proof was necessary.

The ancient rabbis assumed God's existence as well. They argued about God, they argued with God. They were rationalists, mystics, philosophers; some used anthropomorphisms, some believed humans could never truly know God. Their views cover the full spectrum of belief and faith. But they always accepted God and a belief in God as essential ingredients of one's Jewishness. In fact, for the rabbis, study became a sacred vocation because in study they could understand God's will in their lives. Reason and revelation became intertwined. Do you want to know what God wants you to do or demands of you? Go and study. Through study, prayer, and acts of kindness, one could encounter God. Just by looking at the world, one was moved to respond with blessings. In each morning and evening service, one rediscovered God in creation, Torah, and redemption, the three poles of Jewish thought and belief.

Reform Judaism remains loyal to this tradition. Some of us are religious naturalists, rationalists, mystics, traditionalists—our views cover the spectrum. Yet, modern doubts (as well as traditional ones) trouble and challenge us. How can one believe today? How can we respond to God after the Holocaust? How can modern, scientifically inclined people believe in the supernatural? How can we believe in God when we are surrounded by human suffering? Our doubts are real. To be a Jew is to raise doubts, respect them, and force ourselves to live with them and respond to them. Our questions and challenges compel us to move to newer and more profound understandings: that despite the obstacles that stand in the way of belief, somehow God's presence is felt again and again. Sometimes we can only agree to try to let God in. We remain open but questioning, unsure yet listening.

Despite all our questions, we still seek meaning and endow the meaning we seek with religious symbols. The soul of the modern Jew yearns for religion. Not that we reject science and technology, but we have come to understand their limitations. The meaning of person-ness takes us beyond the realm of reason.

Yet some of us are not certain. Our faith lacks certainty. Perhaps what we need to understand is that our faith does not always require certainty. What it requires is an openness of mind, heart, soul, and spirit.

The signals of transcendence are everywhere—in the world around us and in the world within us. One of these signals which emerges in our history is that despite historical forces we are still here, alive, and fairly well. Signals emerge in the redemptive drama of everyday life and in the idea of hope, which is one of our central beliefs.

The doubts we feel and the challenges we confront are real; they are a part of who we are as Jews. Just as real is the openness demanded of us—to the God (however differently perceived) who called us to peoplehood, sacred community, and holiness. God's presence is with us on our journey as a community to sanctify and transform the world. We are the sanctifiers-in-process. We can make the ultimate difference in the journey to fulfill the promise of the day when at last "the Eternal will be one and the Eternal's name will be one."

How Does God Speak to People?

EUGENE B. BOROWITZ

When the Torah scroll is read in the synagogue, again and again we hear, "And *Adonai* spoke to Moses, saying...." In many places in the Bible God appears and talks to people; the prophets specifically credit their speeches to God.

When our religion must fit in with all else we know, we are nonplussed by the notion of revelation. Nothing of that sort has ever happened to us or any responsible individual we know. The people who have declared that God spoke to them have had a message so self-serving, bizarre, or inane that it was self-discrediting. Many, we must judge, have been emotionally deluded.

The critical issue becomes religious authority. With "God spoke" as its central premise, Orthodox Judaism can claim God's own power for its dicta. The rigorous humanistic position argues that all religious commands and teachings were the creations of people. They therefore confront us with nothing more than the genius or fallibility of their human author. Since some people have exceptional spiritual capacity, their teachings can be our best religious guide. For much of the past century and a half, many moderns lived by some such faith.

Most liberal Jews find themselves midway between Orthodoxy and humanism. They do not believe God gave people verbal instructions as the Orthodox do, but they are also not as skeptically unknowing as the humanists. For them, the words "God said" do reveal more about human religious perception than about God's utterances. But these human texts are also responses to the Sacred other, in whatever modern sense we understand God. Some liberals interpret revelation almost exclusively in terms of human religious intuition; they feel on sure ground only when speaking of themselves and their own kind. Others prefer to emphasize God's role. They believe religion's distinctive value lies not in helping us transcend our humanity but in helping us make contact with the Sacred.

God Speaks in Many Ways

Scholars estimate that the various books of the Bible were written in a process that went on for over a thousand years. In all that lengthy record of Jewish faith and anguish we do not find one explicit inquiry about *how* God spoke to people. To the ancient Hebrews revelation may have been special but it was not unnatural, for religion was an organic part of life and God seemed close. We do not, then, find in the Bible any significant discussion of the process by which God communicates.

Scripture does mention many ways in which *Adonai* made contact with people. The most astonishing of these is God's "personal" speaking of Ten Utterances to the people of Israel encamped at the foot of Mt. Sinai. The setting was awesome: "Mt. Sinai was all in smoke for *Adonai* had come down upon it in fire. Smoke rose like the smoke of a kiln and the whole mountain trembled violently. The blare of the horn grew louder and louder. As Moses spoke, God answered him in thunder" (Exodus 19:18–19).

Psalm 29 likewise describes the greatness of God's voice. "The voice of *Adonai* shatters cedars. It makes Mt. Lebanon skip like a calf. The voice of *Adonai* kindles flames of fires. The voice of *Adonai* convulses the wilderness" (Psalms 29:5–8). The prophet's role is aptly described in this passage about Moses and Aaron: "you [Moses] shall speak to him and put the words in his mouth…and he shall speak for you to the people. Thus he will serve you as a mouth and you will serve him, as it were, as God" (Exodus 4:15–16). A true prophet does not originate his message in any way. He only transmits what God has told him.

Varieties of Indirect Communication

Sometimes the disclosure by God comes by way of a vision. Jeremiah (1:13) sees a boiling pot, and "the word of *Adonai*" comes to him with a message of judgment for the people.

In Zechariah the visions are more dreamlike, with flying scrolls or chariots with red horses (5:1; 6:2). The most extraordinary visions come to Daniel, who sees bizarre beasts and dreamlike events (7:1–28).

The Torah proclaims Moses the greatest of all the prophets, explaining that his contact with God was uniquely direct and unmediated. "If there be a prophet among you, I, *Adonai*, make myself known to him in a vision or speak with him in a dream. Not so with Moses, My servant. He is trusted throughout My household. With him I speak mouth to mouth, plainly and not in riddles. He beholds *Adonai*'s likeness" (Numbers 12:6–8).

Sometimes God speaks through what appear to be ordinary people: Samson's mother calls her visitor a "man of God" who looked like "an awesome angel of God" (Judges 13:6). But we are not quite certain how to translate the last term, for the word rendered "angel" is the ordinary Hebrew term for a messenger. So to speak, God can also communicate by messenger.

One last reference to God's speaking cannot be omitted; Elijah challenged the prophets of Baal to a public contest of religious truth and proved them false. Threatened with death if Queen Jezebel's agents can find him, he flees to the Judean wilderness and asks God to take his life. After a miraculous meal, he walks for forty days and nights to a cave at "the mountain of God at Horev," where he spends the night. The next day God asks why he has come and Elijah pours out a bitter complaint. He alone is left of all God's prophets and now they seek his life. " 'Come out,' God called, 'and stand on the mountain before *Adonai*.' And lo, *Adonai* passed by. There was a great and mighty wind, splitting mountains and shattering rocks by *Adonai*'s power. But *Adonai* was not in the earthquake. After the earthquake, fire. But *Adonai* was not in the fire. And after the fire, *kol demamah dakah*" (1 Kings 19:1ff.). The old Jewish translation rendered it as "a still small voice." The new version is "a soft murmuring sound." And that is all the response Elijah gets, except for a command to go back and proceed with God's work.

Medieval Beginnings to a Modern Problem

About a thousand years ago, Jews came into close contact with Moslem philosophy and science. Recognizing the great power of human reason, they began to formulate abstract questions about religion and philosophical responses to them. Special difficulties arose because their "science" used rigorous cause-and-effect reasoning to explain natural phenomena. Specifically, they conceived of the cosmos as a series of utterly transparent crystal spheres, one nesting inside the other. The various stars and planets were suspended in one or another of the spheres, and their odd motions, as observed from earth, were explained by the special motion of their sphere. Everything which happened in the sphere below the moon (and thus on earth) operated in terms of natural cause and effect. God, so to speak, had to operate the universe from outside the total system of spheres. How then could people on earth receive divine communications?

Maimonides responded by taking a current philosophical idea and reformulating it to make it more effective. God, he contended, ordered the world by intellect, which explains why human reason can comprehend nature's laws. When one applies one's mind to the philosophy of religion, metaphysics, one can develop one's reason so that it is open to and activated by God's effecting intellect. Most people do not have the intellectual ability and devotion to rise to this level. Maimonides also believed that everyone could be taught the rudiments of metaphysics, thus insuring them of a lasting link with God. The thoughtful few, by rigorous study and thinking, could become channels for the intellect with which God suffused the universe. The utterly exceptional, in whom mentality was accompanied by morality and complete inner dedication to God, were candidates for the highest religious intimacy, prophecy.

At this point the great rationalist surprises us. He insists that human efforts alone do not produce prophecy. God must grant that culmination; one is a true prophet, Maimonides says, by the grace of God.

Though he did not give a rational explanation for everything, Maimonides made revelation plausible for his generation's questioners. "God speaks" now meant to them a human mind which had reached the stage of being fully influenced by God's activating intellect.

Liberal Jewish thinkers have roughly followed Maimonides' strategy. They have converted "God speaks" into a version of "people understand." I think our challenge is more difficult than Maimonides'. Our scientific world view is much more impenetrable, and a pervasive secularity makes any talk of revelation seem irrational. Yet present-day science also supplies us with metaphors to explain our sense of revelation. God "speaks" like an FM radio transmitter but most people listen to the world via AM. Religion seeks to change our sensitivity so we can get something of the message which surrounds us. And some few religious geniuses are uniquely well tuned in to it.

Contemporary Jewish philosophers go beyond the creation of new metaphors and attempt to explain in detail what they mean by revelation.

Abraham J. Heschel's Theory: Modern but Not Liberal

For Heschel, modern science has robbed us of our instinctive surprise at the wonder that we or anything exists. If we can shed our secular programming, all of us can have a direct, personal appreciation of the incomparable grandeur of the God who created and sustains all being.

The prophets differed from us only in the unusually profound way they had this experience. They had the gift of what Heschel calls "sym-pathy." I have introduced the hyphen to distinguish Heschel's meaning from sympathy as the common sentiment of feeling the distress of a sufferer. Heschel wants us to take the term literally, sym= with, pathos=feeling; the prophet's "sym-pathos" enables him feel along with God. He is totally identified with the divine purposes and that is the source of his message and authority.

Heschel's prophet does not literally hear words addressed to him. He does not have to. He is so intimate with God's "desires" that he can accurately verbalize them. He does this in terms of his personality and situation for he has not surrendered his individuality in this experience. However, Heschel emphasizes that prophets do not invent or create anything they say. Rather their words accurately represent what they felt God was undergoing.

Revelation as the Ethics Reason Discloses

In the last part of the nineteenth century, Hermann Cohen elaborated the first great modern theory of revelation. It was an integral element of his neo-Kantian ideas about God.

For Cohen, using reason is humanity's greatest talent; using it properly enables us to gain an integrated concept of the three distinct realms which comprise mature rationality—science, ethics, and aesthetics. The basis of such a worldview is the integrating idea which people traditionally called God. Thus, for Cohen, true rational philosophy is the same as true religion, a unity he called religion of reason.

Obviously, a god who is understood as an idea cannot "speak." For Cohen, revelation is a term describing the human mind functioning at its best. Cohen attached the highest importance to the creative powers of reason, of the mysterious way a mind originates a new idea, particularly one which extends our unified understanding of the world. To get a fresh comprehensive concept was, in effect, to gain greater knowledge of God, the unique, integrating premise. Equally, to discover the way in which the God-idea rationally requires certain consequences in thought or action may also be termed, for Cohen, a "revelation." All such insight is a perfectly rational and, therefore, natural process.

Cohen becomes quite passionate about the connection between God and ethics. The rational person, he asserted, experienced the commanding power of the ethical as "categorical imperative," to use Kant's famous term. Like all the highest products of the mind, it had the form of law, in this case of moral law. Therefore, a critical sign of one's rationality was one's responsiveness to ethical duty. This is so ordinary a human experience that it seems an exaggeration to call the demands of conscience "revelation." Yet, insofar as they directly instruct us in what the God-concept requires of us, they are everyone's ongoing "revelations."

As liberals popularly came to understand Cohen's theory, "God reveals" means "our conscience requires." Cohen judged Judaism to be the great historical exemplar of religion of reason. He therefore considered its ethics to be its lasting, commanding element. He called for unequivocal abrogation of any Jewish law which conflicted with them, such as, for example, the prohibition against transgressing the Sabbath to save a Gentile life. Where laws were not directly ethical but conducive to ethical behavior, like prayer, he considered them valuable. Where they had no direct or instrumental relation to ethics, one might feel free to keep or discard them as one wished.

Leo Baeck: Revelation and the Religious Sense of Mystery

While Cohen begins with philosophical ideas and then applies them to Judaism, Leo Baeck does the opposite. Baeck, who was a young rabbi in Cohen's later years, starts with the lived experience of Judaism and only afterward looks for concepts to explain its unique genius. Baeck agreed that Cohen had exposed much of Judaism's central truth, but his preoccupation with the intellect prevented his doing justice to its piety. Judaism clearly encompassed more than doctrine and ethics. It taught trust and confidence, dependency and aspiration, resignation yet joyous optimism. These emotions suffused the life of believing Jews as much as did the concept of ethical monotheism.

To bring feelings back into Judaism, Baeck joined the notion of religious consciousness to Cohen's theory of rational religion. Baeck believed faith began with our sense of mystery about human origins and destiny. Paradoxically, our lives, which seem so temporary, also appear to have lasting significance. Though we know we were created by a power far greater than ourselves, yet we share its extraordinary capacity to create, particularly in doing an ethical deed.

For Baeck, revelation derives from our awe at being alive and empowered, as well as from our reason. Sensitivity and not merely conscience instructs us. Baeck's liberal Jew must respond to God in more than intellectual and ethical ways. Prayer and ritual mean much in Baeck's Judaism, for they are appropriate responses to the mystery which surrounds us.

Should intuition and rationality conflict, Baeck insists that ethical judgment be sovereign. Allowing our religious consciousness to be paramount might easily lead us to romantic emotionalism and self-indulgence. That having been said, Baeck quickly reasserts the passionate side of the dialectic. In Judaism the subjective aspect of faith must be a full partner to ethical rationality, lest we create a sterile, moralistic sort of religion.

Baeck's stature as a thinker has been enhanced in recent decades as cultural developments have shown his fears of emotionalism and secularism to be well grounded. We have seen how relying largely on one's feelings can itself dehumanize people, and how conscience without a religious foundation has itself gradually lost our confidence.

Kaplan's Reworking
of Vox Populi, Vox Dei

Both Cohen and Baeck base their thought on the individual. As a result, neither could assign the Jewish people a central place in his thought. Mordecai Kaplan, speaking out of the American immigrant experience, agreed with Cohen's and Baeck's rationalism but rejected its focus. For him, the folk would have to receive greater priority than the individual mind or religious consciousness.

Kaplan's thought derives from American naturalism, which seeks to understand people in terms of their interaction with the world. For Kaplan this meant the way in which culture shaped human individuality. Individual self-fulfillment inevitably involves one's folk, for it gives one's very language and horizon of achievement.

All cultures known to us have a religion. It functions to promote the society's chief values and to help individuals rise to the highest level of development. Thus, the individual, as well as the folk, needs religion to provide a sense that the personal values they cherish are worthy of their trust. Should one lose faith in one's goals, one's humanity begins to die. Healthy people, therefore, manifest an intuitive trust that the best in them is sustained and furthered by many natural processes. Modern Jews should use the word "God" to refer to this unity of the inner and outer thrusts toward human betterment.

Only slowly did higher religious intuitions develop and become part of people's lives. In many places they are barely recognized even today. Religion, like all the other aspects of human life, must be considered a process of growth and discovery. For us, religion must be rational. We will believe only what we can understand.

For Kaplan, then, revelation is the process by which people discover the highest truth about themselves and their world, a largely but not entirely rational matter. Since almost all of us receive our stock of ideas—even our rebellious ones!—from our society, one's people, rather than one's self, is revelation's most reliable source and repository. Consequently when our people honors its individual members by making decisions democratically, we ought to do what it says.

Martin Buber:
Revelation as Relationship

The three preceding liberal theories center on the human role in religion. Martin Buber stands somewhere between Heschel and the liberals. He is more humanistic than Heschel, more God-oriented than the rationalists.

For Buber, God is a reality not ourselves. We can come to know this God, Buber teaches, only if we desist from treating God like an object to be analyzed and learn to relate to God as we do to another subject.

To understand what revelation might mean to us today, Buber utilizes the experience of friendship or love. When you are very close to someone, that person has a powerful effect on your life. You care what they think, want to do what they desire, are fearful of their judgment, and are concerned to make amends for whatever you have done that offends them. Perhaps they specifically spoke to you about these matters, but they need not have. Merely by your intimacy you and they will have a mutual sense of command and responsibility. Indeed, it often happens that they will feel their relationship with you damaged if they must say what deeply concerns them. If you truly cared, you should have known. Even without words, love communicates and demands responsive understanding.

The basic Jewish commandment is not to love our minds, our consciousness, or our highest self, but God. Not everyone is capable of a great passion for God, but all of us can grow into friendly intimacy. Our moments of closeness with God are the basis of our religious life. Whether ours is a great or only an ordinary love, its effect will be the same. Our closeness will increase our understanding and our responsibility. God does not speak words to us, but knowing that God is present with us engenders our knowledge of what we must do to stay close to God.

Heschel disagreed with Buber on one vital matter. Heschel insisted that the prophet's self was radically subordinated to God's greatness and, thus, his message was not creative. Buber had taught that in a true relationship one partner does not sacrifice self to the other. Both partners remain independent selves, although most intricately linked. That individuality can be most fully realized in the most involving relationship is the mystery of mature love.

Buber also believed that nations, like individuals, confronted God in their history. Such experiences formed the ultimate basis of their "nationality" and their culture. For the people of Israel, that had happened at Mt. Sinai and again and again, thanks to the prophets, during the course of biblical history. More important, the Jewish people as a whole came to accept the traditions of these "revelations" as the basis of their folk existence. But against Mordecai Kaplan's later theory, Buber always insisted that individual Jews must give priority to their personal relationship with God, not to what their people says it ought to be.

How Then Might Liberal Jews Read the Bible?

These four liberal thinkers deny that God communicates words. They agree that the statements attributed to God are human creations, arising out of human religious experience.

For liberals, revelation is a human response to God's reality. And it continues today as it did in the past. How then will you find the lasting religious truth of the Bible? If you agree with Hermann Cohen, you will read the Bible with a strong appreciation of its incomparable early understanding of ethical monotheism.

If you follow Leo Baeck, you will also resonate to the sense of personal mystery and exaltation which our ancient forebears felt in relation to God.

If Mordecai Kaplan's rationalism explains things best for you, the Bible will become an incomparable source of your people's decisive early intuitions of nature's support for humankind's proper self-development.

If you share Martin Buber's experience of the power of relationship, you will read the Bible with the same sort of openness you bring to a trusted friend or love, knowing that from its words you may relive now the experience which lies behind the words before you.

If Abraham Heschel has convinced you that in the face of God's greatness we are best off accepting what the prophets have told us, as interpreted by our sages, you will study the texts in an accepting, grateful way.

What you believe about God and humankind and the people of Israel will affect what you believe revelation can mean today. And from that definition will stem your understanding of what constitutes proper authority in contemporary Judaism.

God at Sinai

ALLAN L. SMITH

There is perhaps nothing more challenging to the modern liberal Jew than the question of the existence of God and God's delivery of Jewish law into the hands of the Jewish people. Do we really believe that God came down on Mount Sinai and gave a written and an oral law to Moses? Is it possible to be Jewish and have a meaningful relationship to Judaism without a commanding God who has already given an essentially unchangeable law? How important is it to be kosher or to observe the Sabbath?

There is a very interesting story told within Jewish tradition about ritual purity, which was an extraordinarily important concept in ancient times. Objects could become impure by coming into contact with other objects that were already impure. This concept was serious because certain objects, once tainted, could not be made pure again and had to be discarded. Such was the case with a vessel (that is, anything that could hold water).

A man named Acknai invented an oven which would hold heat but would allow liquid to pass through it. (He used bricks that had sand instead of mortar between them.) Rabbi Eliezer declared that such an oven could not become impure since it was technically not a vessel. The other rabbis out-voted him and said it could become impure. Outraged, Rabbi Eliezer declared, "If I am correct, let that tree get up and walk." All of a sudden the tree he pointed at got up and walked. But the rabbis would not change their minds. "If I am right, let the river flow backwards," Rabbi Eliezer cried. And so the river reversed its course. Still the rabbis were unimpressed. "Let the walls of this house of study collapse," he continued. The walls collapsed out of respect for Rabbi Eliezer. But still the rabbis would not change their minds. Finally, in frustration, Rabbi Eliezer looked to the sky and said, "If I am right, let God speak." And a heavenly voice was heard to say, "The *halachah*—law— is in accordance with Rabbi Eliezer." But the rabbis declared, "You have no place here. The Heavens are the abode of God but the Earth was given unto humankind." "Ah," declared the Holy One. "My children have bested me."

What an enlightened view! If only it were truly under-stood. Even within our tradition there is a recognition that the law is the invention of humankind attempting to make life work in the way it believed God wanted. Reform Judaism does not reject tradition, but it does reserve for itself the right to reinterpret and sometimes even abrogate Jewish law. We might believe in particular standards, but there is no law that is not subject to analysis and rejection as a principle or article of faith. In fact, the question of boundary—*gevul*—is only a question of time and environment. Is there no limit? Not really. There is, however, an orderly process which requires time and understanding.

One should understand that there are many legitimate reasons for observing particular traditions. It is not simply the idea that God commanded a tradition in order to compel modern individuals in their practice. A person may choose a particular form of observance as a discipline or as a way of identifying with a particular group. Just as nothing within the tradition is free from critical examination, so nothing that has been a part of Jewish tradition is, a priori, alien to Reform Judaism.

Still, there needs to be a recognition on the part of all who declare themselves within the Reform sphere that a closer adherence to Jewish law does not make someone more Jewish than someone else. It does not make someone more legitimate or more entitled.

What is God in Reform Judaism?

Theological speculation within Reform Judaism has run the course from the Kantian imperative to religious existentialism. We do not need to rehearse the many ideas of God of our greatest thinkers. They have their parallels in all the arenas of religious thought. You may choose from the widest menu imaginable. What can be said in the simplest form is that Reform Judaism accepts the notion that there is a reality called God, though different societies under different circumstances will determine their own concepts of God. These conceptualizations of God are imitations of the reality. They help us to aspire to the highest. They move us forward in the search.

Within Jewish tradition there is a clue to the methodology one might use in this noble quest. It lies within the outline of Jewish prayer and the official festival cycle. There are three official festivals in our biblical tradition. On Sukot Jews observe the harvest festival and celebrate God's presence in nature. On Passover they celebrate the exodus of the Jews from Egypt and God's presence in history. Finally, on Shavuot they observe the covenant at Sinai and celebrate God's presence in the determination of a moral code of law.

One reads the prayers surrounding the watchword of Israel's faith, the *Shema*. Three paragraphs lead us to praise a God active in nature, a God active in law, and a God active in history. What more useful way to view God is there than as the guide to the creation of a better world, a God who is at one with the natural environment, who works toward moving history forward, and who creates an order that brings actualization and fulfillment to each and every individual?

The idea of God at Sinai and our presence there is to empower humankind to a partnership in creation. What enhances that idea in our world becomes the essence of Reform Jewish tradition.

Worship and Prayer

IRA S. YOUDOVIN

It is often said that "Judaism is a religion of deed, not creed." As with most broad statements, this one is both right and wrong. It is true that Judaism has been less concerned with speculation about what God is than in asserting what God wants of us. While Christian scholars have devoted most of their energies to developing theology, their Jewish counterparts have focused on formulating *halachah*—law.

But this does not mean that Judaism is bereft of theology, any more than it implies that Christianity is indifferent to ethics. The fact that traditional Judaism holds that *halachah* emanates from God is, itself, a powerful theological concept: it is God's nature to demand standards of behavior from all human beings and to command the Jewish people to observe an additional set of ritual practices from which non-Jews are exempt.

The deed/creed dichotomy also reflects differing attitudes toward prayer, particularly as measured by regular service attendance. Ritual piety may have permeated the European *shtetl* and its Sephardic analogue in North Africa and Western Asia. But in Israel, the Jewish state, far more men and women spend Shabbat on the beach than in synagogue. And public opinion polls taken in the United States report that American Jews are far less conscientious about attending services than are their

Protestant and Catholic counterparts. Jewish identity incorporates elements from a diversity of ethnic, cultural, philanthropic, educational, political, and social categories. Religious or spiritual pursuits are not always the most pervasive.

In recent years, a reverse trend seems to be emerging. Jews are increasingly talking about and actively seeking an element of spirituality in their lives. This development originated on college campuses, where students were influenced by Eastern religions and the works of individuals like Martin Buber and other twentieth-century Jewish theologians, who wrote of a numinous, transcendent dimension to human existence.

Though Buber and the others are sometimes mistakenly credited with "inventing" Jewish spirituality, their primary contribution has in fact been to draw attention to the opportunities already inherent in Judaism for living an authentically spiritual life. Our task is to discover and rediscover these many avenues to spirituality, avenues which are open to us if we only search for them.

So what does Judaism mean by "spirituality"? Except for some mystics on the outer fringes of Jewish life and thought, Jewish spirituality is very different from the spirituality defined in other religious and quasi-religious doctrines. Judaism does not promise that the individual or his or her soul will rise until it is in contact with the Oneness of the Universe. Jewish spirituality is far less dramatic and, consequently, far more accessible.

The Hebrew word for holy, *kadosh*, derives from a word meaning "to set apart." Spirituality in Judaism comes from "setting apart" moments in time, taking an otherwise ordinary event and investing it with holiness, elevating life's experiences from the mundane to the holy. It means pausing now and again as you proceed through a normal day's activities and focusing, for just a moment, on the larger implications of what you're doing or what is happening around you.

Private Worship

The classic Jewish vehicle for achieving spirituality is the *berachah*—blessing (meaning prayer of praise). In *Fiddler on the Roof*, Tevye asks his rabbi whether there is a blessing for the czar? "We Jews have a blessing for everything," the rabbi replies. While certainly an exaggeration, the rabbi's point is well taken. Judaism has blessings for a dazzling variety of occasions: before and after eating, seeing lightning, commencing or concluding a journey, waking up in the morning, and going to sleep at night. And, of course, there are many blessings which accompany ritual acts, such as lighting Shabbat candles, reading from the Torah, eating matzah, and affixing a mezuzah to one's residence.

But why so many *berachot* (plural of *berachah*)? Because each *berachah* affords an opportunity to take an otherwise ordinary experience and make it special. For example, let's take a typical college mealtime. As a rule, eating on campus is little more than an occasion for refueling one's engine as quickly as possible before moving on to class or study. Now inject a *Hamotzi*—the prayer over bread. By pausing for just a few seconds after setting down your tray to thank God for "bringing forth bread from the earth," you create an opportunity for remembering that the food we eat originates in the soil of this planet and is part of nature's marvelous bounty.

There are other ways to inject the sacred into everyday life. The morning service contains several brief verses which describe God as "renewing daily the work of creation." These ostensibly have little relevance to college students, who generally awaken after too little sleep, dress hurriedly (unless they've slept in their clothing), and rush off to their first class. But just as you're staggering into a cold shower and fumbling for a hot cup of coffee, the world outside your dorm window is also awakening to a new day. Pausing to recite that *berachah* as you look out at the morning sunshine changes the entire character of how your day begins.

There is even a *berachah* to be recited when using the bathroom. Predictably, this blessing provokes snickers, especially as it thanks God for "opening and closing tubes." One of my teachers in seminary confided that he, too, used to laugh at the *berachah* until one day he had kidney failure and almost died. Having learned the hard way, he now recites this blessing in appreciation for bodily functions he once took for granted.

The opportunities for sanctifying time and experience are virtually unlimited. You can say a *Shehecheyanu* upon returning to campus after a summer's vacation to begin a new academic year or make a simple *Havdalah* in your room at the conclusion of Shabbat before venturing out for a Saturday evening's entertainment. The women's movement within Judaism has developed a number of original rituals for marking the onset and cessation of the monthly menstrual period, which reawaken a woman's appreciation of the marvelous reproductive processes inside her own body.

Of course, this is not to suggest that a *berachah* itself has magical power. But making the effort to recite it and paying attention to its meaning can spiritually elevate the moment.

Communal Worship

Communal worship, which generally takes place on Shabbat and holidays, serves essentially to invest mundane experience with a dimension of holiness. By congregating for prayer, study, and companionship, the group takes what would otherwise be another Friday evening and turns it into Shabbat.

The tradition of fixed public worship in Judaism dates back to biblical times. The Torah commands that specific rituals for sacrificing animals be conducted three times a day, and on Shabbat and on festivals. These rites were performed by Temple priests—*kohanim*—and were accompanied by vocal and instrumental music performed by the Levites (Psalms 150). All other Israelites were either absent or, at most, passive observers.

Sometime during the last two centuries before the common era (B.C.E.), Judaism began moving away from the Temple cult and toward a more participatory form of worship in which prayer replaced sacrifice. The Temple ritual continued, supported by the authority of the Torah and the commitment of religious conservatives. An increasing number of Jews, however, took to congregating in places called synagogues (the word synagogue comes from the Greek *synagoge*, which means "assembly"), where they chanted a communal liturgy, heard the Torah read aloud, and listened to scholars (the forerunners of today's rabbis) interpret and expound on the week's portion. For the past 2,000 years, Jews have marked holy times in their calendar by coming to the synagogue for worship.

Today, congregations everywhere are striving to offer opportunities for worship that best address their members' spiritual needs. While only a decade or two ago most congregations scheduled one service on Friday evening and another on Saturday morning, it is now not uncommon for two or more different types of services to be offered, both affording different segments of the congregation opportunities for finding their own pathway to God. On a typical Shabbat morning, my congregation has one or more of the following: (1) a "tot Shabbat," which is a brief service followed by stories and games for families with preschool-aged children; (2) a lay-led "service in the round," where dress is casual and everybody participates; (3) a beginners' *minyan*, where prayers are taught and explained; (4) a sanctuary service largely conducted by the morning's bar or bat mitzvah.

Creativity

Liturgical creativity is a cherished tradition within Reform Judaism. The pioneers of our movement in Europe made substantial, sometimes radical revisions nearly two centuries ago in the Orthodox service. The two leading rabbis of nineteenth-century American Reform Judaism, Isaac Mayer Wise and David Einhorn, each wrote his own prayer book. Over the years, members of Reform youth groups have compiled vastly original "creative services," drawing upon a variety of sources to achieve relevance and spirituality. This tradition has now expanded beyond youth groups—congregational ritual committees now work with rabbis and cantors to create liturgies that address issues such as gender-biased language.

The college campus is an excellent venue for liturgical creativity. Those of you from a Reform background should feel especially comfortable experimenting with the format and content of their service. A good way to start is by examining our movement's prayer book, *Gates of Prayer*, which includes ten different liturgies for Friday evening. Also consider studying some of the "creative services" mentioned above that have been developed by congregations. Some questions you might want to ask should include the following: What is the structure of the service? What are its grand themes? What does each prayer mean? What ideals are being advocated? Which hopes are being expressed? How can these time-honored values be expressed in a way that best resonates with your group?

Your goal should not be to change the service, although this may be the result of your endeavor. On the other hand, you may find that one of the liturgies currently available meets your needs. Perhaps all you need is consensus for informally neutralizing gender-biased references as you worship, a practice followed by many congregations. What is important is that you and your group achieve a worship experience that will help infuse Friday evening with Shabbat holiness.

Indeed, the mere fact of gathering to welcome Shabbat with even a brief service is significant. Our tradition teaches that when a small group of Jews comes together for prayer, companionship, or study, the *Shechinah* (God's presence) dwells among them. Celebrating Shabbat, even for only an hour or two on Friday evening, not only affords a welcome break from the ongoing rush of campus activities, it is also an opportunity to be with companions who share your common identity and heritage.

The communal aspect of worship is best articulated

by the concept of *minyan*, the traditional requirement that ten Jewish male adults be present for daily, Shabbat, and holiday services. (Reform Judaism counts women in the *minyan* and is flexible about requiring ten people.) Some number of men and women should be present because communication in public worship is not only vertical—that is, between the worshipers and God—but also horizontal. By reciting or chanting a shared liturgy, worshipers are drawn together as a community.

The worshiping community extends beyond normal boundaries of time and space. Liturgical references to the patriarchs and matriarchs connect us to the first generations of Jews nearly 4,000 years ago. Prayers for the future redemption of the Jewish people and all humankind connect us with the future. Ancient words on the printed page make each participant a link in an endless chain of Jewish tradition. Additionally, an awareness that the same prayers are being recited by Jews throughout the world make us conscious of the fact that we are part of a truly international community.

Spirituality is something achieved through a slow process of personal growth. So begin with something simple, such as pausing to make a *Hamotzi* before you eat. Then build from there, making sure that you remain open to further forms of worship and their value. This sense of openness is best expressed in an anecdote told of the great German Jewish theologian, Franz Rosenzweig, who had almost converted to Christianity before deciding to become a more observant Jew. When asked whether he put on *tefilin*, Rosenzweig artfully answered, "Not yet."

Elements of Prayer

Keva and Kavanah

Judaism speaks of two elements present in prayer, *keva* and *kavanah*. It is difficult to translate these words exactly, as there are so many nuances to their meanings. *Keva* is something set, regulated, fixed in form; it is the form itself. *Kavanah* is concentration, devotion, intention, inwardness, direction. *Keva* is the form of the prayer; kavannah is what we bring to prayer. *Keva* is fixed; *kavanah* is fluid. Free-form, directionless prayer is too vague and too transitory; prayers need boundaries and grounding in a degree of reality. Likewise, to speak the written word without personal devotion is mere recitation. The medieval Jewish philosopher Bachya ibn Pekudah suggested that "If you pray with your tongue and your heart is otherwise engaged, your prayer is like a body without a spirit, or a shell without a kernel," adding, "let the words and thoughts of your prayer be directed to God."

In keeping with the idea that one must first develop a feeling of *kavanah*, the first section of the service helps prepare us to pray. The legend is told of a chasidic rabbi who was once asked how he prepared for prayer. He responded, "I pray for an hour that I might be ready to pray." We often read psalms or sing songs to prepare ourselves for prayer.

The traditional morning service, *Shacharit*, begins with *birkot hashachar*, the morning blessings. Originally these blessings were said at home, so they follow the actions we take in the morning of waking, washing, and dressing. (Many of these blessings, however, are no longer found in *Gates of Prayer*.) The Friday evening service begins with a *kabbalat Shabbat*: prayers, songs, and psalms welcoming Shabbat. The *Chatzi Kaddish*— half-*Kaddish*—is also a part of the preparation. It is traditionally recited by the reader and congregation at the end of each section of the prayer service and at the end of the Torah service. When it is included by a Reform congregation, it is usually read or chanted before the *Barechu*.

The second section of the service, encapsulating Jewish history as seen by the rabbis, focuses on three major themes: creation, revelation, and redemption. These themes are reflected in the following prayers:

- The *Barechu*, the call to prayer. It is seen as the gateway to prayer and the formal beginning of the service.

- *Yotzer Or* (morning) and the *Ma'ariv Aravim* (evening) refer to God's creation of the universe. We therefore thank God for the wonders of creation.

- *Ahavah Rabah* (morning) and *Ahavat Olam* (evening) speak of God's great love for the world and remind us that God has given us the Torah. We reaffirm our relationship with God and God's oneness through this prayer.

- The *Shema*, which can be found in Deuteronomy 6:4, has been considered to be the most important statement of a Jew's belief in God. It teaches that

God is One. So when we say this prayer, we affirm our belief that God is One, we are one, and we are God's people.

- *Veahavta* is the checklist for the *Shema*, detailing all the things we should be doing. By following the commandments, we demonstrate our love for God.

- *Geulah* (redemption) speaks of God's freeing of the Israelites from slavery in Egypt, reminding us that there are still people who are not free.

- *Mi Chamocha* is a song of praise which Moses sang at the Red Sea when the Israelites had been saved. (Note: There are different words for *Mi Chamocha* during evening and morning services.)

- *Hashkivenu* is read only in the evening. It asks God to protect us from all adversities during the time we are asleep.

The third part of the service is called the *Amidah*, from the Hebrew *amad* or *omed*, meaning "to stand." It is also known as the *tefilah*, meaning "prayer." And finally, it is also called the *Shemoneh Esreh*, the eighteen benedictions, because the daily morning service consists traditionally of eighteen *berachot*. The Sabbath service, however, has only seven, and the parts and numbers are different on different holidays.

The *Amidah* is broken down into three sections:

1. *Praise:* The first three *berachot* (*Avot*, *Gevurot*, and *Kedushah*) all praise God.

2. *Petition:* The middle *berachot* are all requests. On Shabbat, the middle of the *Amidah* is replaced with a single *beracha*. We are not supposed to ask

anything of God on Shabbat and so, instead of prayers of petition, we include a prayer for the Sabbath.

3. *Thanksgiving:* The last three *berachot* (*Avodah*, *Hoda'ah*, and *Shalom*) all express our appreciation for what God has done for us.

Reading Torah

While study is not the same as prayer, the study of Torah is considered to be of such importance that it was included within the service to ensure that study would not be neglected for more than two days. In traditional synagogues, the Torah is read on Monday, Thursday, and Saturday mornings.

Towards the beginning of the development of the Reform movement, the focus of importance shifted from Saturday morning to Friday night, and Torah was read only on Shabbat evening. While most Reform congregations today read from the Torah on Shabbat morning, some still read it on Friday evening.

After we have finished petitioning God for things (*Amidah*) and have completed the Torah service, we return to praise. The *Aleinu* encompasses many themes previously apparent in the service; God as Creator, Redeemer, and Ruler; the Oneness of God; and our partnership with God. The last part of the prayer expresses our hope for the messianic era, a time when *tikkun olam*, the repairing of the world, will be completed. Until the fourteenth century, this prayer was recited only on Rosh Hashanah. This is how the original read:

It is our duty to praise the Lord of all, to praise the Creator of the universe, for God has not made us like the nations of other lands, nor like the other families of the earth. God has not made our portion like theirs, nor our lot like all the others. For they bow down to vanity and emptiness and pray to a god that cannot save.

By the beginning of the 1700s, however, these sentences had been removed by the Prussian government. They were considered offensive to Christianity, and, although taken from the Book of Isaiah, they were used to show how Jews were prejudiced against Christians. For many centuries, this prayer was cited as one of the reasons for Jewish persecution.

The *Mourners' Kaddish* marks the conclusion of the service. The *Kaddish* is not a prayer for the dead but a prayer in praise of the living. In fact, death is never mentioned; rather, the words praise God. The *Kaddish* is a prayer of hope for the messianic era, of comfort in knowing that we are one with God, and that those we have lost still remain with us in our hearts and our memories. For those familiar with Hebrew, the words seem strange; this is because the *Kaddish* is written in Aramaic.

Although a closing hymn or song is not a part of the traditional service, it helps to bring a sense of closure to the worship experience. This final piece, if carefully chosen, enriches the spirit of *kavanah* of all who worship.

God without Pronouns

DEBBIE FLIEGELMAN

Judaism is particularly sensitive to language and its power. Jews have historically been called the People of the Book, and as the people whose central prayer is the *Shema* (Hear O Israel), the command to hear and heed the words which have shaped our religious beliefs, we cannot underestimate the power of words. Our ancestors, recognizing this power, believed that even to utter or write the name of God was such a powerful act that only the high priests in the Holy of Holies during Yom Kippur could do it. Other people have also seen how important language was to the Jews. Hitler nearly exterminated not just the Jewish people but their culture as well: Books were destroyed, Torahs were desecrated, Yiddish was nearly wiped out.

This all-important language of Judaism has been male-biased for centuries, and it is this bias that needs to be changed. The texts, the liturgy, the stories, the language itself, were written by males for a male audience. Women were literally and figuratively excluded. Regardless of how and why this came to be, if we as Jews are to create a society based on equality, it is our duty to include women in all facets of life.

In 1972 the Reform movement created the Task Force on Equality of Women in Judaism as a step toward achieving religious equality for women. One of its first tasks concerned language; the task force created the

"Glossary of Substitute Terminology." Prayer has a profound emotional impact, and the task force recognized that the impact could be negative if the language did not reflect the reality of those reciting the prayers. As Edith Miller, chairperson of the task force's Liturgy Committee, put it, "Our mission is to help to create an awareness not only of the equal partnership of women in the life and future of the synagogue, but also their desire to be given an opportunity to pray with words which recognize the role of women, as well as the feminine and masculine components of God."

The UAHC and CCAR accepted the task force's work and made many changes to the language of the prayer book, but they did not extend the changes to include God-language. Only later would CCAR publish a gender-sensitive version of *Gates of Prayer*.

Much of the work being done had centered on "people"-language: changing pronouns to a nongender-specific form; changing historical references like "fathers" and "patriarchs" to "ancestors" and "patriarchs and matriarchs"; including references to female as well as male biblical figures. Probably the most recognizable change has been the inclusion of the names of the matriarchs in the prayer known as the *Avot*—Fathers. At first the names of women were included just in the English translations of the prayers, but now many congregations include them in Hebrew as well. Still, while this is a step in the right direction, we should not think that adding some names makes a service truly egalitarian. Some people argue that we should rewrite the prayers entirely instead of just including a short list of women's names. Others feel that changing the Hebrew is altogether wrong. The important thing to remember is the goal—to include women as fully as men in the prayer service. This may mean adding names as well as including references to women (not just as mothers and wives, but as scholars and judges and participants in Judaism).

Making God-Language Gender-Neutral

> All expressions used in the religious enterprise are, in the long run, analogous and metaphorical. Statements about God should not be taken literally…. They contain no inherent finality or unalterable relevance, and convey no ultimate truth. To ignore this limitation by fixating on one set of ideas and thinking that a real correspondence exists between these images of God and God is to be unrealistic, self-aggrandizing, and fundamentally idolatrous.[1]

Feminist theologians and other writers have been addressing the issue of male-centered God language for quite some time. In many different forums and styles, they have analyzed the exclusion of women and the historical and sociological reasons for the continuation of this exclusion, offering in response persuasive arguments for making changes. Much of this article relies on the work of feminists—theologians, rabbis, linguists, writers—such as Rita Gross, Judith Plaskow, Marcia Falk, and Laura Geller, who argue in favor of changing our male-centered God and prayer language. The following section reviews some of the major issues.

Argument #1. There is a strong Jewish philosophical tradition that argues against using anthropomorphisms to describe God, for God ultimately is beyond such labels. In this view, to personify God is to practice a form of idolatry.

One way of coming to terms with the nature of God is to recognize that God is actually beyond our realm of comprehension. Jewish tradition holds that God is so powerful and so great that the true nature of God is unknowable to humans. But as people who think in language, it is inevitable that we should try to describe God in terms that are familiar to us. Modern thinkers, kabbalists, and Jewish philosophers feel that God is a force that cannot be described by our usual terms and that, in fact, God is both male and female and neither one. We do not have words for that, so why choose male-only terms? Instead, we must start to follow the lead of those like the feminist theologian Mary Daly, who argues that "God is not a Being, in fact, not a noun at all. Rather God is Being." [2]

This argument against anthropomorphism is perhaps the strongest argument for our using female imagery in describing or referring to God. Because it is impossible for us to conceive of God without some kind of "metaphor of a divine Person in a covenant relationship of mutual responsibility and love with human persons" [3] (i.e., without some anthropomorphic images), we must use our common pronouns for God. The important thing, therefore, is not to limit ourselves to one gender. Judaism already agrees that whatever God is, God is not limitable, so why limit God by gender? Moreover, use of the word Father to refer to a God that is neither male nor female implies a type of representation that is suggestively idolatrous.

Argument #2. The social patriarchal bias is so strong

that even if we were to use neutral terms, they would still be seen through the filter of male language; we would still imagine a masculine God.

Much of our language has been determined by the patriarchal bias of society. Man was taken as the generic because men were dominant in society. The same is true for theology and prayer language. Elaine Pagels notes, for example, that "theologians…are quick to point out that God is not to be considered in sexual terms at all. Yet the actual language they use daily in worship and prayer conveys a different message and gives the distinct impression that God is thought of in exclusively masculine terms." [4]

Owing to the years of accepting male language as the norm, it has become almost invisible to some. "God's maleness is so deeply and firmly established as part of the Jewish conception of God," according to Judith Plaskow, "that it is almost difficult to document: It is simply part of the lens through which God is seen." [5] In other words, we have become so used to the way things are, that changing it may not even occur to us.

The language we use grows out of the society in which we live, complete with its values and morals. Our language reflects the power structures of that society, so our male-dominated system produced male-dominated language in prayer as well as in everyday speaking. As we have already seen, language denotes attitudes, so "the male images Jews use in speaking to and about God emerge out of and maintain a religious system in which men are normative Jews and women are perceived as Other." [6] This bias in society has begun to change, and so this bias in language must disappear, too. The only way to make sure it disappears, however, is to examine it and challenge it by questioning its relevance in today's society.

Argument #3. While most users of male-biased language claim that the language they use is metaphorical and that such language does not mean that we think of God as male, metaphors have power. What's more, symbols and metaphors lose their symbolic value over time and become descriptive. In effect, the metaphor becomes God, so that any change is seen as an attack on God rather than on language.

When this happens with God language, we lose sight of the multiplicity of God's nature. We begin to conceive of God as a metaphor and only as a metaphor. Then the metaphor itself becomes the object of adoration; it becomes holy and cannot be changed: "The metaphor is no longer simply a way of pointing to God but is identified with God, so that any change in the image seems to defame or disparage God 'himself.' " [7]

Argument #4. Symbols and metaphors are helpful resources, but they are neither binding nor windows to the true nature of God.

We use symbols and metaphors constantly in our speech. They are helpful tools because our language is limited. There are many concepts for which we don't have adequate words—spirituality, depression, springtime, God. Because we don't have specific words for God, we use metaphors and symbols to conjure up images of God, to express those aspects of what we believe to be a part of God's nature. Our tradition is full of examples: "For the Lord God is a sun and a shield," "The Guide of humanity," "You are Peace itself," etc. These few examples have a long history; they have been used for so long that they have ceased to be mere sym-

bols and have become part of our tradition. The weight
of the tradition, therefore, makes it very difficult to
choose new and perhaps more meaningful ways of talking about God. The old ways have become almost
revered, almost holy themselves: "When particular symbols for God become deeply established and familiar,
they lose their transparency as symbols and come to be
seen as descriptions of God that provide unique access to
the nature of divine reality." [8]

It is sometimes hard to remember, then, that our
words for God are just symbols. The old ways of talking
are not binding; they do not necessarily give us any
greater insight into God's nature, nor are we obligated to
use them. Instead, we need to look at them as resources,
as paths to help us find new and more meaningful ways
of talking about God.

Argument #5. If we are to escape the male bias of
God-language, we must change the traditional male
images of power and dominance as well as the pronouns.

Much of the work in changing prayer and God-
language has centered on making pronouns and references to God gender-neutral or gender-inclusive. Many
theologians think that if we are ever truly to get away
from the image of God as male, we must also change the
other kinds of words we use about God.

God is traditionally spoken of as a supreme power
who dominates the world, as a warrior, king, ruler, stern
father, judge. These are stereotypically male attributes;
therefore, even if all pronouns are gender-neutral, we
may still imagine God as a male figure. Judith Plaskow
argues that one way to avoid such a conclusion is to
"disrupt" prayer language:

> For the English speaker, it is quite possible to avoid pronouns for God and to refer to God as the Eternal or source of life and still picture that eternal source as male. Only deliberately disruptive—that is, female—metaphors can break the hold of male metaphors that have been used for millennia. [9]

She does not argue for completely replacing male metaphors with female ones but for mixing the two.

There is a slight danger, however, in categorizing existing images of dominance as male and then trying to incorporate stereotypical female images. It is the danger of reinforcing gender stereotypes of males as powerful and females as nurturers, males as rulers and females as helpers. The trick is to redefine God not as dominance but as empowerment. One way to do this, as a group of women did at a conference, is to call out words that mean God. As that group discovered, many of the words ended with the suffix "-ing": changing, creating, enabling, nurturing, suffering, pushing, touching.

Language and Freedom of Choice

All of this language-changing and freedom of expression raises a very thorny question—what if I want to pray using all masculine language? Isn't that my choice? Just because someone else's worship is more meaningful with these changes doesn't mean my own worship will be more meaningful. In fact, what if I find using that gender-neutral language hinders my worship?

For private worship, you should, of course, feel free to use any kind of language you choose. But when praying publicly, as in a service at your synagogue, you must remember that there are other people praying with you.

And while the freedom of choice is perhaps the most important freedom we can protect, you must remember that there are limits to it. We are free to do what we wish provided our expression or actions do not impose on another person's rights. Ellen Umansky, when asked about this issue, remarked that if, in the Reform movement, prayer language is left up to individual choice, soon women won't be allowed to read from the Torah or count in a *minyan*. In other words, it would be one giant step backward in the fight for equality. What's more, as Rita Gross points out, Judaism insists on equality: "The social destructiveness of the exclusively masculine style of religious expression...is of more concern...than are its theological inadequacies. It would seem that the Jewish sense of justice would demand that such inhumane practices be transformed." [10]

Wrestling with Ritual

MARGARET HOLUB

I once read a story about a family in which a two-year-old boy had outgrown his crib. Seeing how he wept and protested the idea of giving up his bed, his mother devised a ritual to mark the transition. At a special dinner she prepared, the whole family talked about both the sadness of losing his crib and how exciting it would be to sleep in a "big-boy bed." Following the meal, they lovingly took apart the crib and brought it ceremoniously to the garage. The family then assembled the bed, covered it with a new bedspread the young boy had selected, said prayers, and tucked him in.

To be sure, this story, in Gertrud Mueller's *To Dance with God*, has some problems, not the least of which is that mom is now supposed to be the family shaman on top of everything else. But when I first read this story, I found myself crying. I'm no great kid's person or anything, so it took me a while to figure out what had hooked me. I realized that I envied this two-year-old because people around him recognized that something was important to him, and they marked it. How different my childhood, indeed my adulthood, would have been if people around me had celebrated with ritual those moments most meaningful to me!

A year ago I had a terrible kayak accident out in the ocean. Fortunately, it wasn't the end of my life cycle, but it was a life-defining transition for me. When I healed, I found it important to say *Birkat Hagomel* (blessing for deliverance from harm). And when the anniversary of the accident came around, I wished for a marker of some kind.

There are many events in the lives of Jews that don't yet have a marker. Our sages neglected to create rituals for when I was born, when I first began to menstruate, when that cycle ends, and for other landmarks in my life as a woman. I know of no Jewish ritual for lesbians or gay men who come out of the closet. And how do we respond ritually to an abortion?

But even if we enlarge the ritual canon to include all sorts of important moments, there are still the idiosyncratic ones, such as the anniversaries of kayak accidents, which will call for more invention in their commemoration. Once we admit that there will always be new things to mark, then we are drawn into the world of new ritual, and there is no way out.

What makes a ritual work? In a successful ritual, the participant experiences a sense of connection with other people, with "the stream of tradition," and with the source of life itself.

A ritual binds us to others because we share an experience of raw power or because we feel an intimate bond with the group. At a funeral we realize that a whole roomful of people grieves for the loss of one person. After a *kabbalat Shabbat* with a lot of nice singing, we feel like hugging everybody present. As we lift the parsley from the seder plate, we realize that Jews all over the world are doing the same thing at the same moment.

❏

Ritual connects us to the stream of tradition. Rabbi Laura Geller once gave a *derash*—an interpretation of a Torah passage—in which she asked, "Why do people cry at weddings?" What I took from her answer is this: There comes a moment during a wedding when you celebrate not only the union of bride and groom but the coupling of all people, from Adam and Eve in the beginning to God and the *Shechinah* at the end of time. You see all of history and yourself within it. People in the past have made this same commitment, and new generations will do so again and again. By echoing the past and suggesting the future, rituals place us in history, mark the commonness of our humanity, and make us part of the larger story.

Ritual is, most importantly, a tool for highlighting our connection to the great Oneness, the *Ein Sof, El Shaddai*, the animating force behind it all.

I participate in a *chevra kadisha* (burial society). One day, while sitting with the body of a woman, I realized viscerally that something had once inhabited her. Her body was now a shell, left vacant by her self, the person I had known. I began to think that all of us, and not just human beings, are inhabited for a time. Everything is inhabited with something that defines us and keeps us going. The cliffs on the ocean where I live are constantly crumbling and changing. Caves turn into arches and collapse altogether. Everything is moving.

I started thinking that God had inhabited the body of the woman I was now washing and preparing for burial. I recalled the story of a man sitting in a hot pool in the Rio Grande who realized that the Rio Grande is all rivers, all water—that the water constituting 67 percent of our body was once in the river or will be, that it all flows together. It's God that keeps the river flowing and evaporating and raining back down. God is the animating force who connects everything and keeps one thing transforming into the next.

A good ritual makes you feel that energy. It makes you feel alive, full of God. I imagine us sending taproots down into the groundwater, connecting with the one river. Of course, we are all connected anyway. We're all in motion. We're all full of God. If we weren't, we'd be like a frozen image in a photograph. Ritual can open our hearts, enlarge us, elevate us, deepen us.

I do not regard Jewish tradition as a straitjacket of commandments, but rather as a gift, a privilege, an entitlement. I first realized this when I took a job in Los Angeles at a shelter that ran seven days a week. I said, almost flippantly, "I don't work on Saturday." So I got every Sunday shift that year, but Saturday off was my entitlement as a Jew. I see all of Jewish tradition as my inheritance, the things I get that make my life better and connect me with my people, history, and God.

When I was younger and had more energy, I used to say, "I don't need a day a week—I need a month every two years." Shabbat didn't mark a cycle that meant much to me at that time in my life; now that I am getting grey hairs, I find a day of rest and contemplation every week to be a tremendous gift. I have a new understanding of the line in the *Kiddush* that calls Shabbat "our inheritance," and I'm glad to have Shabbat for my own.

When I entered college, I was given a bunch of my grandmother's beautiful beaded cashmere sweaters. I wore them with jeans and Salvation Army suit jackets. Knowing this wouldn't be my grandmother's style, I used to feel a pang, but then I realized, they're my sweaters, and I can do whatever I want with them. Likewise with lighting candles, with saying prayers, with sitting *shivah*. They're mine. I can do what I want with them.

I do ritual excavation and reconfiguration, digging up things my ancestors used in their way and using them in my way. I'm interested in what they used to do, and I know that many traditions have endured because of their effectiveness and beauty. In fact, I use a lot of things just how they came to me. But I also like to mix things up now and then.

My friend Ella Russell loves the *mikveh*—ritual bath. Several years ago, at the end of a difficult romantic relationship, she decided to go to the mikveh. She brought together three woman friends as witnesses. We sat on the edge of the Navarro River and drew from her the bad and the good of the relationship. We spoke of the *mikveh* as a passageway into a holy state, imagining together a future of love and companionship with a more satisfying partner. When she had named and envisioned the holy state she hoped to attain, she said the *Beracha al Hatevilah*—the blessing for immersion—and immersed three times to our cheers.

Largely because of Ella's good teaching, a woman with a chronic illness did a *mikveh* and prayed for healing. And thirty-five women, including my mother, did a *mikveh* on *erev Rosh Hashanah* morning a year ago. *Mikveh* rituals have become part of our community's ritual experience.

One ritual I do not feel comfortable observing is *kashrut*. Dietary laws can create a barrier between Jews and gentiles. I want my home to be full of friends of all kinds, and I want them all to be free to bring dinner. Should I as a rabbi preach against *kashrut*, make sure kids in our Torah school remain oblivious to the "U" on a bottle of salad dressing, say that the only proper Jewish table is one at which anyone can eat without restriction or embarrassment? Or should I simply say, here is *kashrut*, here is what I make of it, here are some other points of view, maybe you can find meaning in it, you decide.

I don't think it's my obligation to tell others what they should believe or do ritually. Of course, my beliefs and preferences matter to me as a leader, some quite strongly. On the other hand, I came to my own beliefs by struggling with the tradition, not because anyone told me it had to be a certain way. I am happiest when people make their own thoughtful Jewish decisions.

What is the point of ritual? Some say good ritual makes you feel high—a luminous, joyful, uplifted emotion full of endorphins. We can all use something that raises our energy without ruining our chromosomes. Others equate ritual with content, using it to affirm certain messages. Our rituals teach us to give praise; to be grateful; to embrace brides and grooms, sick people, and strangers.

For me, the purpose of ritual is not quite any of the above. Through ritual, I seek change in myself, in my community, and beyond. Through ritual, I feel the currents that run between people, back and forward in time, and deep into the groundwater. By traveling along those currents—or, more accurately, by feeling the intersection of these currents within—I try to stem the fragmentation that lies at the root of much of my own pain and which brings so much suffering to others.

When Ella submerged herself in the Navarro River with her three devoted friends as witnesses, her beautiful red curls disappearing into the water, I knew she felt our love and devotion, our desire for her heart to be mended. She also felt many mothers down under there, generations of women in relationships of all kinds who have come and will come out of the water to say *Al Hatevilah*, to find sexual, generative, and romantic renewal. And I know, too, because I saw it, that by immersing herself in *mayim chayim*—the water of life— she was permeated by all water, which is all connected and derived from the One Source.

The point of ritual isn't to follow a law or keep a covenant or to say the words correctly. These are means, not ends. When ritual works, it permeates us, especially at important times, with the real stuff—the love and connection and sensual satisfaction which are the fundamental grace of life. How we achieve this is up to each one of us, a matter of our own personalities, predilections, and personal histories. How fortunate we are to have such an array of treasures to light our way.

How to Be a Truly Spiritual Jew and Avoid the Pitfalls of Quick-Fix Religious Consumerism

JEFFREY K. SALKIN

Everywhere you go in the Reform movement, the word on people's lips is spirituality. It is the religious buzzword of our age.

The trend toward spirituality has greatly enriched Reform Judaism, energizing a movement once perceived as being overly intellectual and rational. Shabbat, festival observance, liturgical experimentation, a new seriousness about Torah study—these are all positive developments. But as with any swing of the pendulum, the rush toward an ill-defined spirituality poses a potential threat.

Mindless Religion

Despite a renewed interest in text study, many Reform Jews equate spiritual with non-intellectual. "I feel Jewish" has replaced "I know Jewish." Thought and the pursuit of knowledge are being sacrificed on the altar of affect.

The author Flannery O'Connor has written: "One of the effects of modern liberal Protestantism has been gradually to turn religion into poetry and therapy, to make truth vaguer and more and more relative, to banish intellectual distinctions, to depend on feeling instead of thought, and gradually to come to believe that God has no power, that he cannot communicate with us, cannot reveal himself to us, indeed, has not done so and that religion is our own sweet invention." Her warning applies to all liberal religions.

The "New Age" Trap

In a Zen parable a man searches for a lost object. He is crawling on his hands and knees when a friend approaches him. "What are you doing?" the friend asks. "I am looking for something that I lost," he replies. "Where did you lose it?" the friend asks. "Over there," the man says, pointing to a nearby place. "Then why are you looking over here?" "Because the light is better here," the man replies. Many Reform Jews are searching for God in a place where the light is rumored to be better—at the intersection of beliefs, philosophies, and techniques called "New Age" religion.

If you visit a Barnes and Noble superstore, you will see what much of American religion has become. There are three bookcases for Judaism; three bookcases for general religion and Christianity; three for general inspiration; two each for Bible, eastern philosophy, and myth; and nine bookcases for New Age. The New Age menu is diverse, including spiritualism, astrology, and psychic phenomena; alchemy, tarot, goddess worship, and Wicca (witchcraft); out-of-body experiences, near-death experiences, and reincarnation; angels, Satanism, and the occult; the channeling of spiritual energy and faith healing; yoga and transcendental meditation; holistic health; unorthodox psychotherapeutic techniques; and healing crystals. New Age follows the time-hallowed American proclivity for creating new religions. It has been called "microwave" religion—instant karma.

Not all New Age religion is incompatible with Judaism. Jewish mysticism is clearly the major point of contact. Long before books about angels became a mega-industry, Judaism taught (or rather sang) about angels. Shabbat opens with a song of welcome to the *malachei ha-shareyt*, the ministering angels. Long before the current healing fad, Judaism recognized the healing power of prayer combined with traditional medicine. Long before New Age speculation, Judaism acknowledged the immortality of the soul, and the Talmud records near-death experiences. Long before New Age, Judaism developed rich traditions of mysticism and meditation. Even astrology is not foreign to the Jewish experience. The Talmud and Midrash discuss the Jewish implications of the zodiac; in Israel tourists can visit a glorious mosaic of the zodiac on the floor of the ancient synagogue at Bet Alpha.

Blurring Boundaries

Despite these cultural and religious parallels, Judaism stands in fundamental opposition to the pantheism that is characteristic of New Age teachings. If God is in everything, then everything is holy and nothing is profane. New Age speaks of "getting in touch with one's inner voice" or "following your bliss." But "following your bliss" is the antithesis of living in covenant.

A Jewishly involved teenager in New Jersey wonders whether it is permissible to observe Lent. "Isn't it about spiritual cleansing?" she asks. A young Jewish woman inquires on the Internet whether she can be a wicca (witch) and still be authentically Jewish.

The multicultural thrust of New Age encourages a smorgasbord approach to ritual. Everyone's traditions, symbols, and stories are mixed into a cauldron and somehow expected to meld into a meaningful universal religion. Such experiments didn't work for medieval alchemists, and it won't work for religious multiculturalists either.

Reb Zalman Schachter-Shalomi, the guru of New Age Judaism, treats mystical Judaism as the Jewish version of universal spirituality, effectively blurring the boundaries between the way of Torah and other religious approaches such as Hinduism, Buddhism, and Sufism. To quote Schachter-Shalomi, "Monotheism was a big step out of polytheism. But now, with our increased access to higher states of consciousness, we have to evolve to pantheism."

Worship of the Self

If spirituality is about "whatever turns you on," then why be Jewish? Appreciating the poetry and devotional intensity of other faiths is commendable, but religious syncretism is a dead end. If "spiritual" is whatever you need it to be, then the entire notion of peoplehood becomes outmoded and parochial.

In a *Doonesbury* cartoon the hip reverend is reviewing the church schedule. "OK, flock, I thought I'd run through this week's activities. This Monday, of course, we have a lecture on nutrition from Kate Moss' personal chef. Tuesday and Thursday will be our regular 12-step nights…. Sex addiction…[is] on Friday at 6:30 pm, right after organic co-gardening. Also, a special treat— Saturday night will be aerobic male-bonding night! So bring your sneaks. Any questions?" "Yes, is there a service?" "Canceled. There was a conflict with the self-esteem workshop."

We Jews may not be running self-esteem workshops in our synagogues, but the cult of "me" is quietly present. Many contemporary Jews find spirituality in the life cycle rather than in the festival cycle. They believe the synagogue exists exclusively for their own life moments—especially bar/bat mitzvah.

Reform Jews who struggle with the meaning of spirituality would do well to hear the cautionary words of writer Cynthia Ozick:

> The Jewish way is to feel responsibility to your fellow-creatures, not to be lifted above them by special intuitive or magical gifts of Divine apprehension; to express the Covenantal relationship by fel-

low-feeling in peoplehood, in duty, and in deed, not to make it secondary to subjective longings; to distinguish between the holy and the profane, not to wash away the holy by finding it everywhere in a great flood of undifferentiated and ubiquitous magical appearance; to attempt to control the self, not to follow the unyoked self's demand for equation with the forces of the universe.

Authentic Reform Spirituality

What, then, is authentic Reform Jewish spirituality? First, spirituality is about God. To speak to God is to acknowledge that we are not about everything, but about something (or Someone). The Jewish spiritual search is about that which is inner, deeper, higher, and historic; the search for that which transcends the moment and individual need. It is simply not enough to speak of inwardness. The inward must connect to God.

Spirituality is about *kedushah*, holiness. *Kedushah* is an attitude towards life. Holiness means to venerate the Divine; to seek out the mystery of God; to sense that some realms are set-apart, unique, linking heaven and earth, and manifesting a shared reality with the Divine. As Rabbi Lawrence Kushner writes, "There are worlds more real than this one. Shabbat is more real than Wednesday. Jerusalem is more real than Chicago. The *sukah* is more real than a garage. *Tzedakah* is more real than income tax."

Holiness means to enter into a conversation about the meaning of life; to ask questions not usually asked in the secular realm; to speak the language of what ought to be, even when it means speaking against the language of what really is.

The following are secular questions: "What are my rights?" "How can I own it?" "What does the world owe me?" "Does it work?" "Will people approve of me?" These are holy questions: "What are my obligations?" "How can I proclaim in my deeds that ultimately God owns everything?" "What do I owe to the world?" "Is this particular behavior right?" "Will God approve of me?"

Reform Judaism must create a lifelong holiness curriculum that speaks of holy places (the home, the synagogue, Jerusalem, the Land of Israel), holy times (Shabbat and festivals, the life cycle), holy relationships (parent/child, husband/wife, teacher/student, sibling/sibling—and even relatively powerful/relatively powerless, which leads us into an involvement with *tikkun olam*), holy ways of speaking (prayer and worship), holy ways of having and giving (*tzedakah* as discipline and life plan), holy ways of eating (an awareness of *kashrut* as a Jewish value), holy ways of reading (Torah and all that flows from it), and holy ways of being (seeing oneself as an inheritor of Jewish history and its lessons). "Holiness" is where "spirituality" becomes "Judaism." Through a disciplined participation in authentic Jewish acts that increase our sense of holiness, we connect ourselves to our people, to our history, to God, and to that ubiquitous, ill-defined thing called spirituality.

Spirituality is about social action. In Judaism there is no dichotomy between the inner and the outer, between action and contemplation. Homelessness, the plight of children, and the loss of compassion and values in our society are spiritual issues. We connect spirituality with social action when "God" becomes more than a cheerleader on the sidelines of our ethical striving. When we legitimately use "God" in a sentence that describes our action, then social action becomes a spiritual path. I am working in this soup kitchen because feeding the hungry is a *mitzvah* ordained by God. I am involved in a black-Jewish dialogue because God created one person at the dawn of creation, and therefore all people are endowed with immeasurable dignity. I am working against violence and pornography in the media because those things violate the image of God.

Spirituality is about study, about an authentic engagement with our people's sacred writings. Study is our way of redeeming ourselves from what the sociologist Peter Berger calls "the homelessness of the mind." Moreover, study is the place where God dwells. The Torah blessing praises God as *Noten Hatorah*—the One Who Gives Torah—in the present tense, rather than the past, teaching us to hear the revealing voice of God through ongoing Torah study.

Spirituality is about the Jewish people. Moments which connect us to the Jewish people are just as holy as moments of prayer, contemplation, and study. I will always remember the shiver down my spine during my first Soviet Jewry rally, realizing at age ten that I was part of a people that transcended my family and synagogue. I feel the same way today walking in Salute to Israel parades, knowing that *am Yisrael chai* (the people of Israel lives) is inextricably linked to *od Avinu chai* (God, our divine parent, lives).

We need to realize what it means to be part of an extended Jewish family. We need to teach others that they are part of a spiritual reality that exists beyond the borders of their own communities, one that reaches back to Abraham and Sarah and forward to the Messianic Age.

Spirituality is about the Land of Israel. Israel must become an integral part of every Jew's spiritual vocabulary. *Eretz Yisrael* is a tangible point of contact between us and God, one of the corporeal signs of the Covenant. When we travel to Israel, Professor Lawrence Hoffman points out, we must go as pilgrims, not as tourists.

Spirituality is about the everyday. We can encounter God in our daily lives, especially in our work. Our workplace, no less than the sanctuary or the place where we study Torah, can become an arena for our spirituality and for the constant demonstration of our deepest values. How do we incorporate Jewish spiritual values into our daily lives? I suggest four ways.

1. *Imitate God.* A doctor imitates God, who is the source of healing. A garment executive imitates God, who made clothing for Adam and Eve in the garden of Eden. Those who console the bereaved imitate God, who buried Moses on Mount Nebo. Parents imitate God's nurturance. Artists imitate God's creativity.

   A weaver told me that when she creates, she goes through the seven days of creation. "First, there is chaos. You hover over your work, just like God did. Then comes the concept, which is the mundane equivalent of 'Let there be light.' As the idea becomes illuminated, you find the form for it. Then you say, 'This is good,' just as God said upon the creation of the world."

2. *Be God's Partner.* Finish the work that God never got around to finishing. Lawyers and judges are God's partners, for "every judge who renders a fair decision is like a partner of the Holy One in the act of creation" (*Shabbat* 119b). Those who work with the frail elderly are God's partners, helping in the restoration of these "broken tablets." Psychotherapists, social workers, and counselors are God's partners in helping people rebuild their lives.

3. *Stand In God's Presence.* Judaism cares more about how you earn your money than what you eat. More than 100 commandments in the Torah are about money; only 24 concern *kashrut*. Caring about ethics at work means refusing to cut corners. It means doing *tzedakah*—leaving the corners of the field for the poor. It means not putting stumbling blocks before the blind, not deceiving those who don't know any better. It means being self-critical, rejecting the vulgarity of, "Hey, it's a jungle out there." To echo Martin Buber, it means treating another person as Thou rather than as It. Even if what you do is not very spiritual, how you do it can be.

4. *Smash False Gods.* Refuse to give into the idols of careerism and workaholism. That means asking aloud: "Why is workaholism the only socially acceptable and laudable addiction in America?" It means not judging ourselves by what we do.

In essence, everything we do in life—whether at home or at work—has spiritual possibilities. Spirituality is about how we talk to and about other people; how we treat our employees; what we eat; how we spend; what we give. The closest Hebrew term for spirituality is *kavanah*—doing things with sacred intentionality. When one lives fully as a Jew, that life becomes a *kiddush Hashem*, a sanctification of the name of God.

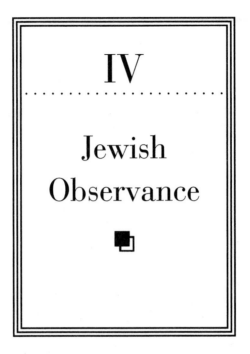

IV

Jewish Observance

How We Celebrate

SIMEON J. MASLIN

The most characteristic element of any religion is its celebration of sacred time. S. R. Hirsch, one of the leaders of nineteenth-century traditional Judaism, wrote: "The catechism of the Jew is the calendar." What he meant was that each of the special days that punctuates the Jewish year teaches us something basic about Judaism. The observance of each of these days is a *mitzvah*, and each one is an essential part of Reform Judaism.

The Jewish calendar that determines the dates of our holy days and festivals today is substantially the same as the calendar that was ordained by the rabbis of the first century. We can find vestiges of earlier lunar months in the Bible, but the months that we generally refer to as the "Hebrew" months originated in about the fifth century B.C.E.

There are twelve months in our religious calendar: Tishri, Cheshvan, Kislev, Tevet, Shevat, Adar, Nisan, Iyar, Sivan, Tamuz, Av, and Elul. The first day of each of these months, Rosh Chodesh, is determined by the appearance of the new moon and is traditionally observed as a semi-holiday. Unlike the Islamic lunar calendar, which disregards the solar seasons, the Jewish calendar is adjusted to the sun by the addition of an extra month, Adar II, approximately every three years.

Each Jewish date and, of course, each Sabbath and festival begins on the eve of the prescribed day. We begin our consideration of sacred time with Shabbat.

Shabbat

Shabbat is the Hebrew word for the Sabbath or Saturday. It is, of course, the only sacred day in Judaism that occurs every week, and it is also the only holy day prescribed by the Ten Commandments. Biblical tradition teaches that human beings must rest on Shabbat because "God blessed the seventh day and declared it holy."

Shabbat is a unique Jewish contribution to our civilization. It is a weekly respite from endless toil and competition. Interrupting the pursuit of wealth and power, it turns the Jew toward the meaning of human existence. Given a day without labor, the individual can concentrate on being a creature fashioned in the divine image.[1]

We observe Shabbat as a day of rest, joy, and holiness. It is a day on which we are encouraged to set aside our daily labors so that we can more fully enjoy our families and our Jewishness.

There are literally scores of *mitzvot* prescribed for Shabbat. Among them are:

- Welcoming Shabbat in our home on Friday evening with a festive dinner, including the blessing of candles, the blessing of family members, *Kiddush* (sanctification of the day) over wine, *Hamotzi* (thanks for food, recited over challah), Shabbat table songs, and *Birkat Hamazon* (grace after meals).

- Refraining from work, shopping, and other workaday activities.

- Joining a congregation in prayer on Friday evening and/or Saturday morning.
- Studying Torah with family or friends.
- Enjoying the day with family or friends.
- Concluding the day with *Havdalah,* a brief ceremony that separates Shabbat from the work week.

Rosh Hashanah

Rosh Hashanah is the Jewish New Year. It is one of the two *Yamim Noraim*—Days of Awe—and it introduces a ten-day period of penitence and introspection. Jewish tradition identifies Rosh Hashanah as the day of divine judgment, and the prayer book metaphorically describes God as sitting in judgment of every human being. Rosh Hashanah emphasizes the concept of individuals as free agents, responsible for the choices that they make and capable of *teshuvah*—repentance.

The theme of Rosh Hashanah is that in spite of human weakness, "the gates of repentance are always open." The struggle for righteousness never ceases. The *mitzvot* and customs of Rosh Hashanah are designed to help Jews enter into the new year with a new spirit so that they might be "inscribed in the Book of Life and Blessing." [2]

Among the *mitzvot* for Rosh Hashanah are:

- Welcoming Rosh Hashanah in our home with the appropriate blessings for the candles, wine, and challah, and a festive dinner.

- Reciting the special prayer for a sweet year over apples dipped in honey.
- Joining a congregation in prayer during Rosh Hashanah services.
- Hearing the *shofar* blown in the synagogue.
- Refraining from work, school, shopping, and other workaday activities.

Yom Kippur

Yom Kippur, the Day of Atonement, is considered by most Jews to be the most sacred day of the year, the "Sabbath of Sabbaths." It is the second of the *Yamim Noraim*, and it concludes the Ten Days of Penitence that begin with Rosh Hashanah.

The grandeur of the liturgy and music adds to the drama and seriousness of the day. From *Kol Nidre*, the first prayer on the eve of Yom Kippur, to the last triumphant note of the *shofar* at the conclusion of *Neilah*, the purpose of Yom Kippur is to move us toward reconciliation with God and our fellow human beings.[3]

Among the *mitzvot* for Yom Kippur are:

- Attempting to reconcile ourselves with friends and family members whom we might have offended in the past year.
- Partaking of a meal before the Yom Kippur Eve service in preparation for the fast day and concluding the meal with the blessing of the festival candles.
- Fasting, if possible, from the eve of Yom Kippur

through the conclusion of services the following evening.

- Joining a congregation in prayer on the eve of Yom Kippur (*Kol Nidre*) and during the several services of the next day.

- Refraining from work, school, shopping, and other workaday activities.

- Attempting to achieve *teshuvah*—repentance for the errors and omissions that alienate us from God.

- Making a gift of *tzedakah,* particularly toward the nurture of the hungry and homeless.

- Memorializing partners and other loved ones during the *Yizkor* memorial service.

Sukot

Sukot, the Feast of Booths (or Tabernacles), is a weeklong holiday that falls just five days after Yom Kippur. It is one of the *Shalosh Regalim*, the Three Pilgrim Festivals, which were celebrated in antiquity by pilgrimages to the Temple of Jerusalem. Like the other two *Regalim*, Pesach and Shavuot, Sukot has both agricultural and historic significance.

The mood of Sukot is particularly joyous. Its beautiful symbolism of the successful harvest provides a welcome change of religious pace from the solemn days of prayer and introspection of Rosh Hashanah and Yom Kippur. Sukot is specifially designated as *Zeman Simchatenu*, the Season of Rejoicing.[4]

Among the *mitzvot* for Sukot are:

- Preparing for the festival by building and decorating a *sukah*—a harvest booth—at home or helping to build and decorate the *sukah* at the synagogue.

- Welcoming Sukot in our home (or in our own *sukah*) with a festive dinner, including appropriate blessings for the candles, wine, and challah and for "dwelling" in the *sukah*.

- Refraining from work, school, shopping, and other workaday activities on the first day of the festival.

- Attending festival services in the synagogue.

- Reciting the blessing over the *lulav* and *etrog*—the palm branch and citron—which, along with the *sukah*, are the symbols of the festival.

- Thanking God for the sustenance that we derive from our bountiful harvests.

Atzeret/Simchat Torah

Atzeret/Simchat Torah concludes the fall festival season and is celebrated as both the last day of Sukot and as a holy day in its own right, "the eighth day of Sacred Assembly." Like Sukot, it, too, is designated as *Zeman Simchatenu*, the Season of Rejoicing. The services for the festival focus on the conclusion and resumption of the annual cycle of Torah readings. In most Reform congregations this holiday is referred to simply as Simchat Torah.

Atzeret/Simchat Torah is the day on which we finish reading the last verses of Deuteronomy and immediately begin again with the first verses of Genesis. The Torah scrolls are removed from the ark and carried around the synagogue. The celebration is one of unbridled joy as we express our happiness at having lived to complete the reading of the Torah yet another time and to begin reading it again.[5]

Among the *mitzvot* for Atzeret/Simchat Torah are:

- Welcoming Atzeret/Simchat Torah in our home with the appropriate blessings for the candles, wine, and challah, and a festive dinner.
- Discussing with family and friends, especially with children, the importance of reading the entire Torah each year.
- Attending festival services in the synagogue.
- Refraining from work, school, shopping, and other workaday activities.
- Participating in the *hakafot*, the joyous procession of Torahs and flags around the synagogue.
- Listening to the final verses of Deuteronomy and the opening verses of Genesis.
- In those congregations where the *Yizkor* memorial service is recited, joining in the remembrance of parents and loved ones.

Chanukah

Chanukah is the eight-day winter festival that commemorates the victories of the Maccabees over the Hellenistic Syrian forces around the year 164 B.C.E. These victories enabled the Jews to reestablish their independence and to rededicate the Temple in Jerusalem to the worship of God. Although Chanukah is traditionally celebrated as a "minor" holiday, it has increased in importance in Western countries due to its proximity to Christmas. Chanukah is a symbol of the eternal struggle of the Jewish people to remain Jewish in a non-Jewish world.

Chanukah celebrates more than the end of an unsuccessful attempt by an outside power to destroy Judaism. The threat to Judaism was both internal and external. The assimilation to Hellenistic culture was so great that certain elements within Jewish society sought to become fully assimilated at the expense of their own unique Judaic culture. The resistance of the Maccabees and their allies to the blandishments of assimilation preserved Judaism.[6]

Among the *mitzvot* for Chanukah are:

- Kindling the Chanukah candles at home on each of the eight nights of Chanukah with the appropriate blessings and readings and discussing the significance of the festival and the lights.

- Displaying the *chanukiyah* (Chanukah menorah) so that it can be seen from outside the house.

- Celebrating the holiday with *dreidel* games and special foods (e.g., *latkes* or doughnuts) cooked in oil.

- Giving modest gifts, especially coins, to children.

Purim

Purim celebrates the events described in the biblical Book of Esther. Central to the religious celebration of the holiday is the reading of the *Megillah* (Scroll of Esther) in the synagogue. But Purim also includes a carnival-like celebration that usually involves masks, costumes, and humorous performances and recitations derived from the victory of Queen Esther and her cousin Mordecai over the nefarious schemes of the wicked Haman. Although it is not certain whether the events described in the Book of Esther are fact, fiction, or a combination of the two, the story provides a powerful annual reminder about the evils of intolerance and blind hatred.

The story of Purim is about hunger for power and about hatred born of the Jews' refusal to assimilate and their unwillingness to compromise religious principle by bowing before secular authority.

Purim recalls the danger of minority status. Hatred of the foreigner and the stranger is still prevalent throughout the world. Anti-Semitism has not disappeared, but despite everything, the Jewish people have survived.[7]

Among the *mitzvot* for Purim are:

- Listening to the reading of the *Megillah* (Scroll of Esther) in the synagogue.
- Rejoicing at Purim carnivals or parties in the synagogue or at home.
- Sending gifts of food—*mishloach manot*—to friends and family.
- Giving *tzedakah* to the poor.

Pesach

Pesach, or Passover, marks the beginning of the spring. It is one of the Three Pilgrim Festivals, and it commemorates the anniversary of the exodus of the Israelites from Egyptian slavery. Its festive family dinner and service, the *seder*, is possibly the most beloved and most observed of all Jewish rituals. Tradition prescribes the eating of unleavened bread, matzah, during the seven days of Pesach, along with other rituals that are intended to remind us we were slaves and God redeemed us, along with our Israelite ancestors.

The liberation of the Jewish people from Egyptian bondage has become a powerful symbol of redemption—not only the redemption of the Jewish people but the redemption of the entire world. Pesach is a constant reminder of our responsibility to those who are oppressed or enslaved physically, intellectually, or ideologically. On Pesach we express our solidarity with other members of the Jewish community who are unable to celebrate Passover in freedom. The experience of redemption in the Passover celebration should inspire all Jews to assist in the future redemption of humanity.[8]

Among the *mitzvot* for Pesach are:

- Preparing the home for the seven-day festival by removing leavened products and substituting matzah and other kosher for Passover foods.

- Reviewing the *Haggadah*—its instructions, dramatic text, and songs—before the *seder* so that the festive occasion will be as meaningful and as beautiful as possible.

- Conducting a *seder* on the first night (some families conduct *sedarim* on the first two nights), with special regard to the traditional symbols, foods, narrative, and songs.

- Paying particular attention to insure the comprehension of the holiday by the children who are present at the *seder*, answering their questions and involving them in the narrative and songs.

- Inviting friends and neighbors to join us at the *seder*.

- Attending festival services in the synagogue on the first and seventh days.

- Eating matzah and avoiding leavened foods through the seven days of the festival.

- Refraining from work, school, shopping, and other workaday activities on the first and seventh days of the festival.

- Observing the seventh day with the appropriate blessings for the candles, wine, and matzah and a festive dinner.

- Joining in the seventh-day *Yizkor* memorial service in those congregations where *Yizkor* is recited.

Shavuot

Shavuot, one of the Three Pilgrim Festivals, means "Weeks." It occurs exactly seven weeks after the beginning of Passover, and it is celebrated as both the anniversary of the Revelation (i.e., the giving of the Torah) and the festival of the early harvest (or "first fruits"). Some people refer to Shavuot as Pentecost, based on its occurrence fifty days after the eve of Passover. Because of Shavuot's relationship to the revelation at Mount Sinai, Reform congregations hold their Confirmation services on this holiday, emphasizing the willingness of Israel, then and now, to enter into a covenant with God.

On Shavuot the Jewish people celebrate their covenantal relationship with God and reaffirm their commitment to a Jewish life of study (*talmud torah*) and of practice (*mitzvah*). The significance of the events at Sinai derives not only from the receiving of *mitzvot* but also from their acceptance, as is illustrated in Israel's response, "*na'aseh venishma*," "we will faithfully do." Sinai represents a constant effort to confront life and history in light of this covenantal relationship.[9]

Among the *mitzvot* for Shavuot are:

- Welcoming Shavuot in our home with the appropriate blessings for the candles, wine, and challah, and a festive dinner.

- Decorating our home and/or synagogue with greenery, fruits, and flowers that represent the early harvest.

- Attending festival services and Confirmation ceremonies at the synagogue.

- Listening to the reading of the Ten Commandments from the Torah and the reading of the Book of Ruth, with its message of love and loyalty to the Jewish people.

- Refraining from work, school, shopping, and other workaday activities.

- In those congregations where the *Yizkor* memorial service is recited, joining in the remembrance of parents and loved ones.

Other Special Days

Tishah Be'Av, the ninth day of Av, is the date assigned by biblical and talmudic traditions to the destruction of Jerusalem and the First Temple by the Babylonians in the year 586 B.C.E. and the destruction of Jerusalem and the Second Temple by the Romans in the year 70 C.E. It is observed by many Jews as a day of mourning, fasting, and the reading of the Book of Lamentations.

Tu Bishvat, the fifteenth day of Shevat, is celebrated as the New Year for Trees, especially in Israel, where the day is devoted to the planting of trees. In recent years reforestation and the protection of the environment have become the focus of the day, and the celebration of the holiday includes eating fruits that grow in Israel.

As a result of the events of the twentieth century, two more special days have been added to the Jewish calendar, one joyous and the other tragic.

Yom Ha'atzmaut is Israel Independence Day. For Jews, Israel is much more than a nation. Its rebirth marks a new era in Jewish history, an era of cultural and national renaissance with profound spiritual significance. As the homeland of the Jewish people, Israel is a symbol of the unity of our people and of the responsibility of each Jew for the welfare and security of every other Jew.

The Reform movement has declared Yom Ha'atzmaut to be a permanent annual festival and has a special service for the day in *Gates of Prayer*. It is a *mitzvah* to mark Yom Ha'atzmaut with prayer, *tzedakah* for Israeli institutions, and participation in communal celebrations of the day.

Yom Hashoah is Holocaust Day, observed on the anniversary of the uprising in the Warsaw Ghetto in

1943. It is a *mitzvah* to remember the 6 million *kedoshim*, martyrs to the inhuman hatred of the Nazis and their anti-Semitic allies, and to mark the day with prayer, *tzedakah*, readings from the literature of the Holocaust, and the kindling of memorial candles. There is a special service for Yom Hashoah in *Gates of Prayer.*

Several other special days appear on the traditional Jewish calendar. References to them can be found in *Gates of the Seasons.*

Origins of Our Symbols

BERNARD M. ZLOTOWITZ

The origin of most Jewish symbols is shrouded in mystery. Scholars agree, however, that Jewish symbols and customs derive from the cultures in which Jews lived.

The Star of David

The Star of David (*Magen David*, literally, "shield of David"), for example, is identified in Western nations exclusively with the Jews, but Muslims regard it as a traditional decorative design. When the Ottoman Sultan Suleiman I (1494–1566) erected the wall around Jerusalem, he put the six-pointed star on the North Wall as one of many designs. In Morocco this popular North African symbol appears on their ten-franc coin.

Dating back to antiquity, the six-pointed star appeared on a column in the Capernaum Synagogue (on the western shore of the Sea of Galilee) of the third century C.E. Some scholars date its first appearance well before that to the second century B.C.E. According to one theory, when the Jews fought the Greeks they adopted the delta, the Greek letter "D," because it stood for David, Israel's great warrior king who brought peace to all Israel and expanded its borders. Then they imposed an inverted delta over the first, representing the Messiah, a descendant of King David, who would bring eternal peace to Israel. The symbol resulting from the two triangles, a symbol of the past combined with a symbol of the future, was an expression of the warriors' belief that David and his descendants would protect them.

In all probability, however, the symbol was merely a geometric design that was adopted by the Jewish people. Nowhere in rabbinic literature is the *Magen David* mentioned. In fact, it did not come into general use as a Jewish symbol until the nineteenth century, when it began to appear on tombstones and synagogues. It was adopted in 1897 by the World Zionist Congress at Basle, Switzerland, as an identifying symbol for Jews.

The Menorah

The menorah, on the other hand, is more easily traceable as a Jewish symbol. We first read about this seven-branched candelabrum in the Torah when Bezalel, the great biblical artisan, is commissioned to design one for the Tabernacle, the portable sanctuary in the Sinai wilderness. This menorah was placed between ten others that Hiram made for Solomon's Temple in Jerusalem. In the Second Temple there was only one menorah; it was destroyed by the Syrian King Antiochus (reigned 175–164 B.C.E.) and was later replaced by Judah Maccabee. This menorah is depicted on the Arch of Titus in Rome, which was built to commemorate the Roman destruction of the Second Temple. The belief that the lights of the menorah stand for the planets or the seven eyes of God wandering over the earth may account for its becoming the symbol adopted by the State of Israel in its wish to be a "light unto the nations." Some scholars have agreed that symbolically the menorah represents the six days of creation, with the center light representing the Sabbath.

Josephus, the Jewish historian of the first century, claimed that in the Jerusalem Temple only the center lamp burned continuously. It was called the *ner hama'aravi* (the western lamp), which in the Book of Samuel was called *ner Elohim* (the lamp of God). When the Temple was destroyed, the rabbis decreed that in remembrance of the center lamp, the synagogue should have a *ner tamid*, a perpetual lamp, burning before the ark. Following the destruction of the Temple, the rabbis forbade the use of the seven-branched menorah in the synagogue so that it would not be confused with the menorah of the Jerusalem Temple, a practice followed today by Orthodox and a number of Conservative congregations but rarely by Reform.

The shape of the menorah suggests a tree. In antiquity its symbolic use was probably influenced by the cosmic tree of the Sumerians, which was the symbol of life and light. But even though in the remote past the menorah may have been borrowed from another culture, it is an authentic Jewish symbol, representing for over two millennia the ideals of Judaism, the giving of light and life.

The Mezuzah

Hardly a Jewish home is without its *mezuzah* on the front doorpost. The Bible enjoins us to write the *Shema* "on the doorpost of your house and your gates" (Deuteronomy 6:9). Within the *mezuzah* is a parchment scroll inscribed with the words from Deuteronomy 6:4–9 and 11:13–21 (not the Ten Commandments as some people believe), written in twenty-two lines by a scribe in the same manner in which a Torah scroll is written. The parchment is then rolled up and put into a wooden, metal, or plastic box and affixed in a slanted vertical position on the right side of the door as you enter. (Rashi claimed it should be vertical, but his grandson Rabbenu Tam claimed it should be in a horizontal position. Thus, the slanted compromise was reached.) On the other side of the parchment the word *Shaddai* (Almighty) is inscribed and can be seen through an opening in the container. The rabbis attached great importance to the *mezuzah* as a physical reminder of the Jew's responsibility to fulfill God's commandments.

Some Jews believe the *mezuzah* can ward off evil spirits. So pervasive was the belief of the potency of the *mezuzah* that, according to an apocryphal account, during the Middle Ages Christians bought them to put on their doorposts to ward off the Black Plague.

Other peoples share this practice of placing the deity's name, or a quote from a sacred text, on the entrance to their homes as a means of protecting them from harm. Muslims put the name of Allah, a verse of the Koran, or something similarly sacred, over their doors. The ancient Egyptians observed a similar custom. It is hard to say which group borrowed from whom.

Tzitzit

Just as the *mezuzah* is a reminder to walk in the right path, so *tzitzit* serve to "remember all the commandments of God and do them" (Numbers 15:39). How do the *tzitzit* serve as reminders of all the commandments? Here we have to revert to *gematria*. The numerical value of *tzitzit* is 600. But there are 613 commandments. The difference is made up by the eight threads and five knots. Originally one of the threads (fringes) was blue "because this color resembles the sea, the sea resembles the sky, and the sky resembles the throne of glory" (*Menachot* 43b). But this was discontinued because the process of getting the proper shading of blue was lost and the rabbis forbade its use. So the blue was introduced as stripes in the *talit*, which later inspired the blue and white colors of the Israeli flag.

The Talit

The Bible requires that men wear fringes on four-cornered garments. When this type of garment went out of style, the wearing of *tzitzit* was endangered. So a special four-cornered garment was introduced to allow observance of this *mitzvah*. Worn under a shirt at all times, this garment is called *talit katan* (a miniature *talit*) or *arba kanfot* (four-cornered garment), not to be confused with the *talit*.

The large *talit* originated as a distinctive garb for the rabbi, much as an academic robe identifies a scholar. In time the lay leaders took a fancy to it and eventually the rest of the male population began to wear it at worship services. In Eastern Europe only married men wore it, enabling the women to know which men were eligible. Today Orthodox Jewish males over thirteen years of age wear the *talit* as a sign of adulthood and, when they die, are buried in it.

The *talit* certainly is a distinctive Jewish symbol. Why it captured the imagination of the Jew remains as mysterious as the adoption of *tefilin* as a unique Jewish symbol. [Editor's note: In the spirit of Reform Judaism, a reexamination and a search for meaning in traditional ways have led many Reform Jews back to the wearing of the *talit*. True to the essence of Reform Judaism, this applies equally to men and women.]

Tefilin

Archaeologists discovered *tefilin* in the Bar-Kochba caves, which makes their use at least two thousand years old. Orthodox and Conservative males are required to put on *tefilin* (leather boxes with straps for head and arm containing parchment scrolls of selected biblical passages) once they reach the age of thirteen years and one day. Though the requirement of wearing *tefilin* is ascribed to four biblical passages (Exodus 13:1–10, 11–16; Deuteronomy 6:4–10, 11:13–21), this *mitzvah* is derived from the commandment "and you shall tie them for a sign upon your hand and they shall be for frontlets [or memorials] between your eyes" (Deuteronomy 6:8).

However, whether this really means *tefilin* as we know it today is a matter of dispute. One scholar has suggested that "[the memorials] between your eyes" meant the placing of ashes upon the forehead as a sign that one had brought an offering to the Temple. [Editor's note: Today, Reform Jewish men and women may choose whether or not they wish to wear *tefilin*.]

The Kipah

Another practice shrouded in mystery is the wearing of a head covering, or *kipah*, a custom that was not enshrined as law until the sixteenth century, when Joseph Karo declared in the *Shulchan Aruch* that a man is not permitted to walk four cubits (about seventy-two inches) with head uncovered.

In biblical times bareheadedness among men was customary. The stories of Samson (Judges 13–16) and of Absalom (2 Samuel 14:26) speak of their hair as a crown of glory, indicating that their heads were uncovered. The priests covered their heads as a sign of dignity, and the High Priest wore a golden diadem on his miter inscribed with the words "Holy unto the Lord."

The wearing of a head covering during worship might have been influenced by the practice of Roman priests, who offered sacrifices with covered heads. Muslims, too, worship with heads covered. The Talmud speaks of the desirability of covering one's head as a sign of fearing God. In one passage Rabbi Huna, son of Rabbi Joshua, would not walk four cubits bareheaded, saying: "The *Shechinah* [Divine Presence] is above my head" (*Kiddushin* 31a).

According to the Talmud (*Berachot* 60b), the morning blessing, "Blessed art Thou, O Lord...who crowns Israel with beauty," was written to add sanctity to the act of covering the head. But the practice of wearing a head covering never fully gained acceptance in the talmudic period, remaining a status symbol and a sign that a man was married. When Rabbi Huna met the great scholar Rabbi Hamnuna, he was amazed that he was not married, as noted by the absence of any head covering (*Kiddushin* 29b).

Centuries passed before the head covering was accepted as a religious symbol. As late as the thirteenth century, it was not customary in France for Jews to cover their heads during worship; yet during the same period in Spain the opposite was true. But by the sixteenth century it became a Jewish law, capturing the imagination of the Jewish people and gaining universal Jewish acceptance. Elijah of Vilna (1720–1797), known as the Vilna Gaon, acknowledged that the practice is based on custom.

Reform Judaism in America (unlike Reform in Europe) adopted the practice of this country: to remove one's hat and stand bareheaded before persons of repute. Thus, Reform congregants worshiped God with heads uncovered as a sign of devotion and faith, respect and awe. Today, however, many Reform Jews wear head coverings in the synagogue as a way of affirming Jewish tradition.

Tradition's Table
Reform Mitzvah

LAWRENCE KUSHNER

The problem is not that God no longer speaks," said my teacher, Arnold Jacob Wolf, many years ago, "it is that God doesn't shut up!" This comment is a penetrating insight into the difference between orthodox and liberal Jewish theology.

For Orthodox Jews, God spoke once and for all at Mount Sinai. Not only did God write the Torah and whisper the Talmud, God included in them the necessary mechanisms to anticipate a relevant response to any future legal contingency. God, in other words, no longer speaks because there is nothing left to say. Like all orthodoxies, this view of God's presence in the world is a total and totally closed system.

Liberals require a higher tolerance for surprises. For us, the unavoidability of novelty and our (occasionally arrogant) assumption that what happens to us could not have been anticipated by previous generations (or God!) require a God who can "keep talking." Each generation poses unimaginable questions which demand new answers. Not even the greatest of our sages foresaw electricity, the liberation of women, nuclear winter, or cholesterol. Or, to put it another way, when we hear the same Torah that was given to our ancestors at Sinai, it sounds different.

Our tradition already anticipates our dilemma by offering two legends which immediately strike us as true.

Unfortunately (like orthodox and liberal theology), they are mutually exclusive. First, we believe that whatever happened at Sinai was an event of supreme and unique importance, never to be repeated. God may continue to speak, but (even for staunch liberal Jews) the Torah remains God's longest and best speech. That is why we get so excited on Shabbat mornings when we read it, on Simchat Torah when we begin it again, and on Shavuot when we remember receiving it.

On the other hand, there is also a tradition which (with an equal measure of accuracy) holds that each and every day the Divine Voice issues from Sinai. What was heard then by our ancestors (even staunch Orthodox Jews maintain) can be heard now, today, by us. Right here and right now, God is saying the very same words which were said at Sinai. Not only, then, is the Torah eternally unchanging (the Orthodox myth), it is also always present, always able to be heard anew (the liberal myth).

Eliyahu KiTov, the great Orthodox Israeli philosopher, poses this problem in two classic religious questions.[1] If the Torah is being spoken all the time, then why can't we hear it clearly now (the great problem for Reform Jews), and if the Torah is being spoken all the time, then what makes the revelation at Sinai so special (the great problem for Orthodox Jews)? In his answers to these questions, KiTov offers a daring solution and a profound insight into the nature of religious consciousness. The reason Sinai is so special, he suggests, and the reason we are unable to hear Torah all the time, is because the background noise, static, tape hiss, and muzak of this world create such a racket that they drown out the sound of God's (ever-speaking) voice.

What made Sinai so important was that it was the only time throughout all history when God "silenced the roar." In the language of modern sound recording technology, God, you might say, switched on the Dolby noise reduction system. When the Torah was given, we could hear what had been there (and continues to be here) all along.

God, then, you might say, is the One who enables us to hear what is continuously being spoken at the most primary level of reality, throughout all creation and all time. For this reason, each act of personal religious focus becomes a miniature Sinai.

For our Orthodox brothers and sisters the problem is how to squeeze coherent responses to contemporary social and technological crises from the Torah—how to hear God's voice anew. For Reform Jews, it is how to ascertain it is really God we hear and not the voice of our own convenience disguised as God—that is to say, how to hold fast to our religious lifeline back to Sinai.

For both liberal and Orthodox Jews, part of the answer comes from the chasidic Rabbi Menachem Mendel of Kotzk. Commenting on the curious word order of the passage in Exodus that reads "we will do and we will hear" (it should say "we will hear and then we will do"), Rabbi Mendel explains that some actions simply cannot be understood (heard) until they are performed (done). We do not know what is commanded of us until we try it. By doing we understand.

Jewish tradition might be thought of, then, as a magnificent banquet table, piled high with everything Jews have ever tried to do in response to God. After 3,000 years, it is a very big table. Some of the dishes are immediately tantalizing; if we are not careful, we could fill up on them and leave room for nothing else. (We don't need

God to tell us to honor our parents.) At first glance, others don't look so good; as when we were children, we need to be persuaded to try them. Often when we do, however, we are surprised and delighted to discover that they are delicious. (It might not occur to us to rest every seventh day.) Others we simply may never enjoy, understand, or even get to at all. (The prohibition against mixing linen and wool remains a mystery, but it also remains on the table.)

We are also permitted to place respectfully on the great table one or two recipes of our own creation. If others agree that they are delicious, word will get around and our offering may (after centuries) gradually move toward the center of the table. (Perhaps it is permissible to drive to the synagogue on Shabbat.) But no one is exempt from trying every dish, just as no one is prohibited from reverently offering an addition. In this way, while we may not resolve the logical tension between a God who spoke once and for all at Sinai and a God who continues to speak, we may be able to endure the paradox.

The Roots of Shabbat

BERNARD M. ZLOTOWITZ

According to traditional Jewish belief, the Sabbath has its origin in God's divine command to observe the seventh day as a day of rest and sanctification. Scholars, on the other hand, are divided in their opinion concerning the origin of the Sabbath, though they all agree it was borrowed from another culture. Some scholars contend its origin is Babylonian. The Babylonians believed the seventh, fourteenth, twenty-first, and twenty-eighth days of the month (following the phases of the moon) were evil days and therefore the physician, the oracular priest, and the king ceased all labor on these days. The cessation of work on the day they called *Sabattu* was based upon fear and had no relation to the biblical concept of the Sabbath as a day of rest, joy, and refreshment of the soul.

Other scholars contend the Hebrews borrowed the concept from the Canaanites, whose primitive agricultural calendar was based on a seven-day week. Here, too, the number seven was regarded as evil and unlucky, a potential source of ill fortune to be avoided at all costs. They viewed this final day of the week as a day when evil spirits abounded, and therefore as a day in which human labor would not prosper.

The ancient Hebrews, however, transformed this negative character of the seventh day into one of joy, refraining from labor because it was a day of gladness of spirit. None of the scholarly theories explain how and why the Jews, who were supposed to have borrowed the Sabbath from the Canaanites or Babylonians, accomplished this transformation.

Traditionally Judaism teaches that the Sabbath was unique to ancient Hebrew culture and not influenced by others. It contends that the Sabbath as a day of rest and joy is our special contribution to the world, a gift from the Jewish people to all humankind.

Understanding Shabbat

STEVEN SCHNUR, BERNARD M. ZLOTOWITZ,
AND ARON HIRT-MANHEIMER

Shabbat embodies the essence of Judaism, symbolizing the relationship of the Jewish people to God and to
humankind. So important is the Sabbath that it alone of
all Jewish festivals is mentioned in the Creation story and
in the Ten Commandments; not even Yom Kippur shares
that privilege.

The Ten Commandments appears twice in the Torah,
once in Exodus and again in Deuteronomy. In the first
instance the Fourth Commandment begins with the
words: "Remember the Sabbath day, to keep it holy."
The Sabbath refers to the day God ceased from the labor
of creation, the seventh day. In imitation of God we are
forbidden to work on the Sabbath. This prohibition
extends to slaves, cattle, and strangers in our midst
(Exodus 20:8–11).

The Fourth Commandment in Deuteronomy differs
in two significant ways from its formulation in Exodus.
First, it begins with "Observe (and not "Remember") the
Sabbath day, to keep it holy" (Deuteronomy 5:12–15).
Second, instead of referring to God's resting on the seventh day as a model for human conduct, it cites the
Israelites' Exodus from Egypt as the basis for observing
the Sabbath. The Jews are reminded: "You were a slave
in the land of Egypt and the Lord your God brought you
out from there with a mighty hand and an outstretched
arm; therefore, the Lord your God commanded you to
observe the Sabbath day" (Deuteronomy 5:15).

Shabbat as Covenant

By referring to the Exodus from Egypt, the Fourth Commandment reminds Jews of their covenant with God, the lessons of their history, and the evils of slavery. The Torah, recognizing the ease with which humans enslave themselves to ideas, routines, and to one another, provided the Sabbath as a weekly counterforce. One who never experiences freedom may neither yearn nor strive for it, but the slave who tastes freedom even one day a week will eventually rebel against enslavement.

How the Sabbath was to be observed by the Israelites was first set forth in the Bible in the context of the forty years of wandering in Sinai. The first practical lesson in Sabbath observance involved the gathering of manna in the desert. Sent by God to feed the wandering Israelites, the dew-like sweet bread fell from the heavens every morning except the morning of the Sabbath. On Friday a double portion was provided to last the entire Shabbat. God, through the Sabbath, taught these former slaves how to plan ahead for their future, how to think like free people.

Following their conquest of Canaan, it became customary for the Israelites to offer animal and grain sacrifices on the Sabbath, in keeping with the laws of the Bible (Numbers 28:9–10). It was also common practice on the seventh day to visit a "man of God" or prophet (2 Kings 4:22–23).

Difficult to Observe

Although the Sabbath was deemed in the Bible to be among the most important of Jewish holy days, second only to Yom Kippur, the Fourth Commandment proved difficult to observe. Repeatedly, the Bible echoes God's angry admonition: "You have despised My holy things and profaned My Sabbaths" (Ezekiel 22:8). The prophets linked Israel's fate to Sabbath observance. The destruction of the First Temple and the subsequent Babylonian Exile, according to Jeremiah, were the result of Israel's failure to keep the Sabbath (Jeremiah 17:21–27). Even after the Jews returned to Jerusalem to rebuild the walls of their holy city about a century and a half after its devastation, they continued to desecrate the Sabbath. Said Nehemiah: "Did not your ancestors thus and did not our God bring all this evil...upon us and upon this city? Yet you bring more wrath upon Israel by profaning the Sabbath" (Nehemiah 13:18). Shifting the emphasis from admonition to reward, Isaiah called the Sabbath a "delight," promising: "If you refrain from trampling the Sabbath..../And call the Sabbath a delight...I will make you ride upon the heights of the earth. /And I will feed you with the heritage of your father Jacob" (Isaiah 58:13–14).

Saving a Life

In the early years of the Maccabean revolt at least one group of Jews refused to defend itself on the seventh day, preferring death to Sabbath desecration (1 Maccabees 2:32–38). Following this tragedy, Mattathias and his sons set a precedent that would be expanded in the Talmud: to save a life or to defend one's life it is permissible to violate the Sabbath (1 Maccabees 2:41).

Many of the Sabbath rituals originated during the

period of the Talmud. Elaborating on the Bible's general and often vague Sabbath prohibitions, the Talmud sought to formalize and thereby protect its observance, listing in detail all acts prohibited on Shabbat. To the thirty-nine types of forbidden labor—modeled on the tasks performed by the priests in constructing the tabernacle (Exodus 31)—the rabbis added "fences" designed to minimize the likelihood of violating the Sabbath. Thus, since the rabbis interpreted the Bible to prohibit writing on Shabbat, they also outlawed the carrying of a writing implement on the seventh day.

In the process of clarifying biblical law, the rabbis sought to lessen its severity; for example: "You shall kindle no fire in all your habitations on the day of Shabbat" (Exodus 35:3). A strict interpretation would have prohibited the use of fire or heat in any form for the duration of the Sabbath. The rabbis, however, permitted the use of fire for light or heat, so long as it had been kindled before the onset of Shabbat.

These laws, collected in the Talmud, formed the blueprint for Shabbat observance. Elaborating both on what should not be done in violation of the Sabbath and what should be done to enhance it, the Talmud provides laws concerning travel, work, lighting candles, eating, praying, caring for the sick, sexual relations, childbirth, circumcision, and virtually every aspect of human endeavor that might occur on the Sabbath.

Honoring the Sabbath

Central to the liturgical practices instituted by the rabbis were the recitation of *Kiddush* at the beginning and

Havdalah at the end of Shabbat. These sanctify the Sabbath by setting it apart from the other six days. Honoring the Sabbath, the rabbis taught, consists of preparing for it as if for a royal visit, bathing oneself, cleaning house, and dressing in one's finest clothes. Delight, they said, consists of eating special foods, taking pleasure in one's spouse, resting, and studying Torah. "One who delights in the Sabbath," the Talmud says, "is given one's heart's desires" (*Shabbat* 18b).

Mixed with these laws are the sayings and legends that have enlivened Jewish culture, folklore, and literature for two thousand years. Never losing sight of the prophet Isaiah's description of the Sabbath as a day of delight, the ancient rabbis spoke repeatedly of it as a special inheritance from God, a gift, a blessing, a Bride, a Queen, a foretaste of the world to come.

The sixteenth-century kabbalists of Safed in northern Israel and the Chasidim of eighteenth-century Eastern Europe enhanced the joy of Sabbath observance by expanding on ideas contained in the talmudic literature. Favorite among these was the concept of the Sabbath as a Bride, which was later incorporated in the Sabbath poem "Lecha Dodi" written by the Safed mystic Solomon Alkabetz:

> Come my beloved to meet the Bride
> Let us welcome the presence of the Sabbath
> Come in peace…and come in joy…
> Come, O Bride! Come, O Bride!

The rabbis viewed the Sabbath as the royal road to redemption, saying, "If Israel were to keep two Sabbaths according to their prescribed law, they would immediately be redeemed" (*Shabbat* 118b). That theme prevails to the present day, whether it be redemption from sin through Sabbath prayer or the redemption of one's humanity through rest and reflection.

This belief in the saving power of Shabbat found modern expression in the writings of Ahad Ha-Am, who in 1898 observed: "More than Israel has kept the Sabbath, the Sabbath has kept Israel. Had it not been for the Sabbath, which weekly restored to the people 'soul' and weekly renewed their spirit, the weekday afflictions would have pulled them further and further downward until they sank to the lowest depths of materialism as well as ethical and intellectual poverty."

Idols of Technical Civilization

"On the seventh day," wrote the modern sage Abraham Heschel, "[one] has no right to tamper with God's world, to change the state of physical things." On that day we should set aside our technological mastery of nature. Believing Shabbat to hold out our best hope for progress, Heschel described the seventh day as "one day a week for freedom, a day on which we would not use the instruments that have been so easily turned into weapons of destruction…a day in which we stop worshiping the idols of technical civilization."

Rabbi Irving Greenberg called Shabbat "the temporary anti-reality of perfection." On the Sabbath, he wrote, "all things are seen through the eyes of love, as if all nature were perfect, in harmony with itself, and with us." In Greenberg's view this foretaste of the redemption is not a substitute for redemptive action. "Thanks to Shabbat," he continued, "there is enough fulfillment in the here and now to keep people in motion toward the final consummation…. The world was meant to be perfect. Says the Shabbat: 'Experience that perfection. Now, go and make it happen!' "

Jewish Text Study

AARON PANKEN

Why Bother to Read Jewish Texts?

Judaism can be traced through its writings. In every age there has been Jewish literature, and by reading this literature we are better able to understand our own history, how our culture developed, and how Jewish life changed over time. We can also learn about different legal and religious practices and how they influenced and were influenced by surrounding cultures.

In the past, decisions affecting the well-being and daily lifestyles of the whole community were made by studying Jewish texts. Today, our texts serve not only as history but as inspiration and guidance. As we study ancient texts, we bring new life to them from our modern perspective, just as their ancient wisdom brings new life to ourselves.

With the advent of the printing press and the invention centuries later of the computer, it has become easier for researchers to publish commentaries on the Bible. Today, it is possible to select from literally hundreds of biblical commentaries, ranging from the scientific and critical to the homiletic and spiritual to the purely homiletical. What follows is a list and short description of a few available commentaries on the Jewish Bible. Remember that these are artificial categories and that most collections include some material from every category.

Scientific/Critical Commentaries

These commentaries concentrate on placing the Bible within its archaeological and historical context by comparing the ancient Israelites with surrounding cultures. These works also focus on the development of the language through the use of variant texts and cognate languages. If you are interested in putting together a program on how modern scholars read the Bible, these books might help you:

The Torah: A Modern Commentary and *The Haftarah Commentary*, edited by W. Gunther Plaut, are standard Reform Jewish study tools. These excellent resources include both critical and historical material. The first covers the Torah thoroughly, touching lightly on some of the prophets, parts of whose books appear as *Haftarah* portions. The latter, which contains a new translation by Chaim Stern, comprises and comments on all of the *Haftarah* portions that accompany the weekly Torah readings. Clearly and concisely written, both are excellent tools for developing programs on the weekly Torah and *Haftarah* portions.

Nahum H. Sarna's *Understanding Genesis* and *Exploring Exodus* are excellent resources for understanding the first two books of the Torah in a scientific light. Sarna writes skillfully and explains the Torah portions in plain English, making even difficult passages understandable. Additionally, he incorporates interesting related material from archaeology and the scientific study of those languages closely related to ancient Hebrew.

The Anchor Bible is a large and exhaustive study tool that now has sections on the entire Hebrew Bible and most of the Christian Bible. This multivolume series has textual notes, a (usually) very literal translation, and some commentary on the text. It is an excellent source in English for the scientific study of the Bible. Its only drawback is that it was written by different authors over the period of many years, so there are tremendous stylistic differences between volumes. This is an excellent source for the study of cognate languages close to ancient Hebrew, since the similarities between the languages are often pointed out in the text and notes.

Used with the *The Anchor Bible* or even another biblical source book, *The Anchor Bible Dictionary*, edited by David Freedman, is an excellent reference on specific biblical topics. It is thorough and offers an excellent bibliography after each topic.

The Prophets by Klaus Koch is a small two-volume set, now available in English. This set provides a good background to the history of the prophetic period and keys itself to the various prophetic texts in a clearly understandable way.

Homiletic/Spiritual Material

A homily is the basic unit of a sermon and, therefore, a good place to begin if you want to write sermons. Also, if you are interested in finding engaging texts from the Jewish tradition that are studied in creative, modern ways, this is the section for you.

The Torah: A Modern Commentary and *The Haftarah Commentary*, as mentioned above, are filled with homiletic and spiritual material, making them excellent sources for the weekly Torah and *Haftarah* readings.

Studies in the Books of Genesis-Deuteronomy by Nehama Leibowitz, now translated into English, is an excellent place to look for English translations of related traditional texts for each of the weekly Torah portions. In this six-volume series, there are usually five or six study sessions for each Torah portion that include medieval and modern commentators in an easy-to-read fashion. It is helpful for both text study sessions and personal study of the commentators.

Five Biblical Portraits and *Messengers of God*, both by Elie Wiesel, bring biblical figures into striking reality. These books cover many individuals of significance in the Bible, including, among others, Joseph, Moses, Jonah, and Saul. They are a good source for new inter-pretations of the biblical characters, not necessarily based strictly on the text. Another book, somewhat akin to these is *Biblical Images: Men and Women of the Book*, by Adin Steinsaltz, a well-known Orthodox rabbi and thinker. His images are not only diverse and fascinating, but they include vivid descriptions of such female bibli-cal characters as Ruth, Deborah, Rebecca, and Rachel, making this volume a recommended resource for modern egalitarian study groups.

Lawrence Kushner's *The River of Light: Spirituality, Judaism, and the Evolution of Consciousness* offers a more spiritual approach to the Bible. It follows Abraham's spiritual development through the use of a modern viewpoint. Rabbi Kushner recently completed another volume with Dr. Kerry Olitzky called *Sparks beneath the Surface: A Spiritual Commentary on the Torah*.

Finally, an exceptional English source for legends and stories about biblical characters is Louis Ginzberg's *Legends of the Jews*. This multivolume work contains a truly astounding set of tales and stories, which may be used for almost any kind of study or sermon. The index is also artfully arranged, making Ginzberg's collection extraordinarily user-friendly. Checking the original source becomes necessary, since the way stories are told in Ginzberg can be incomplete. Whatever its faults, Ginzberg's book remains an excellent source for materials that will flesh out your study sessions.

Modern Rabbinic Responsa

Responsa, or *she'elot u'teshuvot*, are rabbinic answers to Jewish questions. There is a vast array of modern responsa addressing problems from the sublime to the ridiculous. In responsa collections, you can find questions on everything from living wills, euthanasia, abortion, and suicide to the use of elevators on Shabbat and the *kashrut* of dishwashers during Pesach. Responsa collections are organized in two basic ways—by topic and by movement.

Responsa of various movements. These are collections published by the various movements within Judaism. The Central Conference of American Rabbis has published an extensive series of responsa, including *Contemporary American Reform Responsa, American Reform Responsa*, and most recently *Teshuvot for the 1990's: Six Years of Reform Responsa*. Each of these provides answers to relevant questions on topics from who is a Jew to the role of non-Jewish parents in bar and bat mitzvah ceremonies. These are most useful to answer questions about everyday life.

Periodically, the Conservative and Orthodox movements publish responsa and studies of interest to us. *The Ordination of Women as Rabbis: Studies and Responsa*, edited by Simon Greenberg, is a perfect example of a well-rounded, in-depth study of the topic of women rabbis. Another fine example, this time of modern Orthodox responsa in English, is J. David Bleich's *Contemporary Halakhic Problems I, II and III*. This collection is a fascinating, wide-ranging introduction to Orthodox responsa. Although you may have to wade through much quotation and abstruse reasoning, Bleich provides a useful guide to understanding the Orthodox viewpoint on legal matters.

Topical responsa. Topical responsa are often your best source for material on a given subject area, such as biomedical ethics. Since most of the complex issues now surrounding medicine developed long after the medieval period (during which time many of Judaism's greatest rabbis wrote the commentaries that guide much of Jewish life today), experts have had to confront questions on how to handle these issues in modern ways. An example of a valuable collection is *Medicine and Jewish Law*, which is not technically a collection of responsa but gives a good sense of the legal and ethical problems facing contemporary Jews. Two other books that come closer to the actual style of responsa are *Jewish Bioethics* and *Marital Relations, Birth Control and Abortion in Jewish Law*.

The books listed above are just a few of the hundreds, if not thousands, available to Jewish students interested in exploring their Jewish heritage. If you're interested in finding out more about your Judaism, about your people's traditions and history, about why Jews keep kosher or how the structure of the service evolved, then just take a walk over to your campus Hillel or library. Look up some of the volumes mentioned above, which are listed in the bibliography below. Speak to your college's reference librarian. Perhaps your school has a Judaica collection. The books mentioned here are just the beginning of what can be an incredible adventure in Jewish learning. It is up to you to take the first step.

Bibliography

The Anchor Bible. Garden City, NY: Doubleday, 1964.

Bleich, J. David. *Contemporary Halakhic Problems I, II and III*. Hoboken, NJ: Ktav Publishing, 1977.

————, and Rosner, Fred, eds. *Jewish Bioethics*. New York: Sanhedrin Press, 1979.

Feldman, David. *Marital Relations, Birth Control and Abortion in Jewish Law*. New York: Schocken, 1978.

Freedman, David, ed. *The Anchor Bible Dictionary*. Garden City, NY: Doubleday, 1992.

Ginzberg, Louis. *Legends of the Jews*. New York: Simon and Schuster, 1956.

Greenberg, Simon, ed. *The Ordination of Women as Rabbis: Studies and Responsa*. New York: Jewish Theological Seminary Press, 1988.

Jacob, Walter, ed. *American Reform Responsa*. Rev. ed. New York: CCAR Press, 1995.

_____, ed. *Contemporary American Reform Responsa*. New York: CCAR Press, 1995.

Koch, Klaus. *The Prophets*. Philadelphia: Fortress Press, 1983.

Kushner, Lawrence. *The River of Light: Spirituality, Judaism, and the Evolution of Consciousness*. San Francisco: Harper & Row, 1981.

_____, and Kerry Olitzky. *Sparks beneath the Surface: A Spiritual Commentary on the Torah*. Northvale, NJ: Jason Aronson, 1993.

Leibowitz, Nehama. *Studies in the Books of Genesis-Deuteronomy*. Jerusalem: World Zionist Organization, Department of Torah Education, 1972.

Plaut, W. Gunther, ed. *The Haftarah Commentary*. Translated by Chaim Stern. New York: UAHC Press, 1996.

_____, *The Torah: A Modern Commentary*. New York: UAHC Press, 1981.

_____, and Mark Washofsky, eds. *Teshuvot for the 1990's: Six Years of Reform Responsa*. New York: CCAR Press, 1996.

Rosner, Fred, ed. *Medicine and Jewish Law*. Northvale, NJ: Jason Aronson, 1990.

Sarna, Nahum H. *Exploring Exodus*. New York: Schocken, 1986.

_____, *Understanding Genesis*. New York: Schocken, 1966.

Steinsaltz, Adin. *Biblical Images: Men and Women of the Book*. New York: Basic Books, 1984.

Wiesel, Elie. *Five Biblical Portraits*. Notre Dame: University of Notre Dame Press, 1981.

_____, *Messengers of God*. New York: Random House, 1976.

V

. . . .

Israel

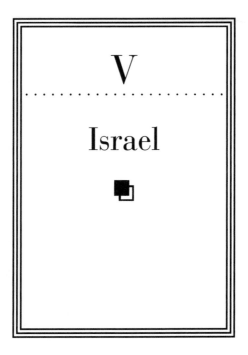

Reform Jews and Israel:
Why We Care

ERIC H. YOFFIE

Terrorist attacks in Jerusalem. Change of government. Middle East peace talks. Hardly a day passes when
these topics are not in the headlines. Israel is news.

Yet whatever our political views on these issues may
be, there are questions that American Jews must face:
Why do we concern ourselves with these matters in the
first place? What does Israel have to do with us? Why
should we care?

The answer is really quite simple. An American Jew
who cares about Judaism and the Jewish people must
care about Israel because Israel helps Jews and strengthens Judaism.

The most dramatic way in which Israel helps Jews is
by providing them with a secure refuge, a place where
they can always go, where they are always welcome, no
questions asked. As American Jews, comfortable and
safe in a democratic country, we often forget how important such a refuge is and how much Jews have suffered
throughout history for not possessing one. The immigra-
tion to Israel of nearly half a million Russian Jews in the
early 1990s and of 15,000 Ethiopian Jews in the 1980s
reminds us that today, as in the past, Jews must have a
place where they can go without first securing the permission of others.

The dramatic rescue of the Ethiopians by the Israeli
government offers an especially compelling example of

this need. These Jews are black and in large measure unskilled and illiterate. Would any government in the world have welcomed them if Israel had not? Clearly not.

Another way of expressing this is to say that for the first time in nearly 2,000 years, Jews have power. In the world in which we live, to be without power is dangerous. Jews outside of Israel must ultimately depend on the good will of others—presidents, kings, dictators—for their survival. Of course, in democratic countries, such as our own, Jews can gain considerable influence through participation in the political process.

But such influence is different in nature and magnitude from the power that is exercised by Israel's Prime Minister as the head of a sovereign Jewish state. Consider the plight of the Ethiopian Jews again. However much American Jews may have wanted to help, they simply did not have the power to open America's shores to the endangered Jewish community of Ethiopia. Nor did any other Jewish community in the world. Only the State of Israel had the power to act on behalf of these Jews, guaranteeing their survival.

It is true, of course, that when one possesses power, one does not always use it wisely. The State of Israel, like other sovereign states, is subject to criticism. Still, rather than coping with being powerless in a dangerous world, Jews are fortunate to be involved in a debate on how Israel's power is to be used.

Another equally important reason for caring about Israel is that Israel strengthens Judaism by offering us the kind of Jewish experience that is not available anywhere else. Israel is the only place in the world where Jews do not have to worry about reconciling their

Judaism with another culture. Only there, where Jews are in the majority, are the problems of assimilation and self-hatred substantially resolved. Only there are the Jews no longer required to explain to non-Jews who they are. Only there can a holiday be fully celebrated as a joyous occasion and not as a strategy for survival. Only there can a Jew live a fully Jewish life without the characteristic self-consciousness of the Diaspora Jew. And only there do we have a setting where the values of our rabbis and prophets can be fully tested against the realities of everyday life.

Judaism can be practiced anywhere, and American Jews have created a vibrant Jewish life. Our Judaism is in no way inferior to the Judaism of Israel, but it is certainly different. If Judaism is to thrive, we need the examples of both communities; we must constantly learn from each other. Israel has many problems. One of the most prominent is the problem of religious fanaticism, a problem that profoundly affects us as Reform Jews. Still, this problem, like so many others that affect Israel and Israel-Diaspora relations, is one that can be solved as long as we offer Israel our caring and loving concern. If the Jewish people are to flourish, both physically and spiritually, the Jewish communities of Israel and the United States must combine their efforts.

If we care only about ourselves and not about Israel, we do not properly serve the Jewish people. If we promote closer ties between our two communities, we assure Jewish survival.

Jerusalem and the Jews

CHAIM RAPHAEL

Why should Jerusalem mean so much to the Jews? It seems enough at first to look at the immensely long historical association between Jerusalem and Jews, something unparalleled in the world. Jerusalem was won as the capital city of the Jewish people three thousand years ago, in the days of King David. For the next thousand years, Jerusalem was the battleground of Jewish experience as recorded in the Bible, the forge of Jewish faith, the rallying point of Jewish identity. When the city was destroyed by the Romans in the year 70 C.E., the loss of the Temple was the symbol of a *galut*—an exile—that was to last for nearly 2,000 years; but this, far from weakening the link, made it even more intense. Centuries of wandering by the Jews gave added poignancy to the memory of their eternal city. Their daily prayers recalled how the psalmists and prophets had sung of its beauty. In joy and sorrow, in legend, folklore, and poetry, Jerusalem was always with them. Life would have become meaningless without the hope that one day they would live again as free people in the city their ancestors had created as "God's dwelling place."

Meaning for Humankind

This extraordinary passion of the Jews for Jerusalem is more than nostalgia. It is a unique way of expressing their feeling that there is some meaning—not only for themselves but for the world at large—in their emergence as a separate people and their survival through the ages.

To understand this, one has to go back to the prophet Isaiah. It was Isaiah, speaking to his fellow Jews more than 700 years before the common era, who saw with extraordinary power how Jewish "distinctiveness," symbolized by the existence of their own Temple at Jerusalem, could give this people a lasting role in world history. To Isaiah, there was a moral principle in the universe that humanity on earth had to grasp. Against the primitive polytheism around them, he argued that the God whom the Jews worshiped at Jerusalem was the creator of all humankind. To "walk in the paths of God" would lead, ultimately, to world kinship. Isaiah's words have rung throughout history: "Nation shall not lift up sword against nation. Neither shall they learn war any more" (Isaiah 2:3–4).

In saying this, he was speaking as a Jew: his vision is announced as "the word of Isaiah concerning Judah and Jerusalem." The two are inextricably linked: "From Zion the Torah will go forth, and the word of God from Jerusalem."

Heart of the People

The idealism of the prophets found its way in later centuries into other religions; but the power of this message would not have come through unless it had been given a national basis in the first place. Even the modern historian Arnold Toynbee, who was not always sympathetic to Jewish ideas, recognized this in his book *The Crucible of Christianity*. It was only when Jerusalem became the undisputed center of Jewish worship, he says, that Jewish identity was given the strength to survive. This will to live emerged triumphantly during the Babylonian Exile. Other nations in these circumstances disappeared. The Jews survived because they had been entrusted, Toynbee writes, with "a unique spiritual treasure." They could not have preserved this "without preserving also the identity of their own community."

Jerusalem was the "home" of this community. In exile the Jews remembered it as the living symbol of what was most precious to them. A famous psalm expresses it movingly:

> By the rivers of Babylon...we wept
> When we remembered Zion...
> We hanged up our harps...
> How shall we sing the Lord's song
> In a foreign country?
> If I forget thee, O Jerusalem,
> Let my right hand forget her cunning.
>
> (Psalm 137)

It was a psalmist also who expressed in one sentence the extraordinary power that the physical presence of Jerusalem has always had over Jews:

> As the mountains are round about Jerusalem,
> So God is round about God's people,
> From this time forth and forever.
>
> (Psalm 125)

Sacred Shrines

The Jews are not alone in having a deep feeling for the majesty of this city. Christians and Muslims have been moved over the centuries by a power that seems to spring, in some mysterious way, from the purity and beauty of its site. Jerusalem became sacred to them as the place where real or legendary events basic to their faiths found enduring expression. Jesus preached in Jerusalem and died there. Muhammad was believed by his followers to have been taken to heaven in a mystic flight from the rock that was once the site of the Temple and is now the site of the great domed Mosque of Omar. Pilgrims and visionaries of the faiths have left powerful evidence of their devotion. The beauty of the city is immeasurably richer because of the churches, mosques, and other historic places that are now part of its tapestry. They have a holiness of their own that the Israelis, ensuring completely free access and protection, deeply respect.

The Only Capital

There is, however, a special element in the Jewish attachment to Jerusalem. The point has been made with great force in a Roman Catholic magazine:

> Jerusalem has always been the only capital for Judaism.... Judaism does not look upon itself exclusively as a people with a religion but as a people who have a religious link with a specific land, the Land of Israel. While Jerusalem has primarily, even exclusively, a religious value for Islam and Christianity, for Judaism it has also a national significance.[1]

The need to hold on physically to Jerusalem never left the Jews. Throughout the long exile there was, in fact, an almost unbroken Jewish presence in the city. Often it was very small, and sometimes nonexistent, as, for example, after the massacres by the Crusaders at the end of the eleventh century. But the urge to set foot on this sacred soil and to live on its hills was too strong to be denied, even though constant persecution made it precarious. From the eighteenth century on, the number of Jewish inhabitants increased steadily. The Jewish quarter of the Old City included many beautiful synagogues. By the middle of the nineteenth century, as the city expanded, the Jews were becoming a majority. Before the outbreak of World War I in 1914, they had risen to 70 percent of the population.

Under British rule, from 1917 on, Jerusalem continued to have a large majority of Jews, though it was a city open to all faiths. How did it happen that when the State of Israel came into being in 1948, the Old City—the most sacred part of Jerusalem—fell into the hands of an unfriendly government, Jordan, which actually barred access to all Jews?

1948–1967: Divided City

It was a tragedy that lies at the heart of the present crisis over the city. After the 1948 Israeli War of Independence, the armistice agreement left each fighting country in possession (broadly) of the areas it was then occupying, but under carefully defined conditions. The kingdom of Jordan, whose forces held the Old City, agreed that access would be granted to all holy places and that the Jews would, in addition, have access to their ancient cemetery on the Mount of Olives and to the great new Hebrew University and hospital buildings on Mount Scopus. Sadly, it has to be recorded that these conditions were not fulfilled. The Jordanians set up barbed wire to keep the Jews out of the Old City. Inside its walls the Jewish quarter was pillaged and sixty-two synagogues were ruined or destroyed. Outside, the old cemetery was desecrated; the precious buildings on Mount Scopus fell into ruins.

For centuries the vision of a return had been expressed in an ancient prayer: "And build Jerusalem, the Holy City, speedily in our days." With an independent state now in existence, Jerusalem in Jewish hands was built up magnificently. By 1967 the population of the city as a whole had risen to almost 300,000, of whom 226,000 (or 76 percent) were Jews. Yet this was a city divided by barbed wire, with the Old City shut off.

In their daily occupations, people are not always aware of the true forces within them. It sometimes takes a crisis to bring them out. There was so much constructive work to be done in Israel in those early years that Jews lived with the paradox of a divided Jerusalem. The full significance emerged, however, during the Six-Day War.

For the soldiers who sprang into battle on the first of the six days—June 5, 1967—the issue could be defined in normal "patriotic" terms. They were fighting for the lives and homes of their people. But when, on the third day, the word came that the Old City was to be liberated, something quite extraordinary seemed to grip these people. Their passion to free the Old City transformed them. For nineteen years exclusion from the Old City had been the price of peace. But now that Jordan had

launched an attack on Israel, the wrong could be right-
ed. The barriers would come down, and Jerusalem
would be whole again. When these Jewish soldiers, after
deeds of incomparable bravery, stood at last facing the
Western Wall, the last surviving relic of the temple, they
knew they had not just won a battle, they had been united with their history. It was a moment of holiness. As the
shofar sounded, many of these tough soldiers found
themselves in tears.

It was the same outside Israel. Jews throughout the
world had trembled for the outcome as the Arab nations
surrounding this little country had mobilized for the
attack. A great sigh of relief went up when the astonishing victories of the first day were announced. But something beyond all this happened when the Holy City was
freed. Jews everywhere left their hearts open as to a
miracle. The prayers of all the Jewish people, past and
present, had been answered. Jerusalem had been
restored to Jewish care and was now once again a united
city.

Open to All

The central purpose of Israeli policy since the Six-Day
War has been to reaffirm the determination that never
again shall Jerusalem be divided, as it had been so tragi-
cally from 1948 to 1967. Politically, Jerusalem is the capital city of the State of Israel; but all who love and revere
this city are completely free to celebrate this feeling. The
holy places of Jerusalem are open to the world under
guarantees that are visibly being kept. As for the administration of the city, it is a matter for the people who live
there, whatever their religious faith. All are given full

democratic rights, not because of "world interest" as expressed by the United Nations but because Israel is a democratic state. Social and economic benefits for all residents are extended equally to all. In effect, the State of Israel is expressing the intention of the U.N. resolutions of 1948–49 that Jerusalem should be a unified, peaceful "open" city. This was frustrated in the intervening years without any action by the U.N. This time the unity of Jerusalem is to be maintained. To preserve the Holy City as a single entity is to preserve civilization.

Living City

But the preservation of Jerusalem, with all its sacred associations, does not mean that the Old City and its immediate surroundings have now to be "frozen" and made unresponsive to human needs. The marvel of Jerusalem is that it is a jewel of the past and, at the same time, a living city of human beings. Its citizens fulfill their role as heirs to a complex tradition, not as "fossils" but with flexibility and imagination. Changes have been taking place all through the centuries. Even in the Old City itself, it is the rich mixture of history and humanity that is so engrossing. The winding streets have a clutter of mixed buildings of all periods. The squares, courtyards, and arches frame vistas of infinite variety. All this bears witness to the adaptability of the many people who have thronged to the city over the years. The settlements and villages outside have also become part of a continuously unfolding scene.

The magic of Jerusalem is that it can absorb and transfuse change. It can continue to grow as a city as long as two absolute priorities are observed. The first is that nothing new must dominate the vision in a crude way. One must still be able to lift up one's eyes unto the hills. The skyline may change, but it must always be a skyline that communicates the peculiar beauty of this area. The other priority is that Jerusalem must never again be divided. It is a city that must exist, and be governed, in unity. When the Israelis in 1967 removed the barbed wire, allowing people of all faiths to walk freely again from one part of the city to another, it was as if the ancient "Destruction" had at last been annealed. In countless numbers the visitors of all nations now turn again toward the city whose stone walls glow golden in the sun. All the visitors have their own memories and receive their own inspiration. For Jews history itself is restored. The psalmist has said it all:

> I was glad when they said unto me:
> "Let us go into the House of God."
> Our feet shall stand within thy gates, O Jerusalem;
> Jerusalem is builded as a city that is
>   compact together....
> Pray for the peace of Jerusalem:
> They shall prosper that love thee.

(Psalm 122)

Don't Hang Up!
Do I Have the Right to Criticize Israel?

DAVID J. FORMAN

During the last year of President Nixon's administration, a rabbi was asked to give the Sunday morning sermon at one of the ecumenical services held at the White House. When word got out that a rabbi had been invited to preach before the President of the United States, the first phone call the rabbi received was from Yitzhak Rabin, Israel's Ambassador to the United States at the time. Rabin proceeded to dictate to the rabbi what he should or should not say about Israel. The rabbi's response was to put the phone down—politely, of course.

When American Jews offer advice to Israel, Israelis do not hang up so politely; they slam the phone down. Israelis believe that Jews living in the Diaspora should not meddle in Israeli affairs—a thesis that, when you think about it, defies all reasonableness.

What is being done in Israel is being done in the name of the Jewish people. Neither Israelis nor Jews can separate themselves from what is happening around them. After all, Israel is the only country in the world for which the Jews are morally and politically responsible. This fact explains why the image of the Jewish people and the perception of Judaism is today determined by how Jews in Israel behave. Israel is the stick by which Jews throughout the world are measured.

Perhaps this is why Rabin felt so free in his attempt to impose his views upon that American rabbi. Israelis are constantly telling Diaspora Jews how to live their Jewish lives—how to educate their children, how to lobby for Israel, how much money to send. Israelis even tell Diaspora Jews who among them can be Jewish! How can Israelis expect American Jews to do their bidding before the U.S. government when they institute policies with which their American counterparts disagree?

Diaspora Jewry and Israel are interdependent. If we Israelis readily issue mandates to Diaspora Jewry, who are we to complain when Diaspora Jews give us advice? Each community may think that the other provides guidance that is not in the other's best interest. And yet each community should feel confident enough in its own ideological commitments and decision-making processes to accept criticism.

If the image of the Jewish people and the perception of Judaism are determined by how Jews in Israel behave, then Diaspora Jews must speak out on issues in Israel, from human rights violations in the territories to minority rights, from religious pluralism to immigrant absorption. In the end, Israel will make its own decisions. But before it does, Israel should at least be aware of the profound effects its actions have upon Diaspora Jewry.

It is painful for Israelis to be criticized by Diaspora Jews. But Jewish moral responsibility compels Jews to urge others not to commit immoral acts. "Whosoever has the capacity to prevent his household from committing a crime, and does not, is accountable for the sins of the entire household" (*Shabbat* 54b). Diaspora Jews have a moral responsibility to challenge those who would compromise Jewish moral principles. It is a responsibility that recognizes no national borders. Moreover, there are practical considerations beyond the moral argument. When the world perceives Israel as a country that abuses human rights, Israel gives anti-Semites outside of its borders greater latitude to receive a public hearing.

At the same time, Diaspora Jews must always keep in mind that they are criticizing another country. Jews abroad must not confuse their existential relationship to Israel with the empirical reality of living there. North American Jews who have not made and do not intend to make *aliyah* ("going up," a term used to refer to emigration to Israel) should at least come to Israel for long stretches of time so that their criticism has the ring of knowledge, integrity, and commitment to it.

Israel, until recently, had been enjoying a wave of worldwide sympathy. Yet even with the recent change in government, Israel continues to take daring risks for peace. As long as Israel stays on this path toward peace, the Diaspora Jewish community will continue to reap the benefits of Israel's positive image. The question is whether Israel is reaping equal benefits from the behavior of Diaspora Jews. Here Diaspora Jews must be prepared to absorb a healthy dose of criticism from Israelis. An incredible lack of Jewish knowledge and commitment, the frightening number of mixed marriages, the spiraling rate of assimilation, the absence (and sometime active flight) from Israel when the Jewish state is endangered all suggest that Diaspora Jewry should reexamine its commitment to Israel before bristling at Israeli criticism.

The Israeli author A. B. Yehoshua once wrote, "Diaspora Jews and Israeli Jews have a common history." In order to adjust to the realities of life in the Diaspora,

Diaspora Jewry had to create a new form of Judaism to fit the American reality. But creating a new Judaism does not mean separating itself from the Jewish past. Israel and Diaspora Jews need each other. If they let their common history splinter, their common destiny may also be sacrificed. Let us not find ourselves in that situation described by our sages: "A man in a boat began to bore a hole under his seat. When his fellow passengers asked him what he was doing, he answered, 'What do you care, am I not boring under my own seat?' " (*Leviticus Rabbah* 4:6).

Israeli and Diaspora Jews have a symbiotic relationship. Both are in the same boat. The way to keep both communities afloat is to be certain that the international phone lines remain open and communication remains honest.

Does Israeli Equal Jew?

RICHARD G. HIRSCH

In modern democracies, where freedom of worship is a basic right, a person's religious identity is not a factor in determining citizenship status. In the United States the principle of separation of church and state prohibits the state from intervening in any matter concerning religion. Therefore, no American law would ever permit, let alone require, government action to define Jewish identity. Indeed, the United States census does not even permit a question about religion.

In only one modern democracy, Israel, is Jewish identity an issue for state discussion. Israel was established as a Jewish state and recognized as such by the United Nations. In July 1950 the new Jewish state enacted one of its first laws—the Law of Return, which states that, upon arriving on Israeli soil, a Jew is entitled to the rights of full citizenship if he or she chooses. On the other hand, for a non-Jew citizenship is not automatic but requires a process of naturalization similar to that in the United States. Related to the Law of Return is the 1949 Law of Population Registration, which requires every inhabitant of Israel over sixteen years old to carry an identity card noting nationality, religion, and citizenship.

The adoption of these two laws generated controversy within Israel, and between Israel and the Diaspora. Initially, each individual upon registration decided how to define himself or herself. In accord with this simple practice, the Minister of Interior, Israel Bar Yehuda, issued a directive in 1958 stating, "Any person declaring in good faith that he is a Jew shall be registered as a Jew and no additional proof shall be required." Regarding children, the directive stated, "If both parents declare that the child is Jewish, the declaration shall be regarded as though it were the legal declaration of the child itself." The Bar Yehuda directive provoked the first major controversy over "Who is a Jew?" The National Religious Party, speaking on behalf of the Orthodox chief rabbinate, contended that the minister of interior's action was contrary to *halachah*, which defines a Jew as a person whose mother is Jewish or who has converted to

Judaism. In protest, the National Religious Party resigned from the coalition government.

Prime Minister David Ben-Gurion established a special ministerial committee to attempt to resolve disputes over registration. At the same time, recognizing that the issue was of intense concern to Diaspora Jewry, Ben-Gurion sent a letter to forty-five of the greatest scholars in the Jewish world, requesting their counsel as to how to deal with the problem. Significantly, more than half the recipients of the prime minister's letter lived in the Diaspora, an implicit recognition that Jews outside Israel have a voice and a stake in actions taken by Israel affecting the personal status of Jews outside Israel's borders. While the responses to Ben-Gurion's questions varied considerably, the vast majority were opposed to separating Jewish national identity from Jewish religion. The government decided, therefore, that it was premature to pass legislation on the subject and issued directives that were not at variance with *halachah*.

The Brother Daniel Case

In 1958 the "Who is a Jew?" issue erupted once again in the famous Brother Daniel case. Brother Daniel, a Carmelite monk living in a monastery on Mount Carmel in Haifa, petitioned the Israel High Court of Justice to become a citizen of Israel according to the Law of Return. Brother Daniel had been born in Poland in 1922 to Jewish parents named Rufeisen, and at his circumcision was given the first name Oswald. He was raised and educated as a Jew in every respect and was active in a Zionist youth movement in preparation for immigrating to Israel. During World War II, he escaped a Nazi prison and evaded recapture by using forged documents certifying that he was a German Christian. Exploiting his Christian identity, he joined the anti-Nazi underground and saved many Jews by warning them of German extermination plans. In fleeing the Nazis, he entered a Christian convent in 1942 and there converted to Christianity. Following the war, he became a monk and entered the Carmelite order, knowing they had a monastery in Palestine. He had never forsaken his aspiration to live in the Land of Israel.

Brother Daniel applied for Israeli citizenship in 1958 under the Law of Return, arguing that, according to Jewish law, a person born a Jew always remains a Jew. His lawyer cited the talmudic dictum: "A Jew, even if he or she has sinned, remains a Jew" (*Sanhedrin* 44a) and contended that even the most Orthodox Jew could not deny that Brother Daniel was a Jew. The Israeli High Court of Justice ruled that the term "Jew" in the Law of Return "has a secular meaning. As it is understood by the ordinary, plain and simple Jew…a Jew who has become a Christian is not called a Jew." In refusing to accept the halachic definition of Jew, the High Court thus gave "Jew" a national definition, reflecting "the healthy instinct of the Jewish people and its thirst for survival."

The Shalit Case

Another landmark decision of Israel's High Court led to the first legislative amendment to the Law of Return. A lieutenant commander in the Israeli navy, Benjamin Shalit, born in Israel, married a non-Jewish woman in Scotland. After the marriage they settled in Israel, where Shalit's wife became a naturalized citizen. Though Mrs.

Shalit never converted to Judaism, the Shalits reared
their two children like other Israeli children, inculcating
in them loyalty to the Jewish people and homeland.
When Commander Shalit filled out the questionnaire for
the Population Registry for his first-born child, in the
space for nationality he entered the word "Jewish" and
left the space for religion blank. The registrar of the
Ministry of Interior struck out the entry for nationality
and in the space for religion he wrote, "Father Jewish,
mother non-Jewish." When the second child was born,
Commander Shalit did not fill in the spaces for religion
or nationality. In the second instance the registrar wrote
in the space for nationality "Father Jewish, mother
non-Jewish." In the space for religion he wrote "not
registered."

Shalit petitioned the High Court of Justice, demanding that the nationality of his children be registered as
Jews and, since both he and his wife regarded themselves as atheists, that in the space for religion the
children be registered as of no religion. Initially the High
Court, understanding the explosive character of the
issue, recommended to the government that it abrogate
the law requiring citizens to enter their nationality and
suggested that only two questions be asked: citizenship
and religion. But the government, concerned about the
internal security problems vis-à-vis Arab citizens of
Israel, rejected the Court's recommendation. The court
had no choice but to render a judgment. On January 23,
1970, in a historic decision and by a 5 to 4 majority, the
court ruled that the registrar had to register the children
as Jewish by nationality even though their mother was
not Jewish.

Law of Return Amended

The decision caused a furor in Orthodox circles. Once again the National Religious Party threatened to withdraw from the coalition government. Prime Minister Golda Meir was besieged by demands to pass legislation nullifying the decision. Even many non-Orthodox Jews feared the decision would be interpreted as sanctioning intermarriage in Israel and abroad. The country, at the time, was engaged in the War of Attrition with Egypt, and a broad coalition government of national unity had been established. Concerned about the stability of the government and the unity of the Jewish people, Prime Minister Meir moved quickly to work out a compromise. After a historic debate in the Knesset, an amendment to the Law of Return was enacted on March 10, 1970, which, for the first time, accepted the definition of the term "Jew" as a person born to a Jewish mother or who has converted to Judaism and is not a member of another religion." The last phrase was to assure that people like Brother Daniel could not be considered as Jews for the purposes of the Law of Return.

During the course of the debate, some of the Orthodox leaders had suggested that the words "according to *halachah*" be inserted after the words "converted to Judaism." Their proposed addition was intended to disqualify recognition of conversions performed by non-Orthodox rabbis outside of Israel. (Since the established Orthodox rabbinate has been given a monopoly in Israel, conversions performed in Israel are registered only if they are performed under Orthodox auspices.) But the Knesset refused to insert the words "according to *halachah*" because it was understood that the majority of conversions outside Israel are performed by Reform and Conservative rabbis. Neither the Knesset nor the government wanted to pass judgment on the religious practices of the major non-Orthodox Diaspora movements abroad, nor did they want to jeopardize the close and interdependent relationship of the Diaspora and Israel. Furthermore, they were keen to keep the gates of Israel open to all potential immigrants, including converts and the progeny of converts of all branches of Judaism.

It was thought that the amendment to the Law of Return would settle once and for all the legal issues of "Who is a Jew?" In effect, the Orthodox view had prevailed against those who preferred a more secular, liberal, nationalistic definition of the term "Jew." However, the State of Israel was to have no respite from the issue. Some Orthodox elements have kept up a steady barrage against the alleged peril of Reform and Conservative conversions. Ever since 1970, the issue of "Who is a Jew?" has come to the forefront after every national election. Why after the election and not before the election? Because no political party has ever won a majority in the Israeli elections for the Knesset. In order to form a government, the party with the largest plurality needs to seek the support of the smaller parties. In almost every case the easiest potential coalition partners are the religious parties. Recognizing that the major party blocs are willing to compromise to gain their support, the religious parties make demands far beyond what their electoral strength would warrant. High on their agenda of demands has been amending the Law of Return. But despite the heavy political pressures exercised by Orthodox Jewry in Israel and abroad, the

Knesset has, to this date, continued to reject all efforts to amend the legislation.

No political body has the right or the capacity to impose a political solution in the area of religious practices. The Knesset has no jurisdiction over Diaspora Jewry and cannot affect the practice of religious movements abroad. The religious differences between Orthodox, Reform, and Conservative Judaism should be reconciled by religious leaders in dialogues based on mutual respect and recognition of a shared Jewish destiny.

If Israel is not a society where all Jews feel at home, then Israel will not remain the spiritual home for all Jews. What is at stake in the "Who is a Jew?" issue is no less than the very character of the Jewish state and its relationship to the Diaspora. Through this struggle Reform Jews are helping to maintain Israel as an open and pluralistic society, one with which all Jews can proudly identify.

The Right to a Homeland
Zionism from the Bible to Balfour to Today

MICHA BALF AND MEIR YOFFE

Nearly 100 years after Theodore Herzl called the First Zionist Congress in Basel to order and 46 years after the founding of the State of Israel, it is ironic that we still need to address the issues of Jewish peoplehood and the Jewish right to a homeland in Israel. Nonetheless, the question of our peoplehood and our right to a homeland are often raised on campuses, particularly where the issue of Palestinian rights has taken hold, and must be addressed because they are such basic elements of every modern Jew's Zionism.

For those Jews in North America who have grown up believing that Judaism is only a religion, the concepts of peoplehood and our right to a homeland are problematic. Clearly, if Judaism were only a faith, its adherents would have no real claim to a homeland. But Judaism is more than a set of beliefs. When Jews use the expression *am echad*—one nation—they are unequivocally stating that the nature of their bond is that of a people bound by a common religion. This concept radically differs from the sense most North American Jews have of themselves as individuals.

Consider, for example, the words of the Declaration of the Establishment of the State of Israel:

Eretz Israel was the birthplace of the Jewish people. Here their spiritual, religious and political identity was shaped. Here they first attained statehood, created cultural values of national and universal significance and gave to the world the eternal Book of Books.

After being forcibly exiled from their land, the people kept faith with it throughout their dispersion and never ceased to hope and pray for their return to it and for the restoration of their political freedom.

Impelled by this historic and traditional attachment, Jews strove in every successive generation to reestablish themselves in their ancient homeland. In recent decades they returned *en masse* as pioneers, *ma'apilim*, and defenders. They made deserts bloom, revived the Hebrew language, built villages and towns, and created a thriving community, controlling its own economy and culture, loving peace but knowing how to defend itself, bringing the blessing of progress to all the country's inhabitants, and aspiring towards independent nationhood.

In these opening words, we find all the threads woven together that constitute the fundamental right of the Jewish people to claim a homeland in Israel. The Declaration itself, however, takes its claim for our right to a Jewish homeland from Genesis 12:1–2 and 12:7:

> God said to Abram, "Go forth from your native land and from your father's house to the land that I will show you. I will make of you a great nation, and I will bless you."…God appeared to Abram and said, "I will give this land to your offspring."

During the centuries of exile from the Holy Land, Jews lost neither the dream of returning to *Eretz Yisrael* nor their sense that return contained within it a spark of redemption. The refrain that Jews have said for years at the Passover seder, "Next year in Jerusalem," is only one example of our yearning for Zion that characterizes so much else in a Jew's life—from our daily prayers to the *Birkat Hamazon* to the direction we face when we pray.

The Emancipation of the eighteenth century irrevocably changed the traditional Jewish world, a world that had prayed for centuries for the coming of the Messiah to relieve its burdens. Emancipation granted Jews equal status before the law. The spread of nationalism in the nineteenth century imbued all the nations of Europe with the intoxicating spirit of liberation. Unfortunately for the Jews, this new freedom was plagued by modern anti-Semitism and xenophobic nationalism.

In the 1880s groups of Jews from Eastern Europe began to return to their ancient homeland. The perilous existence of Jews in the Diaspora inspired many to seek a home that would grant Jews equal status as a nation among the people of the world. Steady persecution by non-Jews also led others to dream of establishing a more perfect society, one that embodied Jewish and universalistic values. *Chalutzim* (pioneers) began to farm the land, pave roads, and build towns and cities Jewish intellectuals revived the Hebrew language, creating a new, vibrant Jewish culture. They were all turning a historical dream into a viable homeland.

Their actions were sanctioned not only by widespread Jewish support but by growing international recognition. The British stated in the famous Balfour Declaration of 1917, "His Majesty's government views favorably the creation of a Jewish Homeland in Palestine."

It was these words that eventually served as the basis

for the international recognition of the League of Nations Mandate in 1920.

By the end of World War II, most of European Jewry had perished in the Holocaust. The survivors turned to Israel for refuge. In response to the overwhelming call for justice, the United Nations and Britain recognized the validity of the Zionist claim and called for the creation of the State of Israel. On May 15, 1948, a Jewish state was officially proclaimed.

Throughout their exile, the Jewish people have always shown some form of allegiance to a Jewish homeland. In this century, when political forces allowed an active resumption of this bond, Jews returned to build, create, and flourish. The reality of a Jewish community in its historical homeland, a community ready for nationhood, was recognized, sanctioned, and endorsed by the international community. It is with this in mind that we affirm our right to the land. As a people with a unique history, culture, language, and tradition, we have a basic right to strengthen and nurture ourselves as a Jewish people in our homeland.

It is a bitter irony that our return to our homeland has placed us in opposition to another people clamoring for its own rights. Zionism has never claimed exclusive nationalistic rights to Israel for Jews. Zionism has simply fought for the right of Jews to be in the one place in the world that cannot be separated from our past, present, or future. Zionism states that there must be one place in the world where Jews can safeguard Jews, a place where the fate of the Jewish people is not dependent on the largesse of others. Our history, both ancient and modern, shows us that this place can only be the land of Israel.

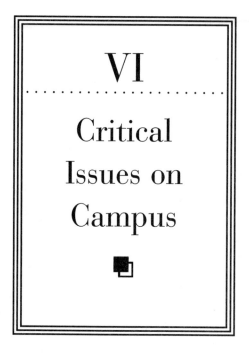

VI

Critical
Issues on
Campus

Reform on Campus

DAVID TERDIMAN

What is college really all about? Is it about academics or socializing? All-night study sessions or all-night parties? Majoring in a particular field or becoming Athlete of the Year? Managing to land a great internship or managing the student union? Making the Dean's list or making lifelong friendships? If we had to pick one word that best summarizes the college experience, that word would have to be "growth." So whether you joined a fraternity or sorority in your freshman year or were elected to an honor society in your senior year, you grow with every experience.

Religious life is another area in which you can grow. Students involve themselves in campus ministries for a number of reasons. Sometimes they seek worship services. Sometimes they have experienced a recent loss and seek consolation. Sometimes they simply want to have around them other students with the same heritage or background. With the ebb and flow in university support of campus religious life, it is often up to the individual religious organization to encourage involvement of the student who wants to grow spiritually.

So what of Judaism on the college campus, specifically Reform Judaism? Are there opportunities for Jewish growth—or life—on the college campus? Most certainly. However, before we discuss the state of Jewish life on the college campus, the phrase "Jewish life" should be defined. Jewish life on the college campus is anything that Jews make it—from services to *tikkun olam* programs, from outings to concerts and lectures, from holiday parties to five Jews sharing a pizza. By Jewish life, what we probably mean is the opportunity for Jews to come together in order to observe and celebrate their religion and the culture that has emerged from it. From the variety of campus programs being offered by various Jewish organizations, we can only hope that the lives of all Jewish college students are being touched in some way by something that has great personal meaning. Why? Because today's Jewish college students are our community's future leaders. In celebrating our religion and culture on college campuses, we ensure Judaism's flourishing tomorrow.

The importance of Jewish life on campus needs little justification. Where to find it and how to create it, however, are not always as easy as they seem. This is why students should know of the many programs that exist on college campuses. There are many organizations on the college campus today. These organizations include Hillel, the United Jewish Appeal, the American Israel Public Affairs Committee, the University Student Department of the World Zionist Organization, KESHER (Reform Movement), KOACH (Conservative Movement), KIRUV (Orthodox Movement), Chabad (Lubavitch), and Jewish fraternities. With so many organizations, there is no reason every Jewish college student should not be able to find an outlet for spiritual growth while in college.

For example, take KESHER, the Reform movement's college outreach network. KESHER empowers groups of students to take ownership of their Judaism by designing their own Reform events at school. Unfortunately, not enough Reform students take as much advantage as they should of the services and programs offered by KESHER. This, of course, does not mean that these students don't feel secure about their Jewish identities. The Union of American Hebrew Congregations knows from a random sampling of Reform college students that 70 percent were members of Temple Youth Groups, 80 percent graduated from religious school, nearly 70 percent attended a Jewishly affiliated camp (UAHC or other), 70 percent attend High Holiday services at their home synagogues or at school, and nearly 70 percent participate in a Passover seder at home or at school.

However we at the UAHC also know from the same random sampling that only 30 percent are involved in a KESHER group on campus, 45 percent participate in Jewish campus organizations such as Hillel, UJA, or a fraternity or sorority, and 35 percent choose to take Jewish Studies courses during their undergraduate careers.[1]

So why the disparity? First many Reform students— with their youth group and camp memories in tow and their Jewish identities secure—choose to explore other areas of campus life. Having participated enthusiastically over the years in NFTY, UAHC camps, and their synagogues, they know that this opportunity away from home is as good a time as any to investigate the wide array of courses and activities on their campuses. Is this unfortunate? Yes. But is telling them to get involved in a Jewish campus activity going to change it? Not necessarily. Instead, roads must be built that awaken and touch the Judaism within these students.

Second, campus Hillels are not always inviting to Reform students. Often Reform students are unfamiliar with different types of observances and, when facing them for the first time, feel their own Judaism may be illegitimate. It is these students who sometimes never return. The UAHC College Education Department nowadays works closely with individual Hillels, sensitizing them to the needs of Reform students by suggesting ways to encourage the participation of Reform students. The College Department's goal is to help Hillels create a pluralistic outlook on Jewish campus by stressing respect for Reform liturgy and forms of practice. But UAHC College Education Department cannot do all of this by itself. Students must be partners in the process; they must put themselves on their local Hillel's agenda and let their Hillel professionals know what they need in order to express their Judaism.

Reform Jewish students should also know that there are Hillels that actively seek the participation of Reform students in their programs. Two in particular that have taken the call for Jewish pluralism to heart are the University of Texas at Austin and Rutgers University in New Jersey. In reaching out to all of his campus's Jewish students, Rabbi Kerry Baker, the director of the Hillel Foundation at University of Texas in Austin, ensures that his Hillel house is *shomer Shabbat* for all denominations. Some parts of the house have lights on timers, other parts allow lights to be turned on and off during Shabbat. This arrangement allows each denomination to respect the observances of the other. Rabbi David Gutterman is an Orthodox rabbi and director of the Hillel Foundation at Rutgers University who took his position in 1995. At Rutgers he found very few Reform students participating in the campus Hillel. With the help of several committed Reform students and the UAHC's College Department, a seat on the Rutgers Hillel student board was quickly created for a KESHER representative and then filled. By the end of that first year, KESHER had become, according to Rabbi Gutterman, one of the most viable communities at Hillel.

Hillels, however, are not the only important institutions that play an important role in the lives of Jewish college students. Rabbis and their synagogues also have an important role to play. They recognize that students' relationship to Judaism often begins at home with the Jewish community they have known for many years. Most synagogues have college committees that keep in touch with students during the year through college newsletters and holiday care packages. These same college committees may also reach out to those students studying in their communities by opening their synagogues' doors for both worship and participation in temple activities during the academic year. Rabbis often teach seminars at local Hillels or travel to other college campuses to visit students from their synagogue. Reform students appreciate the contact and reach back to the synagogues by volunteering in their programs and teaching in their Hebrew and religious schools. Thus a student's Jewish life in college may be just as much off as on campus.

Jewish life on the college campus requires ingenuity, creativity, patience, and, above all, a commitment by students to their Jewish needs and interests. Students who find their Jewish needs not being met must commit themselves to changing Jewish life on their campus. Anything less guarantees a spiritual emptiness no amount of wishful thinking will fulfill. Something more guarantees a Jewish future for themselves and their people.

As Richard Joel, president and international director of Hillel, often says, Jewish campus life is not up in heaven or across the sea. It is in students' hands. Jewish students have to take responsibility for their own Judaism; they have to make it theirs. And while there are many resources to help them take ownership, taking it ultimately hinges on the actions of the students themselves. The college years extend far beyond the four spent on campus, for they lay the groundwork for the path along which life will lead them. If that path is to be a Jewish path, we must have the courage to celebrate our heritage and religion in college today.

Grades Are a Means, Knowledge Is an End

HENRY F. SKIRBALL

The renowned twelfth-century Jewish philosopher Moshe ben Maimon (Maimonides or Rambam),[1] who in his day was the foremost integrator of Aristotelian science and Judaism, wrote of living according to a golden mean by avoiding extremism. A rabbi and a physician, he was responding to the situation in which Jews often found themselves participating in a world where more than one culture and code of values impinged upon them at the same time. Jewish university students today face a similar dilemma, though the decisions they must make about the choices set before them are less often matters of either/or than both/and.

Consider some maxims from the *Pirke Avot (Sayings of the Jewish Fathers),*[2] uttered about a millennium before Maimonides but well known by him, and see how they relate to you. In *Pirke Avot,* we read, "Upon three things the world is based: study, worship and deeds of loving kindness" (Pirke Avot 1:2). To understand the choices confronting college students, we should think about the roles study, worship, and deeds of loving-kindness play in their lives.

Study

> An empty-headed person cannot be a sin-fearing person, nor can an ignorant person be pious. The more academic schooling, the more wisdom. One who adds not to one's store of knowledge, decreases it and one who studies not is deserving of death.
>
> (*Pirke Avot* 2:5; 1:13)

Judaism has always placed a premium on a broad education and accorded status to the learned person. While Europe was still in the Dark Ages, Jews in the Near East were studying in Jewish academies, where they learned not only ritual law but astronomy, botany, civil law, commerce, criminal law, ethics, history, magic, mathematics, medicine, philosophy, psychology, theology, and zoology. Judaism welcomed knowledge from all sources and encouraged its children to learn as broadly as possible. In this day of specialization and the phenomenal increase in empirical knowledge, one can be both overwhelmed and just a bit intimidated. "There is so much to learn! How will I deal with this vast mass of knowledge?" you may say. To this, however, we might answer, quoting our sages, "It is not your obligation to complete the task, nevertheless you are not at liberty to desist from doing your share" (*Pirke Avot* 2:17). Your obligation is not to know everything but to taste a little here and a little there, whether the subject is metallurgy or music, choreography or Chinese history.

With university populations often equaling the size of small cities and the number of students in individual classes totaling hundreds, performance is increasingly measured by a grading system. As such, grades are a means—often inadequate—for self-evaluation and population management. To rewrite a High Holy Day prayer, they are utilized to decide "who shall pass and who shall fail, who shall go on to advanced classes and who shall remain behind, who shall get a scholarship and who will have to wait on tables, who shall be here next year and who shall be sent packing." Often in response to the pressure grades exert upon performance, students turn into "grade-grubbing grinds," trying to outmaneuver their professors for a better grade. Students like these tend to ask themselves such questions as "what will be asked on the exam?" or "what does the professor want me to say when I'm asked for my opinion on an exam?" [3] One of the three cardinal sins of Judaism is idolatry, which is a form of belief that characteristically transforms means into ends. But students should remember that grades are only a means to another end, and that end is knowledge. When students exchange their independent judgment and true intellectual interests for a better grade, they commit a type of idolatry. As our sages wrote, "Whoever labors in study for its own sake merits many things. Be not like servants who serve the master on the condition of receiving a reward, but rather be like servants who serve the master without the condition of receiving a reward" (*Pirke Avot* 6:1).

Closely allied to grade-grubbing is what I call the credit game. In this game, students only study when they know that they will be receiving credits for their schoolwork. Unfortunately, because so many play this game, great lecturers remain unheard, fine books sit on shelves unread, and stirring concerts go unattended. Such a mechanical approach to learning leads to the atrophy of intellectual curiosity. As one of our sages pointed out, "Who is wise? One who learns from all people" (*Pirke Avot* 4:1).

But the credit game isn't the only threat to knowledge during one's college years. Our sages wrote, "The day is short and the work is great. Sleeping late, drinking during the day, immature talk and hanging out at congregating places of the ignorant, drive a person from the world" (*Pirke Avot* 2:15; 3:10). For many students, life in college is different in kind, and not just in degree, from that in high school. For most students, a great deal more freedom—and, consequently, responsibility—is placed squarely on their shoulders. The tasks students once relegated to their parents—from waking them up and getting them to class to making them do their homework— must now become their own. And while it is true that all work and no play can make Jack a dull boy (and Jill a dull girl), this view of things does not justify lack of preparation or the thoughtless pursuit of pleasure during one's college years. Consider again what our sages wrote:

> Who is rich? One who is satisfied with one's portion. One who occupies oneself overmuch in business will not grow wise. The more possessions, the more anxiety. Lessen your toil for worldly goods and busy yourself in Torah. Where there is no satisfaction of material needs, there is no Torah and where there is no Torah, there is no satisfaction of material needs.

> (*Pirke Avot* 4:1; 2:5, 7; 4:10; 3:17)

Here we are warned against pursuing business to the exclusion of everything. So may the same be said of the pursuit of grades and credits. True, both are needed to get us through the formal education system, just as money is needed to get us through life. But to worship grades, credits, or money is to commit a modern form of idolatry. In the end, the question is one of degree. Do we worship the golden calf or the golden mean? Is it worth, say, sacrificing a broad education to the type of narrow training that may make you more money? Chances are that you will spend less than a quarter of your waking hours at work.[4] How are you equipping yourself for the rest of your thinking life? We read in the Torah, "Humankind does not live by bread alone" (Deuteronomy 8:3). College is one of those opportunities to learn how much more there is to life than bread. If the sole end of your education is to make more bread, don't be surprised how flavorless your life may turn out to be.

Worship

The more study of Torah, the more life. If you
have learned much Torah, ascribe no special merit
to yourself, for that is why you were created. If two
sit together and interchange words of Torah, the
Divine Presence abides with them. Knowledge of
Torah takes study, it does not come as an automatic inheritance. Make the study of Torah a fixed
duty at regular times. Do not say, "when I have
time I will study Torah," perchance you will have
no leisure. If you neglect the study of Torah, many
excuses for neglecting it will present themselves to
you. If not now, when?

(*Pirke Avot* 2:7, 8; 3:2; 2:12; 1:15; 2:4; 4:10)

Up until now we have been discussing the traditional
Jewish emphasis on the broadening of one's intellectual
horizons. But what about Jewish studies, long considered
by Judaism as another form of worship? At university you
will both discover new disciplines and fields of study and
add to your store of knowledge in more familiar areas.
However, if you are typical of most Jewish young adults
at university, you have at best an incomplete understanding of Judaism. Thus it behooves you to explore
your heritage as you pursue your other studies. Learning
more about Judaism on campus is not nearly as difficult
as you may think. Indeed, you may be able to study your
Jewish tradition by taking credit courses in your school's
department of religion or Judaic studies. You may also
be able to pursue such studies formally and informally
through your campus Hillel, local synagogue or

chavurah, or regional UAHC office. You may even want to take for credit a summer-, semester-, or year-long university program in Israel.

Surely a tradition that has lasted nearly four millennia and has engaged so many brilliant and sensitive people (sometimes at the cost of their lives) merits your attention and investigation, for this tradition is now yours. The torch has been handed to you and your generation, and you cannot claim it if you know little about your people and your heritage. Do not think that Jewish study is just for those planning careers in Jewish service (cantorate, communal service, education, or rabbinate). It should be integrated into your studies, whatever they are. Our sages speak of this integration in beneficent terms: "Excellent is the study of Torah in combination with some worldly pursuit. All study of the Torah without an occupation must eventually prove futile" (*Pirke Avot* 2:2).

Deeds of Loving-Kindness

Separate yourself not from the community. Not learning but doing is the chief thing. One whose deeds exceed one's wisdom, the wisdom endures; but one whose wisdom exceeds one's deeds, the wisdom does not endure. Let your deeds exceed your learning.

(*Pirke Avot* 2:4; 1:17; 3:9; 6:5)

Judaism has never been interested in pedants, recluses, or aescetics. Your place, therefore, is in the community, irrespective of whether that place is on- or off-campus. Much yet needs to be done. So volunteer your services at a soup kitchen. Involve yourself in a social action initiative. Take part in a political rally. As you learn more, you will be better able to choose your areas of *tikkun olam*—improving the world—and be more competent to make your contribution. You are needed in both the general and Jewish world—locally, nationally and worldwide. Make these years count.

Conclusion

The great nineteenth-century British biologist Thomas Huxley wrote of a phenomenon called social homeostasis. Huxley based this phenomenon on what he believed was an evolutionary mechanism that prevented species from self-destructing. What this mechanism did was alter the evolutionary path of a species' development by bringing it back to a central mean when it veered to some biological extreme. According to Huxley, peoples and societies were also subject to this mechanism. When Western society sailed too far in one direction, social homeostasis brought it back to a social golden mean.

In Judaism, various types of social and intellectual homeostasis have also operated. This homeostasis has emerged repeatedly in the historical tension between universalism and particularism, emancipation and ghettoization, enlightenment and escapism. In the nineteenth-century, Samson Raphael Hirsch's school of neo-Orthodoxy responded to one element of this tension by adding secular studies to Jewish studies. Today we seem to be in need of adding more Jewish studies to our secular studies. Whatever the mix, we certainly need both.

So the parameters are clear: professional training, general education, Jewish education, co-curricular education, informal education, cultural activity, communal action, work, social life and play. All are essential, none dispensable. The art, according to Maimonides, is to achieve that golden mean. By balancing your studies, you can make your college years some of the best years of your life; by diversifying them, you prepare yourself for a productive, satisfying, and fulfilling life as an adult Jew.

Anti-Semitism on Campus

Myth vs. Reality

The Jewish presence on the college and university campus has increased dramatically over the past four decades, to the point where Jewish undergraduate enrollment in private colleges is estimated at between 20 and 30 percent. There is the perception among many in the general Jewish community that anti-Semitism is a significant problem on the campus. This impression has emerged out of an increase in the number of speakers with an anti-Semitic message and the fact that the Middle East debate on campus frequently has an anti-Israel (which is equated with being anti-Jewish) cast to it. The pattern of responses to the set of questions put to campus personnel and students gives a picture that in large measure belies this perception.

To the bottom-line question "How serious do you regard the problem of anti-Semitism on campus?" respondents, including students, generally agreed that anti-Semitism is a problem, sometimes a serious problem, when it occurs, but that anti-Semitic occurrences or situations of anti-Semitism (for example, anti-Israel graffiti, verbal harassment) are infrequent.

For students, the issue is more complicated than for Jewish campus professionals. For one thing, young people may have a different threshold at which they perceive anti-Semitism than do others. Incidents of anti-Semitism have often not yet touched their lives. Therefore, what would be considered by the professionals as being even the most minor anti-Semitic event (for example, a swastika carved on a library desk) may have an unsettling emotional impact on a student. Also, some observers have noted that students have little experience with the way in which Jewish issues are played out over time; they have little experience with the "big picture." Some students' responses expressed great concern over anti-Semitism, with some, for example, identifying criticism of Israel as anti-Semitism. By and large, however, students make an effort to place the importance of anti-Semitism in some larger context of Jewish life on campus—in many cases it is only one of a number of issues that a Jewish student is called upon to face—and students and campus professionals alike tend not to exaggerate its extent.

Without question, there is a difference between the campus and the general community with regard to anti-Semitism, both in terms of incidents and responses. Where the general community may experience rude anti-Jewish events and expressions, campus anti-Semitism is more likely to be linked to the political debate regarding the Middle East. Additionally, dramatic incidents may be more intensely felt on the campus, reverberating on many levels, including the campus press, the radio station, in the dorms, through faculty reaction, and in extracurricular activities. The effect of most incidents, however, is relatively short-term, as students are subject to pressures attendant to the academic calendar and as the cast of characters changes on a yearly cycle. Moreover, the campus has a built-in authority and leadership structure that can and should take action to repudiate anti-Semitism (indeed, all racism and bigotry) and that can set a standard of conduct and civility respecting campus-based political discourse.

Israel and the Middle East

The area most often identified as an issue for Jewish students on the campus—and the one most often articulated in terms of manifest or latent anti-Semitism—is Israel. No longer generally accepted as a democratic "underdog" beleaguered by powerful enemies, Israel is increasingly portrayed as "expansionist" and as a "surrogate for imperialism." This perception plays out in several ways. A number of campuses have reported a significant amount of pro-Palestinian and/or anti-Israel expression and activity. (It should be noted that these two areas of activity are not necessarily the same.) This pro-Palestinian/anti-Israel activity might include displays in student unions and other public areas on campus (often depicting Israeli violence toward Palestinians), and invitations extended to such speakers as Edward Said, a Columbia University professor who sits on the

Palestine National Council, and Clovis Maksoud, until recently the Arab League's Permanent Observer to the United Nations, to name but a few.

There is no area in the discussion of anti-Semitism on the campus—or in the general discussions of anti-Semitism, for that matter—where the distinction between legitimate discussion and anti-Semitic rhetoric and activity is as crucial as in the Middle East debate. Criticism of Israel, as part of legitimate discussion and debate, is obviously constitutionally protected behavior. While some sort of anti-Israel activity is reported on approximately one-third of campuses surveyed, the judgment of most campus observers is that it is the exception rather than the rule for anti-Israel activity on campus to become anti-Semitic in nature. The delegitimizing of Zionism as a national liberation movement of the Jewish people is one example of anti-Israel sentiment spilling over into anti-Semitism.

But even non-anti-Semitic and anti-Israel activity does have the effect of stimulating feelings of discomfort among many Jewish students, who in the face of such activity, may feel isolated and unprotected. And those students who strongly identify with Israel may sometimes experience anti-Israel activity as an "existential attack."

To be sure, the concerted campaign of Arab groups that have identified the campus as a political forum has an impact on Jewish students. On campuses where the Arab student population is significant, anti-Israel activity may be considerable. Yet even in these hyper-political "hotbeds," anti-Semitic rhetoric and activity is sporadic.

Black-Jewish Relations

A large number of universities reported tension between blacks and Jews. It is important to keep this in context: campuses report discernible tension between blacks and whites generally. Moreover, special tension between blacks and Jews arises when outside speakers, such as Louis Farrakhan, Kwame Toure, and Khalid Abdul Mohammed (a Farrakhan lieutenant), are brought in under black organizational sponsorship, and may be heightened when they are funded by the university. Often their speeches include anti-Zionist and blatantly anti-Semitic remarks which may receive a positive response by black students attending the events. Generally, black groups are not inviting speakers because they are anti-Semites, but because they are the spokesmen for black empowerment and achievement. This fact is not sufficiently understood or accepted by some Jewish students, many of whom ascribe anti-Semitic motives to the sponsoring black organizations. It is equally clear that black student leaders who invite these controversial speakers are either unaware of or insensitive to the impact on campus race relations that result from the racist and anti-Semitic undertones in the speakers' addresses.

A number of Hillel directors suggested that black anti-Semitism is not a major threat to Jewish security on campus, nor is it the greatest threat to black-Jewish relations. Rather the relationship may also suffer because many Jewish students stereotype blacks, as do many of their adult models. Additionally, some Jewish students have been described as viewing blacks as "off the map" for inviting speakers with an anti-Semitic message. In the view of these observers, marginalization of blacks on campus in the eyes of white students, including Jews, will contribute to further deterioration of the black-white (including black-Jewish) relationships.

Most respondents believe that anti-black racism is a more prevalent and serious problem than are anti-Semitism or black-Jewish relations generally. Most often cited by survey respondents as larger problems than anti-Semitism were anti-black racism, bigotry against Asians and gays, and sexism toward women.

Other Anti-Semitic Incidents

A number of schools have reported anti-Semitic incidents that appear to be unrelated to either Israel or black-Jewish relations. These include swastikas and other Holocaust-related epithets, various occurrences of "JAP-baiting," and acts related to general racism and bigotry.

The issue of JAP-baiting is a complex one. JAP-baiting, fundamentally a sexist and indeed anti-woman manifestation, is done by many Jewish males (and sometimes even Jewish females) as well as by non-Jews. It is a combination of sexism and anti-Semitism which makes JAP-baiting a particularly difficult and sensitive issue. Its object is often both Jewish and non-Jewish women.

Responding to Anti-Semitism on the Campus: Whose Responsibility?

Generally speaking, university administrators must find a balance between preserving campus freedom of expression on the one hand and countering bigotry and anti-Semitism on the other. In attempting to address this problem, some universities have explored the implementation of campus anti-bias codes (on some campuses referred to as campus conduct and/or disciplinary codes). Though well-intentioned, narrowly drawn codes have been attacked for inhibiting free speech and thereby creating more problems than they solve, even though they are considered to be "P.C." (politically correct). After an examination of the efficacy and constitutionality of campus anti-bias codes, the National Jewish Community Relations Advisory Council (NJCRAC) and its Campus Advisory Committee did not endorse them as an effective means for lessening intergroup tensions. According to NJCRAC, the most effective measure against "bad speech" is not to "limit speech" but to counter it with "good speech" and to implement programs that foster intergroup understanding and prejudice reduction.

Being Proactive Rather than Reactive in the Face of Bigotry

- Become familiar with Jewish and Zionist history. Knowledge about one's roots and heritage gives one power and helps remove some of the feelings of discomfort and isolation a lack of knowledge stimulates in the face of anti-Semitic and/or anti-Israel activity.

- Become involved in Jewish groups on campus.

- Cooperate and work with other Jewish groups on campus. Pool your resources. Try not become bogged down in debating ideological differences with each other. Rather, work together.

- Organize workshops for Jewish students on confronting anti-Semitism.

- Develop a range of programs aimed at increasing students' awareness and knowledge of Israel-related issues and of Jewish issues generally.

- Spend a semester in Israel. If you cannot spend a semester, at least spend a summer getting to know about the land and the people.

- Be aware of the image you portray of your Jewishness. You cannot expect other people to treat you or your beliefs with respect if you constantly make derogatory comments, for example by using the term "JAP."

- Initiate programs directed at healing the rift between blacks and Jews. These can take the form of "celebrate difference" campaigns, anti-racism rallies, and workshops between black and Jewish student leaders.

- Do not exaggerate the extent of anti-Semitism on campus—it will do nothing to help build the Jewish community and Jewish awareness and may, instead, drive Jewish students "underground" by emphasizing negative reasons for Jewish identity.

- Set up assistance programs for victims of all forms of bias and bigotry, including anti-Semitism. Such assistance should include counseling and support of victims as well as outreach to other members of the group at whom the act was targeted.

- Establish a campus-based, student-run mechanism that would function as the campus "address" for a range of campus community relations concerns (including anti-Semitism). Where possible, it should be housed on campus.

- Encourage your home congregation to develop

programs to prepare high school students for the college campus, including pride in their Jewishness and how to respond to incidents of bias.

Institutions

The American Jewish Committee, Institute of Human Relations
    165 East 56th Street
    New York, NY 10022
    (212) 751-4000

The Anti-Defamation League of B'nai Brith
    823 United Nations Plaza
    New York, NY 10017
    (212) 490-2525

National Jewish Community Relations Advisory Council
    (NJCRAC)
    433 Park Avenue South
    New York, NY 10016
    (212) 684-6950

Religious Action Center of Reform Judaism
    2027 Massachusetts Avenue NW
    Washington, DC 20036
    (202) 387-2800

Denying the Holocaust

The Facts about Holocaust Denial

One of the most significant anti-Semitic developments on college campuses today is the effort of a small group of propagandists to place advertisements in student newspapers questioning the established history of the Nazi Holocaust. The first of these ads claimed to call for "open debate on the Holocaust"; it claimed to question not the fact of Nazi anti-Semitism, but merely whether this hatred resulted in an organized killing program. A more recent ad has questioned the authenticity of the U.S. Holocaust Memorial Museum in Washington, D.C.; another has attempted to capitalize on the acclaim for Steven Spielberg's film, *Schindler's List*, by offering for sale "a shocking, absolutely unique video on Auschwitz," which in fact attacks the proven facts of Nazi atrocity at that concentration camp.

Advertisements such as these have appeared in student newspapers on dozens of campuses nationwide. Though there is no evidence that these ads have persuaded large numbers of students to doubt the settled record of events which comprise the Holocaust, their publication has generated acrimony and has frequently caused friction between Jewish and non-Jewish students.

This is precisely the intent of the advertisements: by attacking the facts of the Holocaust, and by framing this attack as merely an unorthodox point of view, the ads encode subtle but hateful anti-Semitic beliefs of Jews as exploiters of non-Jewish guilt and Jews as controllers of academia or the media. These beliefs, in fact, bear comparison to the preachings which brought Hitler to power in prewar Germany.

This essay provides a brief summary of the propaganda campaign known as Holocaust "revisionism"—or, more accurately, Holocaust denial. What follows is (1) a "Q & A" description of the movement, its history, and its leading activists, as well as a review of legal and scholarly responses to this propaganda and (2) a summary of the movement's most common allegations, with brief factual responses

It is highly unlikely that this report will dissuade the Holocaust deniers from their mendacious and hateful campaign. But this information should provide students and educators with the facts to make informed decisions and vigorous responses to these bigoted lies.

The Movement: What You Should Know

What is Holocaust denial?

Holocaust denial is a propaganda movement active in the United States, Canada, and Western Europe which seeks to deny the reality of the Nazi regime's systematic mass murder of nearly 6 million Jews in Europe during World War II.

Who started the movement?

The roots of Holocaust denial can be found in the bureaucratic language of Nazi policy itself, which sought to camouflage the genocidal intent of what the Nazis called the "Final Solution to the Jewish Question," even as these directives were being carried out. After the war, former Nazis and Nazi sympathizers dismissed the overwhelming proof of the Holocaust established at the Nuremberg war crimes trials; similarly, an obscure group of post-War French Trotskyists and anarchists led by Paul Rassinier, seeking to advance their own political agenda, denounced evidence of the genocide as "Stalinist atrocity propaganda."

However, as an organized propaganda movement, Holocaust "revisionism" took root in 1979 when Willis Carto, founder of Liberty Lobby—the largest anti-Jewish propaganda organization in the United States—incorporated the Institute for Historical Review (IHR). The IHR is a pseudo-academic enterprise in which professors with no credentials in history,[1] writers without formal academic certification (such as David Irving, Henri Roques, and Bradley Smith), and career anti-Semites (such as Mark Weber, Ernst Zundel, and the late David McCalden) convene to develop new outlets for their anti-Jewish, anti-Israel, and, for some, pro-Nazi beliefs.

Where is Holocaust denial active today?

IHR has tapped into an international network of propagandists who write for the group's *Journal of Historical Review* (JHR) and meet at its annual conventions. The leading activists affiliated with IHR include Mark Weber, Bradley Smith, and Fred Leuchter (U.S.); Ernst Zundel (Canada); David Irving (England); Robert Faurisson (France); Carlo Mattagno (Italy); and Ahmed Rami (Sweden). Of these activists, Bradley Smith, IHR's "Media Project Director," has attracted the most notoriety in the U.S., due to the series of "revisionist" advertisements which he has placed in college newspapers since 1991 for the Committee for Open Debate on the Holocaust (CODOH).

What is CODOH?

Though Smith claims the "Committee" is an independent entity devoted to promoting "open debate," it is essentially an IHR front. CODOH was founded by Smith and *Journal of Historical Review* editor Mark Weber. Smith's current codirector is Robert Countess, an IHR board member from Huntsville, Alabama. Its other leading representative, David Cole (who claims Jewish parentage), has spoken at IHR meetings and has appeared on talk shows with IHR leaders. CODOH's ads and flyers list the IHR address and cite IHR sources.

Are there laws regulating Bradley Smith's activities?

In Canada and Western Europe, Holocaust deniers have been successfully prosecuted under racial defamation or hate crimes laws. In the United States, however, the First Amendment guarantees the right of free speech, regardless of its political content. Nonetheless, though the First Amendment allows Holocaust deniers to produce and distribute their propaganda, it in no way obligates newspapers or other media outlets to provide them with a forum for their views.

The U.S. Supreme Court ruled in a 1974 decision, *Miami Herald Publishing Company* v. *Tonillo*, that "A newspaper is more than a passive receptacle or conduit for news, comment, and advertising. The choice of material to go into a newspaper…[constitutes] the exercise of editorial control and judgment." Simply stated, to require newspaper editors or broadcasters to provide Smith, or any other individual, with a forum would deny the newspaper or other media its own First Amendment rights to operate a free press, without government coercion; such requirements would also diminish the public's ability to distinguish historical truth from propaganda.

Like the editor of a private newspaper, the editors of all private and most public college newspapers have a First Amendment right to exercise editorial control over which advertisements appear in their newspaper. The only situation in which an editor of a state university newspaper would not have this right would be if the university administration controlled the content of the campus newspaper and set editorial policy for the paper. In such a case, the university would essentially function as an arm of the government, and prohibition of newspaper advertisements based on content would violate the First Amendment. There are a few universities, however, where the administration exercises this type of control over the student paper.

At public elementary and secondary schools, the administration has the right to refuse to print Holocaust denial advertisements in the student newspaper; the U.S. Supreme Court ruled in a 1988 decision, *Hazelwood School District* v. *Kuhlmeier*, that "educators do not offend the First Amendment by exercising editorial control over…the content of student speech in school-sponsored expressive activities so long as their actions are reasonably related to legitimate pedagogical concern." Based on that decision, it is clear that public school officials have the same right as student editors to reject Holocaust denial advertisements, since this propaganda encourages bias and prejudice, offends many individuals, and has a negative educational value.

What have academic authorities said about Holocaust denial?

The History department at Duke University, responding to a CODOH ad, unanimously adopted and published a statement noting: "That historians are constantly engaged in historical revision is certainly correct; however, what historians do is very different from this advertisement. Historical revision of major events…is not concerned with the actuality of these events; rather, it concerns their historical interpretation—their causes and consequences generally. There is no debate among historians about the actuality of the Holocaust…there can be no doubt that the Nazi state systematically put to death millions of Jews, Gypsies, political radicals and other people."

David Oshinsky and Michael Curtis, of Rutgers University, have written, "If one group advertises that the Holocaust never happened, another can buy space to insist that American blacks were never enslaved. The stakes are high because college newspapers may soon be flooded with ads that present discredited assertions as if they were part of normal historical debate. If the Holocaust is not a fact, then nothing is a fact."

Peter Hayes, Associate Professor of History and German at Northwestern University, responded to a Smith ad by stating, "[B]ear in mind that not a single one of the advances in our knowledge since 1945 has been contributed by the self-styled 'Revisionists' whom Smith represents. That is so because contributing to knowledge is decidedly not their purpose. This ad is an assault on the intellectual integrity...of academicians, whom Smith and his ilk wish to browbeat. It is also a throwback to the worst sorts of conspiracy-mongering of anti-Semitic broadsides. Is it plausible that so great and long-standing a conspiracy of repression could really have functioned? That everybody with a Ph.D. active in the field—German, American, Canadian, British, Israeli, etc.—is in on it together? If one suspects it is, might it not be wise to do a bit of checking about Smith, his organization, and his charges before running so implausible an ad?"

Holocaust Denial Themes

The following are summaries of major assertions employed by Holocaust denial propagandists, with brief factual responses.

The Holocaust did not occur because there is no single "master plan" for Jewish annihilation.

There is no single Nazi document that expressly enumerates a "master plan" for the annihilation of European Jewry. Holocaust denial propagandists misrepresent this fact as an exposure of the Holocaust "hoax"; in doing so, they reveal an ignorant and fundamentally misleading approach to the history of the era. That there was no single document does not mean there was no plan. The "final solution"—the Nazis' comprehensive plan to murder all European Jews—was, as the

Encyclopedia of the Holocaust observes, "the culmination of a long evolution of Nazi Jewish policy."[2] The destruction process was shaped gradually: it was borne of many thousands of directives.[3]

The development and implementation of this process was overseen and directed by the highest tier of Nazi leadership, including Heinrich Himmler, Reinhard Heydrich, Adolf Eichmann, Hermann Goering, and Adolph Hitler himself. For the previous two decades, Hitler had relentlessly pondered Jewish annihilation.[4] In a September 16, 1919, letter he wrote that while "the Jewish problem" demanded an "antisemitism of reason"—comprising systematic legal and political sanctions—"the final goal, however, must steadfastly remain the removal of the Jews altogether."[5]

Throughout the 1920s, Hitler maintained that "the Jewish question" was the "pivotal question" for his Party and would be solved "with well-known German thoroughness to the final consequence."[6] With his assumption to power in 1933, Hitler's racial notions were implemented by measures that increasingly excluded Jews from German society.

On January 30, 1939, Hitler warned that if Jewish financiers and Bolsheviks initiated war, "the result will not be the Bolshevization of the earth, and thus the victory of Jewry, but the annihilation of the Jewish race in Europe."[7] On September 21, 1939, after the Germans invaded Poland, SD chief Heydrich ordered the *Einsatzgruppen* (mobile killing units operating in German-occupied territory) to forcibly concentrate Polish Jews into ghettos, alluding to an unspecified "final aim."[8]

In the summer of 1941, with preparation underway

for invading Russia, large-scale mass murder initiatives—already practiced domestically upon the mentally ill and deformed—were broadly enacted against Jews. Heydrich, acting on Hitler's orders, directed the *Einsatzgruppen* to implement the "special tasks" of annihilation in the Soviet Union of Jews and Soviet commissars.[9] On July 31, Heydrich received orders from Goering to prepare plans "for the implementation of the aspired final solution of the Jewish question" in all German-occupied areas.[10] Eichmann, while awaiting trial in Israel in 1960, related that Heydrich had told him in August 1941 that "the Fuhrer has ordered the physical extermination of the Jews."[11] Rudolph Hoess, the Commandant of Auschwitz, wrote in 1946 that "In the summer of 1941…Himmler said to me, 'The Fuhrer has ordered the "Final Solution to the Jewish Question.".… I have chosen the Auschwitz camp for this purpose.' " [12]

On January 20, 1942, Heydrich convened the Wannsee conference to discuss and coordinate implementation of the Final Solution. Eichmann later testified at his trial:

> These gentlemen…were discussing the subject quite bluntly, quite differently from the language that I had to use later in the record. During the conversation they minced no words about it at all…they spoke about methods of killing, about liquidation, about extermination.[13]

Ten days after the conference, while delivering a speech at the Sports Palace in Berlin that was recorded by the Allied monitoring service, Hitler declared: "The result of this war will be the complete annihilation of the Jews...the hour will come when the most evil universal enemy of all time will be finished at least for a thousand years."[14] On February 24, 1943, he stated: "This struggle will not end with the annihilation of Aryan mankind, but with the extermination of the Jewish people in Europe." [15]

Between 5 and 6 million Jews were eventually killed in the course of Hitler's Final Solution.

There were no gas chambers used for mass murder at Auschwitz and other camps.

Death-camp gas chambers were the primary means of execution used against the Jews during the Holocaust. The Nazis issued a directive implementing large-scale gas chambers in the fall of 1941, but by then procedures facilitating mass murder, including the utilization of smaller gas chambers, were already in practice. Before their use in death camps, gas chambers were central to Hitler's "eugenics" program. Between January 1940 and August 1941, 70,273 Germans—most of them physically handicapped or mentally ill—were gassed, 20 to 30 at a time, in hermetically shut chambers disguised as shower rooms.[16]

Meanwhile, mass-shooting of Jews had been extensively practiced on the heels of Germany's eastern campaign. But these actions by murder squads had become an increasingly unwieldy process by October 1941. Three directors of the genocide, Erhard Wetzel, head of the Racial-Policy Office, Alfred Rosenberg, consultant on Jewish affairs for the Occupied Eastern

Territories, and Victor Brack, deputy director of the Chancellory, met at the time with Adolf Eichmann to discuss the use of gas chambers in the genocide program.[17] Thereafter, two technical advisors for the euthanasia gas chambers, *Kriminalkommissar* Christian Wirth and a Dr. Kallmeyer, were sent to the East to begin construction of mass gas chambers.[18] Physicians who had implemented the euthanasia program were also transferred.

Mobile gassing vans, using the exhaust fumes of diesel engines to kill passengers, were used at Chelmno, Belzec, and Treblinka starting in December 1941.[19] Gas chambers were installed and operated at Lublin, Sobibor, Majdanek, and Auschwitz-Birkenau from 1942 until November 1944. Working with chambers measuring an average 225 square feet, the Nazis forced to their deaths 700 to 800 men, women, and children at a time.[20] Two-thirds of this program was completed in 1943–44, and at its height it accounted for 20,000 victims per day.[21] Authorities have estimated that these gas chambers accounted for the deaths of approximately two-and-a-half to three million Jews.

Holocaust scholars rely on the testimony of survivors because there is no objective documentation proving the Nazi genocide.

Another frequent claim of Holocaust "revisionists" concerns what they describe as the lack of objective documentation proving the facts of the Holocaust, and the reliance by scholars on biased and poorly recollected testimonies of survivors. However, the Germans themselves left no shortage of documentation and testimony to these events, and no serious scholar has relied solely on survivor testimony as the conclusive word on Holocaust history. Lucy Dawidowicz, in the preface to her authoritative work, *The War Against the Jews, 1933–1945*, wrote, "The German documents captured by the Allied armies at the war's end have provided an incomparable historical record, which, with regard to volume and accessibility, has been unique in the annals of scholarship…. The National Archives and the American Historical Association jointly have published sixty-seven volumes of *Guides to German Records Microfilmed at Alexandria, VA*. For my work I have limited myself mainly to published German documents." [22] The author then proceeds to list 303 published sources—excluding periodicals—documenting the conclusions of her research. Among these sources are the writings of recognizable Nazi policy makers such as Adolf Hitler, Heinrich Himmler, Rudolf Hoess, and Alfred Rosenberg.

Similarly, Raul Hilberg, in his three-volume edition of *The Destruction of the European Jews*, wrote, "Between 1933 and 1945 the public offices and corporate entities of Nazi Germany generated a large volume of correspondence. Some of these documents were destroyed in Allied bombings, and many more were systematically burned in the course of retreats or in anticipation of surrender. Nevertheless, the accumulated paperwork of the German bureaucracy was vast enough to survive in significant quantities, and even sensitive folders remained." [23]

It is thus largely from these primary sources that the history of the Holocaust has been compiled. A new factor in this process is the sudden availability of innumerable records from the former Soviet Union, many of which had been overlooked or ignored since their capture at war's end by the Red Army. Needless to say, the modification of specific details in this history is certain to continue for a number of years to come, considering the vastness and complexity of the events which comprise the Holocaust. However, it is equally certain that these modifications will only confirm the Holocaust's enormity, rather than—as the "revisionists" would—call it into question.

Bibliography

Arendt, Hannah. *Eichmann in Jerusalem: A Report on the Banality of Evil*. Rev. ed. New York: Penguin, 1964.

Bauer, Yehuda, and Nathan Rotenstreich. *The Holocaust as Historical Experience*. New York: Holmes and Meier Publishers, 1981.

Dawidowicz, Lucy. *The War against the Jews, 1933–1945*. New York: Bantam, 1975.

Gilbert, Martin. *The Holocaust: A History of the Jews of Europe during the Second World War*. New York: Holt, Rinehart, and Winston, 1985.

Gutman, Israel, ed. *Encyclopedia of the Holocaust*. 4 vols. New York: Macmillan Library Reference, 1990.

Hilberg, Raul. *The Destruction of the European Jews*. Rev. ed. 3 vols. New York: Holmes and Meier Publishers, 1985.

Holocaust. Jerusalem: Keter Books, 1974.

Langer, Lawrence L. *Admitting the Holocaust: Collected Essays*. New York: Oxford University Press, 1995.

Levin, Nora. *The Holocaust: The Destruction of European Jewry, 1933–1945*. New York: T. Y. Crowell Co., 1973.

Lifton, Robert J. *The Nazi Doctors: Medical Killings and the Psychology of Genocide.* New York: Basic Books, 1986.

Lipstadt, Deborah. *Denying the Holocaust: The Growing Assault on Truth and Memory.* New York: The Free Press, 1993.

Pressac, Jean-Claude. *Auschwitz: Technique and Operation of the Gas Chambers.* New York: Beate Klarsfeld Foundation, 1989.

Reitlinger, Gerald. *The Final Solution: The Attempt to Exterminate the Jews of Europe, 1939–1945.* 2nd rev. ed. South Brunswick, NJ: T. Yoseloff, 1968.

Wyman, David. *The Abandonment of the Jews.* New York: Pantheon, 1984.

Yahil, Leni. *The Holocaust: The Fate of European Jewry.* New York: Oxford University Press, 1990.

Cults

STEVEN HASSAN, RACHEL ANDRES,

AND JAMES R. LANE

Imagine, if you will, the following scenes:

Saffron-robed men on street corners dancing and chanting with cymbals and drums. Bedraggled teenagers running from car to car selling flowers in the pouring rain. High-strung men in suits and ties confronting people in airport lobbies for money to quarantine AIDS victims and build particle-beam weapons.

Mention "cults" to someone and these are the images you'll evoke. Many of us have seen such images ourselves, either through personal experience or through the mass media. Yet these images do not represent the overall destructive cult phenomenon as it has become today. They are only its visible aspect.

Imagine, then, a different set of images:

Business executives in three-piece suits sitting in hotel ballrooms for company-sponsored "awareness" training, unable to get up to go to the bathroom. Housewives attending "psych-up rallies" so they can recruit friends and neighbors into a pyramid sales organization. Hundreds of students gathering at an accredited university being told they can levitate and "fly" through the air if they only meditate hard enough. Hundreds of people of every description paying huge sums to learn cosmic truths from a "channeled" spirit.

These are some of the forms the destructive cult phenomenon is taking today.

What Is a Destructive Cult?

A destructive cult is a group which violates the rights of its members and damages them through the abusive techniques of unethical mind control. A destructive cult distinguishes itself from a normal social or religious group by subjecting its members to persuasion or other damaging influences to keep them in the group.

"Cults" are not new. Throughout history, groups of enthusiasts have sprung up around charismatic leaders of every possible description. But in recent years, something has been added: the systematic use of modern psychological techniques to reduce a person's will and gain control over his or her thoughts, feelings, and behaviors.

While we usually think of "cults" as being religious (the first definition of "cult" in *Webster's Third New International Dictionary* is "religious practice: worship"), actually they are often completely secular. Webster's also defines "cult" as "a usually small or narrow circle of persons united by devotion or allegiance to some artistic or intellectual program, tendency, or figure (as one of limited popular appeal)." The second definition begins to come close to the meaning of a modern cult but falls a bit short. Modern cults have virtually unlimited popular appeal.

The United States of America has always been a land where freedom of thought and tolerance of differing beliefs have flourished under the protection of the First Amendment of the Constitution. The basis of that diversity (religious and political) is found in the principle of respect for individual rights which is written into our Constitution. Difficult as it may be to believe, in the past twenty-five years we have seen the rise of organizations in our society that systematically violate the rights of their members, subject them to many kinds of abuse, and make them less capable of acting and thinking as responsible adults. For people who stay in these organizations, the result is damage not only to their self-esteem, but often to their whole sense of identity. Their connection with others is also harmed; in some cases they completely lose contact with family and friends for long periods of time.

The damage from living in a cult may not be readily apparent to family members or friends or even—in the early stages—to someone casually meeting such a person for the first time. But many forms of violence, from the very gross to the very subtle, are the inevitable result.

Some members of destructive cults suffer physical abuse during their involvement, in the form of beatings or rape, while others simply suffer the abuse of long hours of grueling, monotonous work—fifteen to eighteen hours a day, year in and year out. In essence, they become slaves with few or no resources, personal or financial, to leave the group, and the group does everything it can to keep them as long as they are productive. When they fall sick or are no longer productive, they are often kicked out.

Groups with such practices often appear, on the surface, to be respectable associations. Cults using mind control appeal to many different human impulses. Religious cults, the best known, are focused on religious dogma. Political cults, often in the news, are organized around a narrow political theory. Psychotherapy/educational cults, which have enjoyed great popularity, purport to give the participant "insight" and "enlightenment." Commercial cults play on people's desires for exciting and lucrative careers. None of these cults deliver what they promise; all, in the long run, entrap their members and destroy their self-esteem.

Destructive cults do many kinds of damage to their members. It is not easy to recover from the damage done by membership in a destructive cult, but it is possible. Cult mind control does not have to be permanent.

Asking Questions: The Key to Protecting Yourself from Destructive Cults

Learning to be an educated consumer can save you time, energy, and money. In the case of destructive cults, being an educated consumer can help save your mind. If you are ever approached by someone who tries to get information from you or invites you to participate in a program, you can ask some very specific questions which will help you avoid over 90 percent of all cult recruiters. These questions work best if you ask them in a very direct yet friendly manner and demand very specific answers. Although most groups use deception, it is important to realize that most cult members don't realize they are lying to you in the process of recruitment. For that reason, by asking these direct questions one after another, you can usually discover that either you are not being told a straight story, or that the cult member doesn't have the straight story to begin with.

Because members have been trained to avoid thinking negatively about the group, you will often receive less than direct responses. Among the more common strategies of cult recruiters are vague generalities, evasive remarks, and attempts to change the subject. Vague generalities such as "We're just trying to help people to overcome their problems" or "We're having a free dinner tonight to discuss some world problems" or "We're just getting together to study the Word of God" should make you suspicious. Evasive remarks such as "I understand you are feeling skeptical; I was too before I really came to understand" or "Is that what you really want to know?" should also ring warning bells for you.

Another common technique used by cult recruiters is to change the subject. For example, when you ask a question about whether or not a cult leader has a criminal background, you may hear a long monologue about how all the world's greatest religious leaders have been persecuted. If the recruiter does not answer in a clear, concise, direct way, you may be sure that there is something wrong with his answer. There is always one reply that no recruiter can respond to: you can simply walk away.

You should never give your address or phone number to someone you suspect might be involved with a cult. (Perhaps you might not have even given this particular person the time of day except for the fact that he or she is particularly attractive.) Instead, take the individual's name, number and address, and initiate contact yourself if you wish. Stay in control! Don't allow yourself to be pressured into revealing personal information. People who have released their addresses and phone numbers have learned the hard way the unbelievable nuisance that can result.

Most of all, though, you will find that the best possible advantage over a cult recruiter is the ability to ask direct penetrating questions.

Examples of questions to ask include:

Are you trying to recruit me into any type of organization? Can you tell me the names of other organizations that are affiliated with this group?

Who is the top leader? What are his background and qualifications? Does he have a criminal record?

What does your group believe? Does it believe that the ends justify the means? Is deception allowed in certain circumstances? Is your group considered to be controversial by anyone? If people are critical of your group, what are their main objections?

What are members expected to do once they join? Do I have to quit school or work, donate my money and property, or cut myself off from family members and friends who might oppose my membership?

How do you feel about former members of your group? Does your group impose restrictions on communicating with former members?

What are the three things you like least about the group and organization?

What else would you rather do in your life than be a member of the group? The answer is likely to be "Nothing."

If you make it through all the above questions and feel reasonably comfortable that the person you spoke with was being straight with you, and you are still interested in learning more about the group, there are several other things it is strongly suggested that you do. You can ask other members of the group the same questions and see if you get consistent answers. If there are vast differences, you might want to confront them with the fact and see what kind of response you get.

Before you attend any program, be advised that you should still research the group independently. Contact the Cult Awareness Network (CAN) to see if it has any information on this group. It never hurts to be cautious.

If CAN does not have any information on the group, and you are still interested, go to the program with a trusted friend. In this way, you will have someone you can trust to discuss what you see and hear. Destructive cults, as a rule, will always try to find some convenient way to split you from your friend. "Divide and conquer" is the rule here. Don't let anyone split you up. Demand to stay with your friend. If you are pressured to conform or are confronted by group leaders, simply walk out.

If you find yourself in an indoctrination session, stand up and announce that you don't like being manipulated and controlled. The louder you speak, the faster you will be escorted from the room.

Don't let your curiosity get the best of you. Curiosity and overconfidence have been the downfall of many people, including myself. Placing yourself in a potentially dangerous situation just isn't worth it.[1]

Judaism and Cults

Although as Jews we are concerned about religious questions, our disagreement with cults does not focus on the content of their beliefs. Rather, we are concerned with what is, in our opinion, deceptive proselytizing and unethical conduct (i.e., front organizations, mind-control practices). We expect these groups to accept the same social and legal accountability as do mainstream religious organizations. We expect openness in accessibility of information and an honest declaration of goals and principles to potential new members.

We are also concerned about the political activities of these organizations, since many seem to view the First Amendment guarantee of freedom of religion as granting license to function in any manner they choose. They expect their proclamation of religious belief sufficient to obviate any criticism or investigation. We believe that the First Amendment was not established to protect religious organizations, but rather to insure the freedom of individuals to hold and express their own religious ideas and to congregate so that those ideas can be furthered. The constitutional guarantee of freedom of religion was not created to protect the business dealings of religious organizations (thereby granting tax-exempt status for non-church related business income), nor was it created to give them the right to enter, in any means they see fit, the lives of individuals in ways that violate freedom of religion and freedom of thought.

We cannot blindly protect destructive organizations at the expense of the rights of the individuals involved. We are concerned with the need to educate individuals to protect themselves from manipulative and coercive techniques by religious organizations and cults which claim to bring salvation without effort.

In conclusion, anyone can be recruited into a cult. The desires that lead people to join cults are desires that each of us has: to feel loved, to be included, to be part of a committed community working to improve the world, to have a sense of life's meaning, and to feel closer to God. The major difference between individuals in cults and those outside cults is the way those desires have been fulfilled. One may have entered a cult with a profound commitment to bettering the world and improving oneself—without realizing the potential dangers of the path chosen. We do not judge or blame those individuals for their involvement in these groups or their desire (be it secret or overt) to leave. Today's lifestyle options are numerous. The pressures that drive individuals to take refuge in religious cults will not abate, since they are a product of natural desires for social support and religious meaning.

As a people, we have survived far more hostile challenges than those posed by destructive cults and we have thrived. In fact, challenges to the Jewish community have always stimulated movement and growth for us as a people. By realizing that the needs which cult members want to have met can in fact be answered by Judaism—whether we answer them by returning to our tradition or by reinterpreting the tradition for modern times—we find that we do in fact have the resources to meet the challenges of these destructive cults.

If you, a close friend, or a relative are involved in a destructive cult, seek professional advice as soon as possible.[2]

Bibliography

Andres, Rachel, and James R. Lane, eds. *Cults and Consequences: The Definitive Handbook*. Los Angeles: The Jewish Federation of Greater Los Angeles, 1988.

Hassan, Steven. *Combating Cult Mind Control*. Vermont: Park Street Press 1988.

Institutions

American Family Foundation
    (AFF).
P.O. Box 336
Weston, MA 02193
(617) 893-0930

Council on Mind Abuse
P.O. Box 575, Station Z
Toronto M5N 2Z6
    Canada
(416) 484-1112

Cult Awareness Network
    (CAN)
2421 West Pratt Boulevard
Suite 1173
Chicago, IL 60643
(312) 267-7777

International Cult Education
    Program (ICEP)
P.O. Box 1232, Gracie Station
New York, NY 10028
(212) 439-1550

Task Force on Missionaries
    and Cults of the Jewish
    Community Relations
    Council of New York
111 West 40th Street
New York, NY 10018
(212) 860-8533

Union of American Hebrew
    Congregations (UAHC)
838 Fifth Avenue
New York, NY 10021
 (212) 650-4000

Missionaries

STUART FEDEROW

Few people join a cult or convert to Christianity solely because they find its theology appealing or full of Divine Truth. Rather, people do so because they have needs that are not being met by either their own religious community or their usual support system of family and friends. Their needs may stem from feelings of loneliness, crises in their lives, or a lack of spirituality that they feel within their own religious tradition. Whatever the reason, when individuals in need experience a void that they feel unable to fill, they will search for answers that fill that empty space—even if it means accepting a different theology. This is one of the main reasons why college students, away from their support systems back home, are such easy targets for cults and missionaries.

Cults and missionary Christianity offer another attraction—an apparent spiritual connection with God that many Jews feel has been missing from their personal experience with organized Judaism. Many Jews complain that the religious services of the Jewish community are cold and that their congregations are too large, overly formal, and without conviction that God is present in their life. By contrast, cultic and Christian services often seem very spiritual, and the community of believers appear to be loving and accepting of potential or new members.

Since the 1960s, Christian missionaries have incorporated a new tactic into their recruiting practices, and that tactic is telling Jews that they can remain Jewish even after they have converted to Christianity. Jews are enticed by this notion because it lets them believe that they can convert without severing their ties to Judaism and the Jewish people. But this simply is not true. Once one adopts the doctrine of a religion other than Judaism, that individual is no longer regarded as a Jew.

It is impossible to believe in more than one religion at a time when the beliefs of the two religions are mutually exclusive. This point, in fact, is made in I Kings 21, when Elijah the prophet tells those Israelites who have begun to follow the pagan god Baal, "How long will you go limping with two different opinions? If the Eternal is God, follow God. But if it is Baal, then follow him." One may believe in one or the other, Elijah asserts, but not both. Even today, despite their many differences, all modern denominations of Judaism agree that one cannot be a Jew and a Christian at the same time.

In his book *The Real Messiah*, Aryeh Kaplan, an Orthodox rabbi, argues that a "Jew who accepts Christianity might call himself a 'Jewish Christian,' but he is no longer a Jew." This argument of Rabbi Kaplan's is based on his interpretation of a passage from Maimonides' *Mishneh Torah*, in which Maimonides asserts: "An Israelite who worshiped an idol is an idolater in all respects and not like an Israelite who committed a transgression" (*Avodat Kochavim* 2:5).

Nor has Maimonides' view dimmed with the centuries. In *Contemporary American Reform Responsa*, we read the following:

"Messianic Jews" claim that they are Jews, but we must ask ourselves whether we identify them as Jews. We cannot do so as they consider Jesus of Nazareth as the Messiah who has fulfilled the Messianic promises. In this way they have clearly placed themselves with Christianity.... The theology and underlying beliefs of "Messianic Jews" remove them from Judaism and make them Christians.... We would, therefore, be stricter with [voluntary apostates] than with individuals who were forced into a position of becoming Christian.... For us such a modern willing apostate is a non-Jew.[1]

There are many means Christian missionaries use to convince others that one can be a Jew and a Christian at the same time. One method is that of changing their own names to something that sounds more Jewish. Those who converted from Judaism, for example, simply adopt the Hebrew name given to them at birth. Another tactic to convince others that Judaism and Christianity can mix comfortably is to refer to characters in the New Testament by their Hebrew names. Jesus is thus called Yeshua, Paul is Shaul, Mary is Miriam, and so on. A third tactic used by missionaries is to place in their literature photos and illustrations of "Jewish-looking" individuals performing Christian ceremonies. A photo, for example, may show a bearded man with a yarmulke on his head and a cross around his neck leading what appears to be *Kiddush*. A fourth tactic adopted by missionaries is to take Jewish symbols, Jewish rituals, and Jewish ritual objects and imbue them with Christian meanings. Thus, they explain the Passover ritual of dividing the matzah into two pieces, hiding the *afikoman*, and finding it again as a symbolic reenactment of the death, burial, and resurrection of Jesus.

All of these techniques are used to make it appear as if one can remain Jewish after converting to Christianity. Their goal is simple: to make the targeted individual more likely to adopt Christian theology by concealing the Christian content beneath a Jewish form. Though the system of belief the missionaries describe may appear Jewish, the theological content is clearly Christian.

Once their targets become comfortable, missionaries prepare for the next step in the conversion process by directing conversation towards religion, faith, and the Bible. The missionaries may invite their targets to a Bible study group or engage them in a series of one-on-one Bible study sessions. Their intent is to teach their targets to read the Bible from a Christian perspective, through Christian eyes. Biblical passages that, according to the Jewish tradition, have nothing to do with the Messiah are shown, in fact, to be Messianic. Generally these passages are treated as prefigurations of Jesus' coming. This mode of argumentation is known as "proof-texting." Almost since the beginning of Christianity, Christians have quoted portions of the Hebrew Bible as proof of Jesus' fulfilment of all the Messianic prophecies. And yet, we should not forget that for the same 2,000 years we Jews have also quoted the Hebrew Bible and even the New Testament as evidence that Jesus did not fulfill any Messianic prophecy and could not have been the Messiah.

The Jewish community tends to be reluctant to debate theology with Christian missionaries. It is easy to criticize the theology of the cults because our Christian friends have no reason to be insulted by our asserting that some cult leader is not God. But once we assert to a Christian missionary that Jesus was neither God nor the Messiah—that, in fact, Jesus was no more a child of God than any other human being—we find ourselves in the embarrassing situation of having insulted the faith of Christians with no interest at all in missionizing Jews. Many in the Jewish community will, therefore, only criticize the deceptive missionary practice of telling Jews that they can become a Christian and still remain Jewish. They will also protest the practices of missionaries who imbue Jewish ceremonies and symbols with Christian meanings. And though you may feel uncomfortable arguing theology with someone trying to convert you, you should at least be aware of some of the prooftexting techniques that person is likely to use.

For example, did you know that tennis is mentioned in the Bible? In Genesis 41:46 the text reads, "And Joseph served in Pharaoh's court."

We laugh at this statement because we know that tennis was invented more than a thousand years after the story of Joseph took place, so this obviously is not a reference to tennis. What the verse actually says is that Joseph worked as a servant in Pharaoh's royal court. The point is, however, that in order to get the first inter-pretation, the statement must be *taken out of context*.

This humorous example illustrates how Christian missionaries use quotations from the Hebrew Bible to prove that Jesus was the Messiah. For example, Matthew 2:14–15 makes it appear as if a prophecy has been fulfilled by Jesus when he writes, "And he rose and took the child and his mother by night, and departed to Egypt, and remained there until the death of Herod.

This was to fulfill what the Lord had spoken by the prophet, 'Out of Egypt have I called my son.' " The quotation, "Out of Egypt have I called my son," is taken from Hosea 11:1. But Matthew uses only half of the verse. The whole verse reads, "When Israel was a child, I loved him, and out of Egypt I called my son." Hosea tells us, very specifically, that Israel was the son whom God called out of Egypt. But how can Hosea call Israel the son of God? Well, one just has to remember that Hosea is referring to Exodus 4:22–23, in which God tells Moses during the Exodus from Egypt, "Then you shall say to Pharaoh, 'Thus says the Lord: "Israel is my first-born son. I have said to you, 'let My son go, that he may worship me.' " ' "

The point here is that to prove that Jesus fulfilled the prophecy concerning the Messiah, missionaries must take the Biblical verse that they use as evidence *out of context*.

Christian missionaries also rely on *mistranslations* of the Hebrew Bible in their attempts to prove that Jesus was the Messiah. For example, Matthew 1:22–25 makes it appear as though the birth of Jesus fulfills a prophecy concerning the Messiah: "All this took place to fulfill what the Lord had spoken by the prophet: 'Behold a virgin shall conceive and bear a son and his name shall be Emmanuel, which means "God is with us." ' "

But Matthew here is misquoting Isaiah 7:14, where we find a very different translation from the Hebrew: "Therefore the Lord himself will give you a sign: Behold, the young woman is pregnant. She will bear a son, and shall call his name Emmanuel." The birth of Emmanuel was a sign from God to King Ahaz to show that he had nothing to fear from two enemy kings. This took place more than 600 years before Jesus was born. (Again, *check the context!*) The Hebrew word for virgin is *betu-lah*. In this passage from Isaiah, however, the word used is *almah*, which means young woman. *Almah*, properly translated, makes no reference to her sexual status. (As further evidence of the fact that the *almah* cannot mean virgin, see Proverbs 30:18–20, in which an *almah* is likened to an adulterous woman.) In addition, at no time in the entire New Testament is Jesus ever called Emmanuel. And finally, not once does Judaism ever claim that the Messiah had to be born of a virgin. The Messiah must be able to trace his lineage back to King David through King Solomon down to the Messiah's own biological father (Isaiah 11:1; II Samuel 7:12–16; I Chronicles 28:5–7. Cf. Luke 3:31–32). To have been born of a virgin would have meant Jesus had no human father. But this would have prevented his having been the Messiah, for no lineage could then be traced back to King David through a human father.

So next time missionaries try to use prooftexts in their efforts to proselytize you, say quickly, "Thank you for your concern," and move on. If, however, they press you for a response to their prooftexts, be sure to do the following:

Check the context. What is the purpose of the verse they quote in the context of the story in which it is found? What are the verses that come before and after it?

Check the original Hebrew or a reliable translation. Does the verse they quote actually say what they claim it says?

You may also want to ask yourself, "Can these proof-texts be used to describe anyone else in history?" If they can, then Jesus was not alone in "fulfilling" these verses. (See the bibliography for more information on how to respond to prooftexting.)

College life can be fun, exciting, and challenging. There are many people on whom you can count and who truly know and care about you; there are people who love you and will support you when life is difficult. But there are also those out there waiting to take advantage of this transitional moment in your life. Don't let them. Instead, let those who love you for who you already are and what you already believe know how you are feeling. Let them know that you need their help so that they can extend their hearts and hands to you. And don't be scared to look through the books mentioned in the reading list below for a better understanding of your own faith and the issues raised in this article.

Bibliography

Andres, Rachel, and James R. Lane, eds. *Cults and Consequences: The Definitive Handbook*, Los Angeles: The Jewish Federation of Greater Los Angeles, 1988.

ben Avraham, Isaac of Troki. *Faith Strengthened: 1,200 Biblical Refutations to Christian Missionaries.* New York: Hermon Press, 1970.

Cohen, Arthur A. *The Myth of the Judeo-Christian Tradition.* New York: Harper and Row, 1969.

Kaplan, Aryeh. *The Real Messiah.* New York: National Conference of Synagogue Youth and the Union of Orthodox Jewish Congregations of America, 1985.

"Missionaries." *Keeping Posted*, February 1987.

Prager, Dennis, and Joseph Telushkin. *The Nine Questions People Ask about Judaism: The Intelligent Skeptic's Guide*. New York: Simon and Schuster, 1981.

Rudin, A. James, and Marcia R. Rudin. *Prison or Paradise? The New Religious Cults*. Cleveland: Collins, 1980.

Sigal, Gerald. *The Jew and the Christian Missionary: A Jewish Response to Missionary Christianity*. Hoboken, NJ: Ktav Publishing, 1981.

Syme, Daniel. *The Jewish Home*. New York: UAHC Press, 1988.

Weiss-Rosmarin, Trude. *Judaism & Christianity: The Differences*. New York: Jonathan David Publishers, 1965.

Looking Ahead
An Introduction to Black-Jewish Relations

ALBERT VORSPAN AND DAVID SAPERSTEIN

The Jewish Role in the Civil Rights Struggle

Jews have been in the forefront of the struggle to achieve equality of opportunity for African Americans (Blacks), Hispanics, Asians, and members of all groups suffering from discrimination. Jews recognize that discrimination against any racial or religious group in American life threatens the ultimate security of the Jew.

More important for our purposes is the view that Judaism, to fulfill itself, must exert the full weight of its moral prestige towards the achievement of equal rights and opportunities for all persons, regardless of race or national origin. For this principle is the essence of our religious faith, as it is the essence of democracy itself.

It is not surprising that Jews responded powerfully to the fight against racial segregation and discrimination in America. After all, no group in history has been so frequently the victim of racial hatred.

Jews, more than any other segment of the white population, played an active role in the dramatic civil rights struggles of the 1950s and 1960s, when the Black-Jewish alliance was at the heart of the civil rights movement.

When the Mississippi Summer of 1964 was organized to break the back of legal segregation in the then most stubbornly resistant state of the Union, more than half of the young people who volunteered from all parts of the United States were Jews. In that struggle, two of the three martyrs killed by white extremists in Philadelphia, Mississippi, Andrew Goodman and Michael Schwerner, were Jewish; the third, James Earl Chaney, was black.

Jews contributed substantially to the funds raised by such organizations as the National Association for the Advancement of Colored People, the Southern Christian Leadership Conference, and the Student Non-Violent Coordinating Committee.

For many years, Kivie Kaplan (a vice-chair of the Reform Jewish movement) was the national president of the NAACP; Arnie Aronson and Joe Rauh, Jr., served as secretary and general counsel, respectively, to the Leadership Conference on Civil Rights (LCCR); Jack Greenberg was a key leader of the NAACP Legal Defense Fund (all of them Jews).

Rabbis marched with Martin Luther King, Jr., throughout the South; many were jailed, some were beaten. Prominent among these were Rabbi Abraham Joshua Heschel, who was a spiritual partner to King in the struggle against racism.

Jewish political leverage contributed to passage of landmark civil rights laws, nationally and locally.

The Civil Rights Act of 1964 and the Voting Rights Act of 1965 were drafted in the conference room of Reform Judaism's Emily and Kivie Kaplan Religious Action Center Building in Washington, D.C., under the aegis of the Leadership Conference on Civil Rights, which for decades was housed in the center.

We have seen the relationship between Blacks and Jews at a high point during the Civil Rights Movement. However, the bloody Crown Heights confrontation in Brooklyn, New York, certainly brought the two groups to a historical low point. But there are still substantial grounds for hope. Many Blacks and Jews still share a vision of a just, generous, and open society. Despite our dramatic economic differences, public opinion polls show that our attitudes and values are remarkably alike: we both recoil against bigotry and advocate a primary role for government in solving social inequity; and we are essential partners in virtually every successful coalition for social justice.

In presidential, congressional, and local elections, Jews and Blacks vote alike more than any other identifiable groups. Approximately 70 percent of Jews and 90 percent of Blacks opposed the 1984 Reagan and the 1988 Bush candidacies. No other groups gave the Democratic candidates a majority. An even higher percentage of Jews supported Bill Clinton in 1992.

In fact, in communities across America, Blacks and Jews are working together daily to address their common concerns. In 1991, the Religious Action Center of Reform Judaism, through its Marjorie Kovler Institute for Black-Jewish Relations, published a manual on cooperative programming in black churches and Jewish synagogues based on existing successful programs from across the country. Over 250 such programs are described at length. Consider the following:

- In Los Angeles, black and Jewish doctors, nurses, and congregants sponsor an annual health fair that serves over three hundred people with basic checkups, bloodwork, referrals to city agencies, and follow-ups with local clinics.

- In Hamden, Connecticut, a black church and Jewish synagogue have founded an interfaith AIDS network that provides financial and emotional support for people living with AIDS.

- In Plainfield, New Jersey, a black Episcopal church and a Reform Jewish synagogue jointly bought a dilapidated building and, with their own hands, rehabilitated it to house low-income families.

- In Manhasset and Great Neck, Long Island (in New York), the black and Jewish communities created a summer employment workshop to teach teens job-hunting skills. The same coalition also closed down a crack house that threatened the safety of a local housing project.

Such mutual efforts promote better Black-Jewish relations. But lasting improvement will require Blacks and Jews to change their perceptions of each other. This generation of Blacks (especially young people) has little awareness of past Jewish contributions to human equality. And even those who are aware question where the Jewish community stands today. However, Jews want to feel some appreciation for sacrifices they have made to achieve equal rights for Blacks and other minorities, which they feel they are not receiving from this generation of Blacks.

Black youths will have to understand recent history, including the Holocaust and its profound impact on the Jewish psyche, if any new relationship is to be forged. And Jews, too, will have to modulate injured feelings and stop expecting constant gratitude. Jews must understand that Blacks see us as more often blocking their hopes for progress than advancing them (in affirmative action, in minority housing, as well as in Jewish support for the death penalty, which many Blacks see as code words for "get tough with Blacks").

Can this drift be arrested? It is difficult to look ahead with confidence at this time, but we must try because both Jews and Blacks have a common stake in an open and compassionate society. When Jews and Blacks square off against each other, we elate our common enemies (Nazis, the KKK, and other foes of equality in America). Whether we like it or not, Blacks and Jews are joined together in a common destiny. It is time to join together to renew that special relationship and to unite in the struggle against poverty, ignorance, bigotry, crime, and an ineffective welfare system.

Bibliography

Landsberg, Lynne F., and David Saperstein, eds. *Common Road to Justice: A Programming Manual for Blacks and Jews*, Washington, D.C.: The Marjorie Kovler Institute for Black-Jewish Relations of the Religious Action Center of Reform Judaism, 1991.

Salzman, Jack, ed. *Bridges and Boundaries: African Americans and American Jews*. New York: The Jewish Museum, 1992.

Vorspan, Albert, and David Saperstein. *Tough Choices: Jewish Perspectives on Social Justice*. New York: UAHC Press, 1992.

Feminism and Judaism

DEBBIE FLIEGELMAN

> Like any other successful revolution, and
> like the broader woman's movement,
> Jewish Feminism ought to look toward
> the day when it can self-destruct.[1]

There are many people who claim that the Jewish
feminist movement is no longer needed, that Jewish
feminism can, in fact, go ahead and self-destruct, having
served its purpose well. They often point to the ordination of women as rabbis in both the Reform and
Conservative movements; the growing acceptance of
gender-neutral language in prayer; the equality in
religious education for boys and girls, men and women.
While it is true that great strides have been made, it is
not yet time for Jewish feminists to sit back and survey
their completed project. It seems that the closer we get
to our larger goal of true equality, the more apparent all
of the seemingly minor inequalities become.

Jewish feminism has historically been divided into
two camps: the prove-Judaism-is-a-sexist-religion group
and the reclaimer group. There has also emerged a
show-the-sexism-and-then-learn-how-to-adapt-it group,
which combines the research and ideas of the first two.

"Prove Judaism Is a Sexist Religion"

Biblical religion (and theology) is sexist to the
core. It is not retrievable for women, since it

265

ignores women's experience, speaks of the god-
head in male terms, legitimizes women's subordi-
nate positions of powerlessness, and promotes
male dominance and violence against women.
Therefore, feminists must move beyond the
boundaries of biblical religion and reject the patriarchal authority of biblical revelation.[2]

Sadly, it is too easy to point out the sexism in Judaism.
From text to practice, women and women's experiences
are barely visible. Although apologists will trot out a few
female role models (Ruth, Esther, Deborah), there is
little debate that women and men do not receive equal
attention or treatment in our tradition. Feminist scholarship in this area tends to focus on the exclusion of
women from and the blatantly sexist attitude toward
women in Jewish texts. One area that is consistently cited
as an example of women's exclusion from the community of Jews is the prayer in the morning service thanking
God for not having created the sayer of the prayer a
woman.[3] And there are numerous other examples in the
Bible, such as when God commands the Israelites at
Sinai not to go near a woman, an injunction that obviously refers only to the men.

But those who wish to prove that Judaism is a sexist
religion do not just concentrate on demonstrating the
sexism of the Bible; not only is such an approach obvious, but such sexism can also be explained (and
excused?) by taking into account the times in which the
Bible was written. It is clear that women had in that
society roles and responsibilities many of which no
longer exist. This is why those who argue that Judaism is
sexist must also demonstrate the presence of sexism in
contemporary Judaism.

There has also been discussion about the glass ceiling in the hiring of female rabbis. The prove-it group acknowledges the great strides women have made in the rabbinate but argues that women are still not treated equally. There are far fewer women leading very large congregations in the United States, and while some assert that women rabbis were ordained too recently to receive such positions, many have responded that, if this is the case, then why are men with whom they were ordained leading such congregations.

Reclaimers

If you think something is missing from Judaism, it is in Judaism that you have to look for the answer.[4]

While the reclaimers recognize the sexism in Judaism, they want to be able to practice Judaism and feel good about it; they want to find positive female role models and emphasize those elements of and instances in Judaism where women are included. As Alice Bloch says, "I take pride in my Jewish heritage, and I am tired of hearing women dismiss Jewish identity as 'oppressive' and 'patriarchal,' without knowing anything about it. I am tired of feminist books that sum up all Jewish thought in that one stupid prayer, 'Blessed art Thou...who did not make me a woman.'... Jewish identity is important to me because being Jewish is an integral part of myself; it's my inheritance, my roots." [5]

So instead of focusing on sexist imagery and liturgy, reclaimers look for that which is positive, sometimes reinterpreting what is negative in a positive light. For example, Lilith is traditionally considered a demon who tempts men and kills babies. The reclaimers turn the story around and look at Lilith as a strong independent woman with healthy sexual values. They portray her as a role model for women, attributing her demise to the inability of men to deal with strong women.

Vashti is another example for the reclaimers of a "bad girl" (because of disobedience to her king and husband) whose image needs to be reinterpreted. According to the reclaimers, Vashti is not a disobedient wife but a woman with a strong sense of self-worth. It is this sense of self-worth that explains her refusal to be used as a sexual plaything. In fact, they argue, she shares many of the same qualities as Mordecai, who is honored for his strong sense of values.

The reclaimers also reinterpret traditional laws and customs. While the prove-it group often points to the laws of *niddah* (concerning women, menstruation, and purity) as examples of female oppression, the reclaimers demonstrate how women can use these laws in their favor. The *mikveh*, for example, can be a spiritual place, one where women can share experience exclusive to women. The recent feminist impetus to celebrate menstruation also comes from the reclaimers, who see the menstrual period as moment in time when abstention from sex can double as time for personal reflection and getting in touch with one's body.

"Show the Sexism and Then Learn to Adapt It"

This last group is a synthesis of the first two. It is, in fact, something of an endpoint in the most modern versions of Jewish feminist thought. Members of this group take a hard and critical look at Judaism, exposing its sexist attitudes toward women. But they do not abandon Judaism altogether. Instead they insist on adapting and claiming whatever can be used from Judaism and discarding that which has no place in the modern world.

The following two excerpts are from articles that fall into this category. The common theme is the recognition that Judaism is sexist in some ways. But this recognition is combined with a deep love and respect for Judaism and the desire to remain a part of the community. Read them, and think hard about what they say.

> And so the tasks of Jewish feminism is not as simple as it seemed ten years ago. It is not merely a matter of changing and reinterpreting *halachah* and gaining inclusion in the *minyan*; rather, it is a much more complex process, bringing with it the hope (and threat) of profound change. Feminism challenges the patriarchal nature of Judaism and demands recognition of women as full persons rather than only in male-defined roles…. My own examination of my life as a feminist is my identity as a Jew. But the irony here is that I affirm my Jewishness in a way Judaism seems unable and unwilling to accept or return.[6]

> Surely, if she had the choice, any self-respecting Jewish woman (let alone feminist) would disavow herself from such a self-negating structure. But even after all that has been realized (and much, much more) is integrated into our consciousness, it is difficult for us to break our ties…. How can we, after all that has come before us, break the chain?

And, we do not want to stop being Jews. In spite
of all, many Jewish feminists are feminists because
we are Jews. Our Jewish heritage is one of activism
in the cause of freedom and justice. Paradoxically,
our Jewish experience has taught us the importance of feminist issues. Stripped of male dominance, the Jewish world view may not be so different from the feminist world view.[7]

Bibliography

Aarons, Victoria. "The Outsider within Women in
Contemporary Jewish-American Fiction." *Contemporary
Literature* 28 (1987): 378–393.

Baum, Charlotte, Paula Hyman, and Sonya Michel. *The Jewish
Woman in America*. New York: Plume, 1975.

Biale, Rachel. *Women and Jewish Law: An Exploration of
Women's Issues in Halakhic Sources*. New York: Schocken,
1984.

Birnbaum, Philip. *Daily Prayer Book: Ha-Siddur Ha-Shalem*.
New York: Hebrew Publishing Company, 1949.

Broner, E.M. *Her Mothers*. Bloomington: Indiana University
Press, 1975.

_____. *A Weave of Women*. Bloomington: Indiana University
Press, 1978.

Bulkin, Elly. "Hard Ground: Jewish Identity, Racism, and Anti-
Semitism." In *Yours in Struggle: Three Feminist
Perspectives on Anti-Semitism and Racism*, edited by Elly
Bulkin, Minnie Bruce Pratt, and Barbara Smith. Ithaca, NY:
Firebrand Books, 1988.

Cantor, Aviva. *The Jewish Woman, 1900–1985*: A Bibliography.
Fresh Meadows, NY: Biblio Press, 1987.

Christ, Carol P., and Judith Plaskow, eds. *Womanspirit Rising:
A Feminist Reader in Religion*. San Francisco: Harper and
Row, 1979.

Daum, Annette. "Responses in Reform Judaism to the Use of Sexist Language." Paper presented at the American Psychological Association in Montreal, Quebec, Canada, on September 2, 1980.

Greenberg, Blu. *On Women and Judaism: A View from Tradition*. Philadelphia: Jewish Publication Society, 1981.

Heschel, Susannah, ed. *On Being a Jewish Feminist*. New York: Schocken, 1983.

Henry, Sondra, and Emily Taitz. *Written Out of History: A Hidden Legacy of Jewish Women Revealed through Their Writings and Letters*. New York: Bloch, 1978.

Kaye/Kantrowitz, Melanie, and Irena Klepfisz, eds. *The Tribe of Dina: A Jewish Woman's Anthology*. Boston: Beacon Press, 1989.

Klagsbrun, Francine. *Voices of Wisdom*. Middle Village, NY: Jonathan David, 1980.

Kotrun, Elizabeth, ed. *The Jewish Woman: New Perspectives*. New York: Schocken, 1976.

Mazow, Julia Wolf, ed. *The Woman Who Lost Her Names*. San Francisco: Harper and Row, 1980.

Moore, Deborah Dash. "Defining American Jewish Ethnicity." *Prospects: The Annual of American Cultural Studies 6* (1981): 387–409.

Ozick, Cynthia. *The Messiah of Stockholm*. New York: Vintage, 1988.

Plaskow, Judith. *Standing Again at Sinai: Judaism from a Feminist Perspective*. San Francisco: Harper and Row, 1990.

_____, and Carol P. Christ, eds. *Weaving the Visitors: New Patterns in Feminist Spirituality*. San Francisco: Harper and Row, 1989.

Rapoport, Nessa. *Preparing for Sabbath*. Sunnyside, NY: Biblio Press, 1981.

Schneider, Susan Weidman. *Jewish and Female: A Guide and Sourcebook for Today's Jewish Woman*. New York: Simon and Schuster, 1985.

Shulman, Gail. "A Feminist Path to Judaism." In *On Being a Jewish Feminist,* edited by Susannah Heschel. New York: Schocken, 1983.

Task Force on Equality of Women in Judaism. *Out of the House of Bondage: Supplement to the New Union Haggadah.* New York: UAHC Press, 1983.

A Turning Point in Interfaith Relations?

A. JAMES RUDIN

The development of positive Christian-Jewish relations is one of the great success stories of this century.

This extraordinary undertaking began after World War II, when Christians and Jews found themselves literally and spiritually in the ashes of the *Shoah*. After Auschwitz, Jews realized that all outside sources of protection had failed, most notably the Christian Church.

Because the *Shoah* took place in Christian Europe, Jews looked at their neighbors in a radically new way and asked: "What did they do to save Jews?" And to those Christians who were too young or not involved, Jews ask: "Would Christians today take action to avert another *Shoah*?" And Jews ask themselves: "Does the *Shoah* have any meaning?"

For some Christians the *Shoah* created severe theological problems. If Christian moral restraints were unable to prevent the *Shoah*, of what use are such ethics and values? If they are only for theologically "sunny days," and not "stormy days," why bother with being a Christian?

Neither community has satisfactorily answered these probing questions, and perhaps they never will. But the need for a new relationship between Christians and Jews was clear. In 1948 the World Council of Churches publicly condemned anti-Semitism, and in 1965, the Roman Catholic Church achieved a historic breakthrough at the Second Vatican Council with the adoption of the Nostra Aetate Declaration.

Since then many denominations, bishops' conferences, and church bodies have spoken out forcefully on Jews, Judaism, anti-Semitism, and the *Shoah*. There have been more positive Christian-Jewish encounters since 1965 than there were in the first 1,900 years of Christianity.

But sadly, what we are attempting in the United States is not the norm throughout the world. There are many areas, including the former Soviet Union, where religious and ethnic rivalries are being acted out with bloody results. What we are striving for is authentic religious pluralism, something that must never be taken for granted.

Building on Our Success

As a result of the growing positive relationship between Christians and Jews, each group now has high expectations of the other. Today, Jews expect responsible Christian leaders, both clergy and lay, to publicly condemn all anti-Semitic statements and actions. We expect Christians to establish courses in churches, colleges, universities, and seminaries that address the pathology of anti-Semitism. We expect programs aimed at eradicating anti-Semitism from church life, including education, liturgy, seminary training, and a host of other activities.

And Christians now expect more as well, including the removal of anti-Christian material from Jewish educational material along with a condemnation of those who use stereotypes and caricatures to misrepresent Christians and Christianity. Of course, the historical parallel between Christians and Jews is unequal, but Jews need to recognize that profound and irrevocable changes have taken place within parts of the Christian community. It is unfair to demand that Christians recognize the permanent validity of Jews and Judaism, without also demanding that Jews overcome their prejudices towards Christians and Christianity.

At this point, Christian-Jewish relations would be perceived as a success needing only some further enhancement. But that would be only part of the picture. Christian-Jewish relations are at a critical turning point, and if we are not prudent in our actions, many of the recent positive achievements will be weakened or even lost.

Seizing the Moment

There are two reasons for this defining moment. One is the calendar and the other is today's ideological climate. After 1945, many interreligious pioneers were Christians and Jews who personally experienced Nazism. But the Jewish and Christian pioneers are passing from the scene, succeeded by younger leaders for whom the *Shoah* is not a personal experience. This is inevitable, but it does mean a difference. As the new generation assumes leadership, the *Shoah* will remain central in Christian-Jewish relations, but it will no longer be the only major force.

The second reason for this critical moment in Christian-Jewish relations is the climate of the times. After 1945, the United States was the unchallenged political, military, and economic leader of what we call the free world. Americans, already victors over Nazism, were determined to defeat Communism while still maintaining the legendary openness of the American spirit.

The U.S. opposed an atheistic and anti-Jewish Soviet regime, and welcomed positive Christian-Jewish relations. Overcoming bigotry was a worthwhile goal that enhanced our national image as the champion of human rights and religious liberty.

The early gains in Christian-Jewish relations took place against the backdrop of a religiously benign America. President Eisenhower supposedly said it "didn't matter what anyone believed as long as they believed in something." But a funny thing happened in the last decade. Religious fundamentalism has entered the public arena with power and influence, and now it matters to many Americans what other Americans believe.

There are no more fevered issues than abortion, bioethics, moral values in the public schools, sexual equality, and the flood of "rights" concerns including homosexuals, African-Americans, Asians, Hispanics, Native Americans, the disabled, the young, the old, and even animals. With so many other causes, the struggle against anti-Semitism and the need for Christian-Jewish dialogue is often perceived as just another worthy conversionary Christianity. It is clear why Christian-Jewish relations can no longer depend upon the post-World War II momentum.

Defining the Issues

There are three critical areas in today's Christian-Jewish relations. The first is how the *Shoah* will be remembered. The second relates to Christian and Jewish understandings of the State of Israel, and the final area is the theological issue of conversion, mission, witness, and proselytizing.

Jews will always remember the *Shoah*, but how will Christians remember it after the survivors die? Will it be cited morally as an example of "man's inhumanity to man"? Will the Nazis' war against the Jews be blanched out and replaced by a universalism emptied of the uniqueness of Jewish suffering? Will it be only a sidecar in future history books? Or will it be taught as a catastrophic example of what happened when murderous anti-Semitism became the national policy of a modern state?

This was painfully illustrated by the 1993 controversy surrounding the location of the Carmelite convent at Auschwitz. One major Christian misunderstanding was the belief that the root problem was that Jews did not want nuns to pray for the victims of Nazism. But the actual issue was the convent's inappropriate location in the very building where the poison gas was stored. Jews and many Christians strongly believe that Auschwitz must remain intact. To change the camp's character is wrong because Auschwitz represents the ultimate symbol of evil and Jewish suffering. Jews did not object to the Carmelites or their prayers. And to prove this point, the Jewish community welcomed the new convent that is nearing completion just 600 yards outside the camp.

On the other hand, it was difficult for Jews to recognize that Auschwitz is also a center of martyrdom for Polish Catholics. During the crisis, people played an obscene numbers game in which each community claimed it had suffered more from the Nazis than the other.

The Auschwitz convent crisis, which is on the way to a satisfactory resolution, was a lightning flash that illumined the charred *Shoah* terrain that still separates Christians and Jews. Many Christians believe that the *Shoah* is just another example of depravity in a sinful world. But for Jews, the *Shoah* was a radical act of evil; the nearly successful attempt to murder an entire people. The convent crisis revealed that much work remains to assure that the *Shoah* is not minimized or relativized in Christian teaching.

Israel in the Christian Mind

A second critical issue is the Christian attitude towards the State of Israel. Today many theologians are exploring what a reborn Jewish state means for Christianity. For example, some Christians still believe that God has cursed the Jews for not accepting Jesus as Messiah, and as a result they are condemned to be perpetual pariahs.

But Jews are no longer the eternal refugee. Israel is the one place where Jews are free to work out their destiny as the majority in their own land, and this has dramatically altered the relationship between Christians and Jews. Although we are not equal in numbers, Israel provides an equilibrium in Christian-Jewish relations.

Christians must not employ a double standard when they judge Israeli actions and policies. There are many Western Christians who support and even celebrate all the national liberation movements that have emerged since 1945 except one—Zionism. The double standard is often used to decry alleged Israeli human rights violations. Like every other state, Israel is imperfect, but as a democracy, it acknowledges its shortcomings. However, when Christians unfairly single out Israel for criticism, they weaken their professed concern for justice and equity.

Redefining Basic Terms

The final issue relates to witness, mission, conversion, and proselytizing. These terms are heavily charged with history and theology. As positive Christian-Jewish relations unfold, Christians must ask how one remains faithful to the authenticity of Christianity while affirming theological space for Jews and Judaism. It is a profound question for Christians as they engage Jews in dialogue.

Why do Christians often relate to Muslims, Hindus, Buddhists, Shintoists, and other religions in a more benevolent manner than they have historically related to Jews? What is in the Christian relationship to Jews and Judaism that has inspired such hostility?

There is a difference between Christian mission and Christian witness. Mission means the singling out of Jews as candidates for conversion, while witness means the quality of one's spiritual life. Jews and Christians can "compete" with one another in witnessing. It means abandoning all covert and overt attempts to missionize and letting God's spirit move people along diverse religious paths.

But proselytizing is religious coercion, the heavy-handed and insulting attempts by Christians to convert Jews. And conversion is best understood by *teshuvah*, a turning towards God, something not induced by pressure and manipulation. But with the current rise of an aggressive Christian fundamentalism, positive Christian-Jewish relations could become a casualty. Christians who are committed to the dialogue must develop some clear working definitions for mission, witness, conversion, and proselytism. If they do not do so, fundamentalists will do it for them, and we will all be the losers.

The Boundaries of Pluralism

GARY BRETTON-GRANATOOR

In the last three decades, interreligious dialogue has suffered many ups and downs. Yet the very fact that interreligious dialogue has become a priority within

Judaism and almost every major faith gives us hope for the future. I suggest that in these past three decades, there have been three distinct stages in our dialogue.

The first stage began in those years during the design and implementation of the Catholic Church's Vatican II Reforms and the parallel reforms that took place within the Protestant communities. This period could be called the Age of Tea and Sympathy. For during those years, interreligious dialogue was primarily focused on faith communities introducing themselves to one another (often over tea and sandwiches) and learning to shed their mutual fears.

The second stage could be called the Age of Education, during which we actively learned about our neighbors' faiths and taught them about our own. This education was at times superficial as individuals focused on liturgical/holiday calendars and basic tenets. It was also during this Age that nascent attempts were made at joint worship, often centering around the holiday of Thanksgiving or Brotherhood Week. During this stage, we discovered the common threads that ran through our traditions and sometimes even tried to piece together shared services. (Unfortunately, these services were designed to offend no one, such that, more often than not, they also inspired no one.)

We are now at the third stage as we direct our educational resources toward some of the more profound questions that lie at the heart of our dialogue. At the same time, we are working with other faiths in the area of social justice. The best examples of these joint actions are the tremendous efforts that many of our congregations have made on behalf of the homeless and the hungry.

One of the constant themes during these many years of dialogue has been the security of our people. We have worked hard through education and dialogue to contain the scourge of anti-Semitism. And yet, though we have often been thwarted in our attempts, still we have found that the best avenue for eradicating anti-Semitism has been to conduct and maintain an open dialogue with our neighboring faiths. Because of this dialogue, incidents of anti-Semitism, although they are still with us, have waned in number and intensity.

Our successes in dialogue with the Catholic, Protestant, Muslim, and other communities suggest that we are heading in the right direction. Yes, we have our failures, and, yes, there are many faiths that do not understand the importance of certain issues to the Jewish people. But we must not be put off by these setbacks. Instead, let us see these problems as guide-posts on the route we must chart in our future course. This third stage is still in the making, which is why we must be attentive to the five areas that serve as the foundation for this stage.

1. *Theology*. Many modern Jews are uniquely situated to engage in theological dialogue with those of other faith communities. Unfortunately, this is an area we Jews are not as adept as we should be at discussing. For too long, most Jews have been cowed by the memories of past disputes. Today, theological dialogue is an expressed need on the part of Catholic and Protestant communities, as well as other communities, and most traditional Jews are barred from engaging in such dialogue due to the *teshuvah* (answer) of Rav Soloveitchik.

In response to the question of whether Jews should participate in interfaith dialogue, Rav Soloveitchik responded that only in those instances where dialogue will accrue to the safety and security benefit of the Jewish people, with the strong proviso that no theological discussion ever ensue. The advantage for the Jewish community of participating in theological dialogue is understanding the basis of the Christian community's faith, and, thus, a better understanding of what makes us different and what binds us together. The outward manifestations of difference, such as modalities of prayer, architecture, and decor, are only of secondary importance—we must understand what makes our faiths different at their very core if we are to understand each other at all.

2. *Roots of Spirituality.* We need to learn not only about our own notions of spirituality but those of our brothers and sisters in other faiths. While we are more than willing to share our *midrashim* and other rabbinic tales with our neighbors, we seem reticent to discuss those sources that describe our spiritual experience of Judaism. We need to expose ourselves to those materials so we can help our fellow Jews find deeper meaning in their own Jewish experience, even if it means learning of them from non-Jewish sources.

3. *Challenges of Pluralism.* Here we face a number of questions. For Americans and others who live in democratic and pluralistic societies, to what extent are we willing to say that there is truth in other religious positions? At what point do the mandates of our own religious faith need to be set aside for

"the common good"? What does it do to our own core of faith to say that what we believe is correct and true but that others are entitled to believe that their faiths are true also? These are the challenges of pluralism that those of deep religious conviction must confront to live peacefully in modern democratic society.

4. *Challenges to Pluralism.* In the challenge of pluralism, we faced one set of questions. In the challenge to pluralism, we confront a different set. For example, if we accept all faith communities, what about those faiths which insist that what we profess is wrong and what they profess is right? Additionally, what of those placed in the public trust by election or appointment who feel compelled to enact or support legislation dictated by their religious beliefs? As Americans today, we may be witnessing the slow but steady demolition of the wall of separation between church and state articulated by Jefferson. As the right of prayer in the public schools is more readily accepted and religious symbols are allowed to stand on public property, how do we respond to this reduction in the separation of church and state?

5. *Understanding Living Religion.* For more than a quarter of a century, we have been either the guests or the hosts of other religions, but how well do we really understand our neighbors? What impact do their religious beliefs have on their day-to-day existence? How does faith translate into practice outside of church and pew? For that matter, how seriously have we considered the impact of our own religious principles on our

day-to-day life? For example, do Jewish ethics come into play when a business decision needs to be made? How loudly does our liturgical calendar speak to us when we are also tempted to celebrate events in our day-to-day lives?

These five areas need to be placed in the forefront of our minds as we set the future agenda for our participation in interfaith activities. Dialogue is critical to our own survival, which is why we must teach all of our followers not only the beauty of our tradition and what makes us different but how to articulate that difference to those who do not share our faith. Should we fail to do so, the price we pay could be higher than we wish.

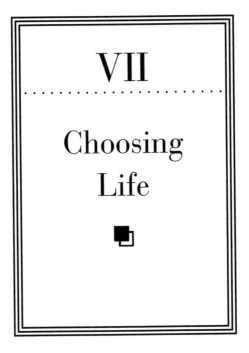

VII

Choosing
Life

To Do or Not To Do
Peer Pressure

BARBARA COHEN

For some of you, going to college is your first long-term experience away from home, and the carefully planned values and self-discipline your parents spent so many years instilling in you are, for the first time, now open to question. The place is new, the faces different, and the free time unstructured. You are free to choose your own activities; you can even choose not to do any at all. Your curfews are up to you—as are your study habits, your diet and personal hygiene, even who you will date or spend time with. If you haven't already, you will probably spend much of your first year asking some of the most basic questions about life: Who am I? What do I like to do? With whom? What are my beliefs? What kind of person do I want to be?

Given all these new freedoms and new pressures, how then do you avoid situations that may force you to compromise your values? Judaism teaches us a great deal about resisting temptation and remaining true to ourselves. Ben Zoma says, "Who is wise? One who learns from everyone. Who is strong? One who controls his own impulses. Who is rich? One who is happy with his portion" (*Pirke Avot* 4:1). Now while this passage acknowledges the influence those around have and should have on you, you must take care not be so easily swayed by the desires of others. By making plans before the weekend and learning to appreciate quiet evenings as a treat rather than a bore, you can avoid resisting the pressure to "party" that is so common to college life. The lesson Ben Zoma teaches us is that we need to find ways to be "happy with our portion."

Despite the large amount of unstructured time available to you, you should know that college students have very hectic schedules. Academics take up (or should take up) most of that time, whether it's writing papers, reading your textbook, or studying for midterms and finals. Alongside other extracurricular and social commitments, making time for everything can seem like an overwhelming, if not impossible, task.

As hard as it may be just to meet our academic obligations, it is even more difficult to prioritize a schedule when our friends have a different agenda for us. How should a student with a midterm or large paper due respond when friends encourage him or her to "blow it off" for a while and go to a party or cafe instead? For disorganized students or those who are just not clear about their priorities, the temptation to put socializing before studying may be too difficult to resist.

Certainly, a student needs time for social activities. But it is important to be able to determine when there is time for such activities. Balancing the solitude of study against the need for companionship is the source of most conflicts college students feel. Our rabbis understood this conflict, which is why they taught us, "If I am not for myself, who will be for me? But if I am for myself alone, what am I? And if not now, when?" (*Pirke Avot* 1:2). This three-part guideline can be quite helpful to college students still learning to prioritize their objectives.

College is clearly a time for self-growth, and it is of the utmost importance to act in our own best interest.

Only we know what is best for ourselves. Only by remembering our needs and acting on our own beliefs will we avoid caving in to those pressures urging us to do things that are not right.

I remember my first week of college. All the women who lived on my dorm floor gathered in one woman's room for a little "girl talk." The conversation eventually turned to sex and the status of everyone's virginity. Several people revealed that they were not yet sexually active, while others joked, saying "You probably won't be a virgin by the end of this year!" Even though this talk was among good friends, there was still a type of pressure being placed on those who were not yet sexually active by those who automatically assumed that everyone in college is sexually active.

It is at moments like these that those feeling pressured by others should recall what Rabbi Zusya of Hanipol said before he died, "In the world to come they will not ask me, 'Why were you not Moses?' They will ask me, 'Why were you not Zusya?' " In other words, the only standards we should hold ourselves to are our own. Sexual decisions should never be a matter of group consensus, as in the example above. What individuals decide to do or not to do with their body is a very private matter.

Identifying the sources of peer pressure at college is often difficult, especially when we start becoming interested in participating in campus groups or enter a new social circle. So some questions to keep in mind when you join a group or make new friends should include the following: Am I engaging in activities in which I am truly interested and for which I have the time, or am I merely participating because I feel pressured by the group to take part? Am I joining this organization because I believe in its vision or because of its status? If I do not ultimately end up joining a group, have I considered alternative ways of getting involved and making friends on campus? Am I willing and able to stay true to my beliefs if they differ from those of my friends? What do I truly believe?

Ultimately, we must answer for our own actions. While it is understandably difficult to overcome the pressures of people we like and want to impress, we alone will be responsible for the choices we make under the influence of others. This is why we must, therefore, also be able to identify those conditions in which we become more vulnerable to peer pressure. These conditions emerge when we have too much unstructured free time on our hands or find ourselves in a situation where it is easier to lose ourselves in mindless behavior rather than explore our deepest values. College affords the opportunity of a lifetime. It is a time when we can focus on ourselves and grow, learn, explore, and develop as individuals. It is a time when we need social contact, for social contact is what gives us our humanity. But our ability to think independently and make personal choices must remain paramount in the four years or more that we have to figure out who we really are.

Suicide

RAMIE ARIAN

Suicide is a difficult topic to avoid on the college campus. It is natural during college to ponder the meaning of one's life and to test the notion that there is no meaning. At one point or another, most college students give some thought to taking their own life.

In the last twenty-five years the rate of completed suicide among college-age people has tripled. Suicide is the second leading cause of death (after accidents) among 19- to 24-year-olds. Its prominence as a leading cause of death on the college campus is why we must explore the subject in some detail.

This section is divided into three parts. The first part is a brief statement of the official Reform Jewish position on suicide: This statement links the traditional view and the reality of our lives today. The second part is a more detailed description of the traditional Jewish view of suicide and how that view developed. (This section thus is carefully footnoted to serve as a starting point for anyone wishing to pursue the subject further.) The third part contains some practical advice if someone you know (it could be you) is contemplating suicide.

The Value of Life:
The Reform Jewish View of Suicide [1]

Judaism has always considered human life to be sacred and the taking of one's life as a *chet*—a sin. Suicide is forbidden except under specific, tragic circumstances, such as the choice between forced conversion and death, which has occured time and again throughout our people's history.

According to Jewish law, when a Jew commits suicide, he or she is to be interred on the periphery of the cemetery, a fair distance from the other grave sites. Moreover, no mourning rites are to be observed for the individual. However, if the suicide victim is considered *lo lada'at*—mentally incompetent—these rules are suspended.

Reform Judaism does not condone the taking of one's own life. In keeping with Jewish tradition, however, which emphasizes compassion and concern for the surviving family, the rites of burial and mourning customs are observed. Survivors of suicide attempts are urged to seek appropriate therapy.

Reform Jews are deeply concerned with the recent epidemic of completed and attempted suicides. In an effort to reverse these alarming trends, the Union of American Hebrew Congregations has determined to use its resources to teach and emphasize the value and holiness of life as a God-given gift to be held in sacred trust. We seek to teach each of our children to recognize the uniqueness of their own lives. The saving of a life, including one's own, is tantamount to saving the world.

The Traditional Jewish Position on Suicide: A Summary [2]

In Jewish tradition, intentional suicide is forbidden and is punishable by the withholding of those traditional burial and mourning rites whose function is to honor the deceased. [3]

Rabbinic tradition focuses a great deal of attention on the issue of "intention." In practical application, this question of "intention" is often dealt with in terms of technical legal competence. Although forbidden, suicide is only punishable if the act was "intentionally" committed by a person judged to be legally competent to have such intent. In the absence of clear evidence of intent and competence, there is a presumption of innocence (that is, of lack of intent and/or competence), and penalties are not applied. [4]

There is no clearly articulated prohibition against suicide in the Bible, the *Mishnah*, or the Talmud. [5] In fact, the Bible records several instances of suicide (e.g., Samson, King Saul) without any hint of blame (and even with a tone of praise). The Talmud records numerous instances of suicide, generally without laying any blame whatsoever on the suicide victim.

Without challenging the general prohibition against suicide, later rabbinic authorities cite these biblical and talmudic cases as precedents for clarifying and extending the instances in which suicide is judged blameless because intention or legal competence are determined to be lacking. The suicide of King Saul, [6] in particular, is frequently cited as a precedent for excusing suicide in a wide variety of situations.

Although there is no unanimity among rabbinic authorities, there has evolved a broad range of circumstances in which a suicide may be declared blameless because of lack of intent or legal competence. In each of these cases, the penalties for committing the sin (or crime) of suicide would not be applied: [7]

1. Suicide by a minor. [8]

2. Suicide as an act of repentance.

3. Suicide under conditions of incarceration.

4. Suicide as a consequence of poverty.

5. Suicide in response to intense humiliation.

6. Suicide committed under the extreme influence of alcohol.

7. Suicide by the mentally ill.[9]

8. Suicide as an act of empathy.

9. Suicide as an act of martyrdom.[10]

By gradually extending the grounds for exempting suicides from traditional penalties, Jewish tradition arrived at the following situation: suicide is clearly prohibited, but the penalties are practically never applied. Many rabbis view this as precisely the correct stance for tradition to take. By maintaining a clear prohibition against suicide, a strong religious taboo against the act is established. By granting case-by-case exceptions in almost any imaginable circumstance, the support of the community is not withheld from the mourners of suicide victims.

There are, however, those who argue that the tradition's position on suicide has become too lenient. Modern halachic debate on the permissibility of suicide has been rekindled by the climbing suicide rate for Jews in the nineteenth and twentieth centuries. At least one contemporary halachic authority has argued for a more concerted effort to deter suicidal behavior by bringing the full weight of Jewish tradition to bear on the would-be suicide.[11]

If Someone You Know
Is Contemplating Suicide

As strange as it may seem, most people with suicidal feelings actually want to live. More correctly, these people are ambivalent: A part of them wants to live while another part of them wants to die. What most suicidal people really want is to be relieved of emotional pain, itself the likely result of many conscious and unconscious causes.

Suicidal people often give warnings of their intent. They may indicate that they are depressed by talking about death, dropping comments about not being needed or important, or by making final arrangements. Generally, a person will show more than one sign at a time.

People who talk about suicide are seriously considering ending their own lives. These people are crying out for help, and this warning should not be ignored. You should ask them directly if they have suicidal feelings or if they plan to harm themselves. Asking may make them feel relieved that someone has finally recognized their emotional pain. However, make sure you can handle an affirmative answer.

If someone you know is seriously considering suicide, you should do whatever is necessary to get help from trained professionals—even at the risk of betraying that person's confidence. Ask for help from your parents, a teacher, counselor, rabbi, cantor, youth advisor, or any other adult you trust. Most cities and many universities have suicide hotlines, and most campuses have health services, where there are medical professionals trained to help. You can call anonymously on behalf of your friend, and you will be informed how best to help that person.

Resources

For information on the warning signs of suicide, contact the UAHC Task Force on Youth Suicide Prevention, 1330 Beacon Street, Suite 355, Brookline, MA 02146 (617) 277-1655.

An excellent book to read if you want to help someone who is thinking about committing suicide is *When Living Hurts* by Sol Gordon. You can find it in paperback in most large bookstores, or you can order it from the UAHC Press, 838 Fifth Avenue, New York, NY 10021 (212) 249-0100.

A Jewish Way of Eating

ALLEN ROSS AND STUART COPANS

Eating has always held a central place in Jewish life. Indeed, the essence of our faith has been to discover and foster a personal relationship with God through the seemingly mundane events of daily living. While the Reform movement has not required its members to keep kosher, the values underlying traditional dietary laws are certainly worth our consideration. Reciting *berachot* before and after every meal and applying the laws of *kashrut* create daily opportunities to elevate one's consciousness about our relationship to God.

Maimonides suggested that one of the functions of Jewish dietary laws was to increase our consciousness of what we ate. Whether we are eating vegetables that others have grown or the flesh of animals who have given their lives for our growth, it is important that we be aware of how much is involved in our meals. In this world of supermarkets and cellophane-packaged meats, it is easy to eat without thinking about where our food comes from. In traditional Jewish communities, the *shochet*—ritual slaughterer—was expected to be almost as learned and as holy as the rabbi because of the sacredness of his occupation.

Some Jews express their consciousness about what they eat by being vegetarians. In Genesis 1:29 there is a strong suggestion that humans were supposed to be vegetarians: "God said, 'See, I give you every seed-bearing plant that is upon all the earth, and every tree that has seed-bearing fruit; they shall be yours for food.' " In fact, according to Jewish writings, people were not only vegetarians before Noah but will be again during the messianic age. In the meantime, eating a vegetarian diet is a remarkably simple way to keep kosher.

Whatever form our diet takes, whether it's keeping kosher or eating vegetarian, our sense of why we eat what we eat can become hollow if we do not see it primarily as a means for elevating our reverence for life. Sharing our lives together over food strengthens our social bonds as Jews. From the morning brunch of bagels and lox to the Passover seder to a *Kiddush* after services, there are many occasions in our tradition for pleasurable eating. There is also the tradition of discussing Torah whenever Jews gather for a meal. In Judaism, eating is a multileveled event, combining the best aspects of what is supposed to be a social, educational, and spiritual experience.

In today's secular world, the elevation of daily simple tasks to a higher, more spiritual level is constantly being challenged. It may often feel as though there is hardly enough time for anything. Grabbing ten minutes for lunch may seem a luxury in college as you run from your dormitory to a class to the library and back again; remembering to get ketchup to go with your Big Mac and fries may be your highest level of consciousness during lunch. But should eating only be a way to get food into your system in order to satisfy bodily needs? If so, you will have missed a significant opportunity to enhance your life as a Jew.

As a college student, you are in the position to test your values outside the boundaries of your family. Your parents can't see or hear what you say or do. What sort of Jewish identity you wish to establish or maintain is clearly your choice. Whether you examine that identity or let it atrophy is up to you. The act of eating, however, is an ideal area for exploring what role your Judaism will have in how you live your life.

Jewish attitudes toward food reveal several important values. Gluttony and asceticism are both frowned upon, while moderation is praised. One is expected to gain pleasure through eating; to celebrate holy occasions through the use of eating and drinking, and to thank God for our generous bounty of food. Maimonides held the view that virtue was the mean between two extremes, that eating in moderation was a positive behavior, and that ascetic behavior was "counter to the divine will."

Unfortunately, moderation has never been so tested as in today's society. Extreme behaviors in the act of eating are all too prevalent, from the self-starvation of anorexia to the binging and purging of bulimia. The restrictions of eating disorders are the antithesis of the guidelines established for eating as Jews. There is no joy in food, no pleasure of social contact, and no sanctification of God. The desperate attempt to take "control" of one's life by manipulating food turns a person inward, away from social and spiritual connections. You can't get enough of what you don't need when you are overeating or undereating.

Recapturing a sense of value and meaning with food can be an important ingredient in resolving an eating problem. In addition, Jewish teachings and medical ethics emphasize the responsibility of each person to maintain a healthy life. It is incumbent on us as Jews to utilize medical and therapeutic help in order to recover from these disorders. Most colleges and universities have excellent counseling and medical resources with trained professionals to help students address eating problems. If you have problems with food and your diet practices, don't keep it a secret! Let people help you and work with you toward recovery. If treated, people can go on to live healthy, full lives. If not treated, these illnesses can be fatal.

In Judaism, each life is precious. What affects one affects us all. We have a responsibility to help those in need. So if your roommate or friend at college has eating problems, talk to them about it and encourage them to get help. Let your dorm leader know of your concerns. Get assistance from professionals for your friend. There are also a number of good publications to help you understand eating problems and what to do about them, such as Susan Kano's *Making Peace with Food*.

Spiritual considerations are a part of effective treatment to help poeple recover a more healthy approach to eating. Twelve-step programs, such as Overeaters Anonymous, emphasize self-help, the benefit of supportive groups, and the spiritual aspects of recovery for eating problems. The values inherent in the twelve steps are compatible with, and in part derived from, Jewish ethics and values.

In contemporary American life, it is easy for us to focus on what we want, rather than what we have; on what we think is owed to us, rather than what is given to us; and on the pleasures we hope to have in the future, rather than the pleasures we have every day in our lives. If we eat with attention and care, if we take our meals as times to appreciate the presence of holiness in the necessary aspects of our daily lives, then our meals can help prepare us for the rest of our lives not only by providing us with physical sustenance, but by providing us with social and spiritual sustenance as well.

Bibliography

Heschel, Abraham Joshua. *The Wisdom of Heschel*. New York: Farrar, Straus and Giroux, 1975.

Kano, Susan. *Making Peace with Food: Freeing Yourself from the Diet/Weight Obsession*. New York: Harper and Row, 1989.

Substance Abuse
in the Jewish Community
A Historical Perspective

KERRY M. OLITZKY

It would be too easy to claim that the Jewish community does not need to face the problem of addiction. Few even acknowledge that the problem exists within the community. Jewish institutions, for the most part, have not opened their doors (until very recently) to twelve-step programs of any sort. Prior to the modern period (with some obvious exceptions), individual Jewish communities were segregated from the rest of the world. Social problems were addressed within them and seldom discussed in public. While we are free to question the findings of the few classic studies on the problem, those findings do seem to bear out the claim that the historical Jewish community has been relatively free from alcoholism.[1]

To explain this phenomenon, some scholars have suggested that the use of alcohol in the Jewish community was not related to the development of self-esteem, as it was in other ethnic subgroups. It was not part of the Jewish communal subculture.[2] Fifty years ago, one researcher wrote, "We are dealing with a highly developed superego of the exile…. Implicit in the culture of the Jewish people is a taboo against conspicuous deviation from the conduct norms within an alien community… an emotionally sustaining tradition and family organization preclude the status-giving effects for alcohol." [3] Because the use of alcohol (primarily in the form of wine) was sanctified in the strong institutional context of synagogue and family, the potential for alcohol abuse was kept under control. Still there is no denying that substance abuse among Jews exists.[4]

For example, while many addictive behaviors are seldom discussed at length in sacred literature, the abuse of alcohol is described, sometimes at length, in its pages. Drinking to excess was even mandated on certain festivals. On Purim, for example, Jews are instructed to drink until they cannot tell the difference between the exclamations "Blessed be Mordecai" and "Cursed be Haman," the hero and villain respectively of the Book of Esther upon which the holiday is based (*Megillah* 7b). One text in the Babylonian Talmud even recounts the death of one rabbi at the hands of another, the result of a round of Purim drinking. According to the text, it seems that Rabbah and Rabbi Zeira were celebrating Purim together when all of a sudden, in a drunken stupor, Rabbah slit Rabbi Zeira's throat. The next morning, Rabbah prayed to God that Zeira's life be restored, which it was. The following year, Rabbah invited Rabbi Zeira again to his Purim feast, but Zeira replied, "No, thank you. A miracle may not happen a second time" (*Megillah* 7b).

In the rabbinic literature, one finds careful distinctions continually being drawn between use and abuse, suggesting that the rabbis were well aware of the dangers of substance abuse and addiction. Commenting on a text from Proverbs 23:31a, "Look not upon the wine when it is red," the sage Rava, for example, indulges in a bit of wordplay when he writes, "Look not upon the wine, for its end is blood" (*Sanhedrin* 70a). Even the Temple priests recognized the mind-altering effects of alcohol, prohibiting its use during sacrifices. (Indeed, according to biblical theology, one error in the use of alcohol could subject the entire Israelite community to the wrath of God.) Alcohol was also forbidden to the Sanhedrin when decisions were being made. (The Sanhedrin was the ancient rabbinic legal body which held in the balance the life of individuals and the welfare of the community.) And while total abstinence was not encouraged, one could not drink during prayers.

Yet though our tradition acknowledged the deleterious effects of alcohol, the Jewish view of alcohol remained ambiguous. This ambiguity is captured by Ben Sira, the author of a book of Hebrew wisdom literature, who asserts, "Wine is life-giving water to a man, if he drink it in moderation. What life has a man who lacks new wine, seeing that it was created for rejoicing from the beginning?" (*Ben Sira* 31:27).

No doubt there is much room for debate on the effect of alcoholism on the Jewish community. Like statistics, sacred texts are easily manipulated to present a continuum of views on the use of alcohol: from the drunkenness of Noah in Genesis 9:20–24 to the deaths of Aaron's priestly sons Nadav and Avihu in Leviticus 10:1–13 (which according to one rabbinic perspective was a result of their intoxication) to the idealized vows of the Nazirite in Numbers 6 (which included total abstention from wine and strong drink). Rabbinic sages like Rabbi Meir went so far as to say that "The tree of which Adam ate was actually a grapevine, for nothing brings as much woe to the human species as has wine" (*Sanhedrin* 70a, b).

Whether they explicitly stated it or not, the rabbis of old recognized the compulsive behavior and potential for abuse alcohol could induce. They had witnessed such conduct among the members of their community and codified their response within the texts of Jewish law, such as the *Shulchan Aruch*, the traditional code of Jewish Law:

> Since it is a requirement from God that the body of a human being be healthy and perfect, because it is impossible for a human being when ill to comprehend the knowledge concerning the Creator, it is therefore necessary to shun all things that tend to injure the body and acquire habits that make the body healthy and sound.

Both body and soul are divine gifts to us. The soul is eternal, but the body exists only for a time. The idea that we must care for everything in our world was thus meant to apply to our bodies as well as our souls. We are, in short, banned from ruining the work of our Creator.

Over the centuries, we Jews have convinced ourselves that we are not like the other nations. We are free from the problems of alcoholism and drug abuse that plague other communities. But, as our tradition makes clear, it does not matter whether there are or are not large numbers of alcoholics or drug addicts within the Jewish community. Every life is precious; none should waste itself in the throes of alcohol or drugs.

Indeed, the idea that Jews don't drink or take drugs may be part of a myth generated by the Jewish community in order to conceal its own flaws from the non-Jewish community. No amount of myth, however, can veil the fact that alcohol abuse exists—as do other addictive behaviors—in the Jewish community. And while alcohol abuse may be less common among Jews than non-Jews, Jews do have a strong tendency to use drugs to foster self-esteem. We saw this especially in the 1960s drug culture, where Jews were highly represented.[4] Moreover, the abuse of legal drugs remains very high among Jews. Food addictions also continue to plague the Jewish community, epitomized in the stereotypic Jewish mother fussily telling her child to "eat just a little more." And we know that Jews are overrepresented among compulsive gamblers.[5] (Note that gambling is not prohibited, even according to the strictest interpretation of Jewish law.) Run away as much as we might from the problem, eventually we will have to recognize that many members of the Jewish community—especially on the college campus where the constant pressure to drink heavily is strong—are in pain and need our help. As one friend in recovery once put it, "I felt like I had a hole inside of me. I tried to fill the hole with alcohol and drugs. It didn't work!"

Saving a Life
A Jewish Response to AIDS

HOWARD I. BOGOT

In 1985, the Union of American Hebrew Congregations issued a summons to action on AIDS. This landmark resolution called for increased financial and human resources to be used for prevention, treatment, and public education, and for an end to discrimination against those with AIDS or related illnesses. Since then the death toll has increased several-fold. An estimated one to one and a half million Americans are already infected with the Human Immunodeficiency Virus (HIV): many, if not most, may be expected to suffer chronic immunological or neurological problems throughout their lifetimes. Without strong educational and public policy efforts, millions more will be infected. How are we, as Jews, responding to the AIDS crisis?

AIDS (Acquired Immune Deficiency Syndrome) is a viral disease which breaks down a part of the body's immune system. This breakdown leaves the body vulnerable to a variety of unusual, life-threatening illnesses. It is these illnesses, not the AIDS virus itself, which can result in death. Physical illness is often just the beginning of the suffering faced by people with AIDS or ARC (AIDS-Related Complex) and their families.

Many people with AIDS, or those suspected of carrying the virus which causes AIDS, have lost their jobs, been evicted from their homes, or been abandoned by frightened friends and family. Often this discrimination is based on homophobia or an unfounded fear of infection. Medical research continues to prove that the HIV virus is not transmitted through casual contact, such as shaking hands or touching, eating in restaurants, working in the same office, or living in the same household. Although scientists do not yet know how AIDS first developed, Jewish religious leaders have been firm in repudiating the suggestion that AIDS is a form of divine retribution for sin. AIDS is no more a punishment of those it has touched than an earthquake or a famine. The loving and compassionate God whom Judaism teaches us to revere does not command us to judge our fellow humans, but to share in the divine task of healing and comforting. The Jewish people's historical experience of being blamed for other epidemics in the past deepens our ability to empathize with people affected by AIDS today and reinforces our commitment to counteract dangerous misinformation and scapegoating.

Shituf Betsa'ar (Empathy)

Contracting AIDS is not a judgment of character regarding those with AIDS or an assessment of their family and friends. It is a disease in which a degree of cause/effect predictability may exist. However, this awareness does not change the fact that, as Jews, we do not define AIDS as a punishment levied against a "sinner" by an angry deity whose vindictive justice cancels out all compassionate and merciful action.

Unfortunately, many people, family and friends, do not accept these opinions and the person with AIDS is often isolated, avoided, and evaluated as pitiful, inadequate, misled, or evil. Jews, in response to the *mitzvah* of *shituf betsa'ar* (empathy), must be sensitive to these dynamics and act in such a way as to nurture in those with AIDS, their family, and their friends, a feeling of self-worth and dignity.

Pikuach Nefesh (Saving a Life)

In our Jewish way of life, *pikuach nefesh* is an ultimate value. This Hebrew concept asserts that any behavior devoted to saving a life is unparalleled. Only being forced to commit murder, adultery, or idolatry can modify a person's dedication to life. Lifesaving is a *mitzvah* (responsibility) that is so important it must be pursued relentlessly—even if other religious mandates must be set aside. (*Pikuach nefesh* is the Jewish priority which captures the drama of the *lechayim* when one completes the Shabbat *Kiddush*); highlights the description of Torah as a Tree of Life; and reminds all students of Judaism that *Adonai* is the living God.

The AIDS epidemic challenges the concept of *pikuach nefesh*. It has brought death and dying into the lives of individuals, families, and communities to such a degree that lifesaving seems an impossibility. Nevertheless, adopting a more educated style of personal sexual activity, supporting a variety of efforts to provide people with honest and realistic information on AIDS, treating every person with AIDS as a life-equal-to-all-life, and participating in projects designed to further AIDS research are assertions of *pikuach nefesh* which can make a difference in the quality of life.

Perhaps the most significant relationship between the concept of *pikuach nefesh* and AIDS is best expressed by the word "relevancy." Because a Jew must strive to save life, praise life, cherish life, and nurture life, threats to life—such as the AIDS epidemic—should be treated as an enemy, and the fight to control AIDS as a major battle.

The Jewish concern about AIDS is more than a response to the media or a reaction prompted by personal fear. It is a logical advertisement of Judaism's valuing of every human person and the quality of life which makes the individual unique.

Bikur Cholim (Visiting the Sick)

Implied in the *mitzvah* of *bikur cholim* is the value of active caring in contrast to well-expressed intention.

Bikur cholim demonstrates to the patients that illness has not cut them off from the world. Although they might feel and, indeed, be imprisoned by the limitations of their own bodies, medical apparatus, and the "doctor's orders," *bikur cholim* can provide a sustaining sense of connectedness.

AIDS imposes multiple levels of isolation. Social judgments, ever-increasing physical helplessness, (generally) a lack of hope, and a lack of self-control combine to create an environment in which *bikur cholim* may be the most significant act of intervention from which the person with AIDS can derive benefit.

Accurate information about the AIDS virus and an awareness of its impact on an individual are important aspects of one's involvement in the *mitzvah* of *bikur cholim.*

For the person with AIDS, family members, friends, and the caring visitor, *bikur cholim* is an extension of Judaism, a declaration of a Jew's privilege to imitate the image of *Adonai.*

Adonai is *Tzur Yisrael*—the Rock of Israel—thus, the *mitzvah* of visiting the person with AIDS can generate similar feelings of stability and safety.

As with all *mitzvot*, *bikur cholim* is not a one-time "good deed." The true reward for performing any *mitzvah* is the opportunity to do another. For the person with AIDS, the ability to rely on *bikur cholim*, as an ongoing example of Jewish activism, can result in a "healing" sense of belonging to a unique family, *am kedushah* (the Jewish people)—a people who really care.

Kol Yisrael Arevim Zeh Bazeh (Each Jew Is Responsible for Every Jew)

As members of the Jewish people, we are taught that "each Jew is responsible for every Jew," and that this *mitzvah* should condition our concerns for Jews in particular and all humanity in general. The AIDS epidemic tests this valued rabbinic principle in unparalleled ways:

1. As we make love with another person, educated behavior is an absolute requirement. The casual, temporary relationship could seduce one or both individuals into unsafe acts. Loving demands responsible sex in which people are treated as the end rather than the means to the end. (The use of condoms and total rejection of medically unsupervised use of narcotics are some of these responsible behaviors.)

2. Each individual is responsible for knowing up-to-date facts about AIDS and its treatment. This information can be the basis for constructive

and meaningful relationships among individuals involved with a person with AIDS.

3. Each of us is responsible for providing others with assertive perspectives on safe lovemaking. It is a *mitzvah* to say "no!" when encouraged to become involved in high-risk sexual behavior. Holding, hugging, caressing, kissing—indeed, enjoying each other's company—must be reaffirmed as serious, satisfying, and romantic expressions of passionate feelings.

Chesed Ve'emet (Compassion and Truth)

The biblical concept of *chesed ve'emet* has special significance in relation to the death of a person with AIDS.

Chesed ve'emet reflects the concern in Judaism that Jews respond to an individual's death with loving kindness and integrity, expectations not unlike those mandated for a Jew's lifetime dealings with others.

Death—resulting from AIDS—often promotes denial, misrepresentation, and cruelty. Rather than experience kindness and honest confrontation, the person dying of AIDS, as well as his/her loved ones and friends, are often ignored, judged as flawed individuals and forced to construct fantasies or mysteries about their relationship with AIDS.

The *mitzvah* of *chesed ve'emet* requires that we reject even the slightest expression of prejudice and/or naive judgment regarding AIDS or the person who has died of AIDS. Jews must demand that sophisticated AIDS education combined with an aggressive campaign for human dignity inspire all of society with a perspective on AIDS which reflects compassion and truth.

Chesed ve'emet calls on the Jewish community to provide meaningful settings and liturgies in which the family and friends of a person who has died of AIDS can express their grief and receive ongoing comfort.

Of greatest significance, however, is each Jew's relationship with the person dying of AIDS. The *mitzvah* of *chesed ve'emet* calls on Jews to reach out to the individual and discover ways in which to support his/her confrontation with death: a quiet but dependable presence, an offer to facilitate a wish or special need, careful listening, and other behaviors designed to communicate respect for an important life and a brave struggle to survive.

Tikkun Olam (Repairing the World)

Tikkun olam reflects a Jewish mystical perspective on creation. This interpretation suggests that, when time began, *Adonai* filled all space with divine light. Indeed, God was everywhere. Subsequently *Adonai* experienced self-imposed contraction or withdrawal in order to leave space in which creation could take place. This ongoing process, bathed in divine light, resulted in our world being created. However, according to the mystics, the negative effect is that the divine light becomes fragmented and the sparks are scattered throughout the universe. Thus the lifelong challenge of each individual is to gather the sparks together (*tikkun olam*) so that *Adonai's* divine light can be unified.

To the extent that *tikkun olam* implies repairing an

imperfect world, the AIDS epidemic provides every Jew with a demanding agenda:

1. Financial support for medical research.

2. Initiation of, commitment to, and participation in AIDS education programs for young people and adults.

3. Advocating the legal, economic, occupational, and social rights of persons with AIDS and those diagnosed as "carrying" the AIDS virus.

4. Organizing a wide range of programs for one's synagogue, including family counseling, *bikur cholim*, *chavurot*, religious school, youth group education projects, and specially sensitized *minyan* (worship) support groups for families and loved ones mourning the death of a person with AIDS.

5. Support of and participation in blood bank projects.

Resources

UAHC-CCAR Committee on AIDS. UAHC-CCAR Committee on AIDS has a variety of resources available to help educate you and your community in order to organize a Jewish response to this epidemic. For information contact: Ms. Randi Locke, Projects Coordinator, UAHC, 838 Fifth Avenue, New York NY, 10021-7064, (212) 249-0100.

Audio Visual Materials

"Common Threads: Stories Form the Quilt." This video tells the dramatic story of the first decade of AIDS in

America through the profile of five people commemorated in five panels of the Names Project AIDS Memorial Quilt. Contact: The Names Project, 2362 Market Street, San Francisco, CA 94114. (415) 863-1966.

"The Los Altos Story." This documentary is an award-winning, sensitive portrayal of the effects of AIDS on three members of the Rotary Club in this California community. Contact the Rotary AIDS Project, P.O. Box 794, Los Altos, CA 94023. (415) 688-6164.

Publications

"Confronting the AIDS Crisis: A Manual for Synagogue Leaders." This newly revised publication provides guidance and facts in dealing with AIDS. It contains a wide range of material, including "Helping People with AIDS and Their Families," by Robert M. Rankin; "AIDS Havdalah Service: A Prayer of Memory and Hope"; "AIDS Insights and Strategies: A Resource for Religious School and Congregational Program Development"; "Recommendations for Children & Employees with AIDS/HIV Infection in the Synagogue Setting"; "AIDS: A Glossary of Jewish Values," by Howard I. Bogot; "An Annotated Bibliography of AIDS," prepared by Joseph Edelheit and Lisa B. Schwartz.

A Note on New Resources

New resources are constantly being developed. Inquiries should be directed to the UAHC-CCAR Committee on AIDS, 838 Fifth Avenue, New York, NY 10021 (212) 650-4000; Rabbi Janet Marder, Co-Director, UAHC-CCAR Committee on AIDS, 6300 Wilshire Boulevard, Suite #1475, Los Angeles, CA 90048 (213) 653-9962.

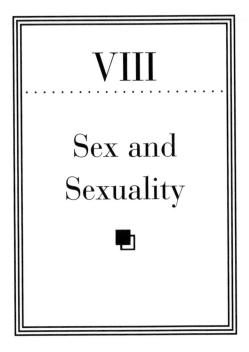

VIII

. . . .

Sex and Sexuality

Jewish Sexual Ethics

MARK GLICKMAN

> There are three things that are a fore-
> taste of the world to come: Shabbat, a
> sunny day, and sexual intercourse
> (*Berachot* 17a).

It's hard to be more up front about sex than in the
above line. This in fact is one of the reasons why I like it
so much. But, its boldness aside, another reason I like
this line so much is because it so succinctly sums up
much of the Jewish view of sex. But let's be more specific. If we had to summarize the Jewish view of sexuality in
just one sentence, it would probably go something like
this: According to Jewish tradition, sex is a great and holy
act—so holy, in fact, that it should never be trivialized or
cheapened.

The Holiness of Sex

Unlike many other religions, Judaism does not view sex
as something inherently sinful. On the contrary, a Jew is
commanded to marry and, once married, to engage in
sexual intercourse. In fact, a male Jew who is unem-
ployed is commanded to perform his "marital duty" at
least once a day, while working men are only required to
have intercourse twice a week. Even sailors who travel
for months at a time are required to have sex with their
wives once every six months. So you are probably asking,
why does Judaism view sex so favorably? There are two
reasons:

1. *Sex is the best way we know to produce children.* The first commandment in the Torah is to "Be fruitful and multiply," and Jews are commanded to do just that by having children. Jewish law considers a couple to have completed this *mitzvah* only after it has had two children. This, however, does not mean that the couple doesn't have an obligation keep on having as many children as it can. While this requirement may be tempered today by the difficulties families often face in providing for their children's physical and emotional needs, this does not alter the fact that Jews have traditionally seen themselves as commanded by God to have children. As a command from God, sex is a holy act.

2. *Sex feels good.* The classical rabbis weren't prudes. They were aware that having sex is a pleasurable and enjoyable activity—which explains why they permitted married couples to have sex despite the possible infertility of either partner (as in the case of older and barren couples). We are commanded to enjoy the pleasures of God's world, and the rabbis included sex as one of those pleasures.

Sex Shouldn't Be Trivialized or Cheapened

Since sex is something Judaism sees as holy, our tradition holds that it is an act that must be taken very seriously. Sexual intercourse is, after all, one of the most intimate ways in which two people interact. And while intercourse can be a source of pleasure and affection, it can also cause much harm. In addition to the risk of unwanted pregnancy and venereal disease, sexual intercourse involving people who are psychologically unprepared can end in a great deal of emotional pain. That sex is something not to be treated lightly is illustrated by how Judaism handles the prohibition on premarital sex and sex during a woman's menstrual period:

1. *The prohibition against premarital sex.* Although Jews are commanded to have sex, we are forbidden to do so with anyone but our spouse. Anyone who has spent time with ultra-Orthodox Jews knows the rigor with which they follow this prohibition. During prayer, men and women are separated so they cannot see each other. At weddings and other simchas, men and women dance only with members of their own sex. Finally, ultra-Orthodox men and women will not even touch a member of the opposite sex (except for their husband or wife). Although these rules seem extreme and, at times, sexist, they also illustrate just how seriously traditional Judaism views sexual relations.

2. *Regulations regarding when Jews are permitted to have sex.* Jewish law forbids a married couple from having sex during and seven days after the wife's menstrual period. This prohibition stems from a notion, which Reform Judaism rejects, that a menstruating woman is "impure" and must be "cleansed" in a *mikveh* (Jewish ritual bath) before she has further contact with her husband. But the fact remains that Judaism views sex as something that is not to be indulged in a wanton manner at any time. Sexual intercourse, like much else in Judaism, is controlled by ritual law for a reason, and that reason is to maintain the holiness of the

act. Many Orthodox Jewish couples have commented that these rules enhance instead of detract from their sex life by transforming the act of intercourse into something pleasurable *and* holy.

Judaism sees sex as something that is very holy—and holy things always carry the potential for greatness and danger. Thus the Jewish tradition, even as it impels us to explore our own sexuality, asks us to be careful about how we approach it. It asks us to appreciate the wonder and the seriousness, the glory and the danger, the beauty and the majesty of sexual affection between two people.

Bibliography

Biale, David. *Eros and the Jews: From Biblical Israel to Contemporary America.* New York: HarperCollins, 1992.

Feldman, David M. *Marital Relations, Birth Control and Abortion in Jewish Law.* New York: Schocken, 1978.

Klein, Isaac. *A Guide to Jewish Religious Practice.* Hoboken, NJ: Ktav Publishing, 1979.

Abortion

GLYNIS CONYER REISS

Abortion rights has been and continues to be one of the most controversial issues in American society. The controversy arises over the right of the government to be involved in decisions relating to a woman's right to choose. In 1991, the Religious Coalition for Abortion Rights issued the following statement:

> Abortion rights opponents are attempting to place into secular law restrictions on abortion rights based on their theological belief that human life or personhood begins at conception. Such laws prohibit people who do not share that theological belief from making decisions concerning unplanned pregnancies according to the teachings of their faiths. These laws also violate the religious freedom of people who believe abortion may be a moral alternative to a problem pregnancy.
>
> The diversity of religious views in this country, on the sensitive issue of abortion, requires that abortion decisions must remain with the individual, to be made on the basis of conscience and personal religious principles and free from government interference.[1]

Defining a Person

One of those religious views is that shared by many of the 4,000,000 Jews who live in America. Now, while not every Jew may agree with the above statement, there are many who do, and do so on the basis of Jewish law. According to commentaries on tractate *Sanhedrin* in the Talmud, a fetus is not considered to be a full human being and for this reason has no juridical personality of its own: "The fetus in the womb is not a person [*lav nefesh hu*] until it is born" (*Sanhedrin* 72b).

According to Jewish law, therefore, a child is considered a person only when it has come into the world. Until then, there is no capital liability for destroying a fetus. By this reasoning, abortion cannot be considered murder. The basis for this decision is scriptural.

> If men strive, and wound a pregnant woman so that her fruit be expelled, but no harm befall her, then shall he be fined as her husband shall assess, and the matter placed before the judges. But if harm befall her, then thou shalt give life for life.
>
> (Exodus 21:22)

Talmudic commentators, as they explain this biblical passage, assert that only monetary compensation can be exacted of the person who causes a woman to miscarry. No prohibition is evident from this scriptural passage against destroying the unborn fetus. Clearly, and here the major rabbinic commentators on the Bible agree, the one who was responsible for destroying the unborn fetus is not culpable for murder. Rabbinic writings reiterate this concept in many different instances and in many

different places. The classic source for this Jewish attitude toward the status of the fetus and thus toward abortion is found in the *Mishnah*:

> A woman who is having difficulty in giving birth,
> it is permitted to cut up the child inside her womb
> and take it out limb by limb because her life
> takes precedence. However, if the greater part of
> the child has come out, it must not be touched,
> because one life must not be taken to save
> another.
>
> (*Mishnah Ohalot* 7:6)

Rashi, the preeminent commentator on the Bible and
the Talmud, gives the following explanation of this
Talmudic passage: "As long as the child did not come out
into the world, it is not called a living being and it is
therefore permissible to take its life in order to save the
life of its mother. Once the head of the child has come
out, the child may not be harmed because it is considered as fully born, and one life may not be taken to save
another."

Now there are, to be sure, laws relating to fetuses
more than 40 days old. Laws of ritual uncleanliness, for
example, must be observed for fetuses older than 40 days
(*Mishnah Niddah* 3:5). Such laws suggest that the
unborn fetus, though not a living person (*nefesh*), still
has some status. However, nowhere does it state that
destroying this fetus by premature artificial termination
of pregnancy is prohibited.

It is clear that Jewish law does not equate abortion
with murder because Jewish law does not view a fetus as
a person or a human being. Jewish law essentially agrees

with the majority Supreme Court opinion in *Roe* v. *Wade* that "the Constitution does not define 'person' in so many words. The use of the word is such that it has application only postnatally."

Alternate Views

Despite this plethora of evidence from Judaism recognizing the legality of abortion, Orthodox Jewish authorities continue to hold a negative view of abortion. Indeed, most Orthodox rabbis prohibit abortion except in special instances, such as when a woman is impregnated through rape or incest, or when it is clear that continuing the pregnancy to birth would constitute a clear danger to the life and/or health of the mother.

The reasons traditional Judaism generally prohibits abortion, despite the rabbinic literature permitting therapeutic abortion, are complex and diverse. Some Orthodox rabbis are more lenient than others in this area. Conservative and Reform Judaism, drawing from this long tradition, take the more liberal stance. As Balfour Brickner stated on March 24, 1976, in testimony before the U.S. House of Representatives Judiciary Committee's sub-committee on Civil and Constitutional Rights, "While Jewish law teaches a reverent and responsible attitude to the question of life and, therefore, views abortion with great concern, there may be circumstances that sanction or even require therapeutic abortion. Were the beliefs of another religion concerning abortion to be enacted into law, our right to follow our religious convictions as we understand them would be abrogated."

In her book *On Women and Judaism: A View from Tradition*, Blu Greenberg suggests that the issue is really one of abortion on demand. Because the Jewish tradition sets precedents only on therapeutic abortion, "...one way to maintain some integrity within the halachic framework would be to broaden the interpretation of therapeutic abortion, to extend the principles of precedence of the mother's actual life and health to include serious regard for the quality of life as well." [2]

Within this context, one needs to give consideration to the emotional as well as the physical well-being of the mother. The many demands that society makes on us today, the financial hardship of raising a child, the need to complete one's schooling, responsibilities to other children, and so forth may be so burdensome as to place the mother's mental health at jeopardy. In these cases, writes Greenberg, "abortion should be seen as a necessity rather than an evil. Indeed, many *mitzvot* are interdependent functions of timing and the conditions they regulate." [3]

Making a Choice

Abortion is an intensely complex and personal decision, one which raises profound moral and religious questions that the government cannot and should not attempt to answer for every individual.[4]

This statement speaks to the heart of the abortion issue and its politicization. The Constitution promises freedom of religion. Any law which either prohibits or mandates abortion undermines that promise by compelling people to compromise strictly held beliefs. There will never be widespread agreement on whether abortion is an unacceptable decision in any circumstance or a moral alternative to a dangerous or unwanted pregnancy.

Our tradition makes it very clear that "a woman's life, her pain, and her concerns take precedence over those of the fetus; existing life is always sacred and takes precedence over a potential life." [5] When the government intervenes in the personal lives of the citizens of its country, it runs the risk of violating the very freedom which they proclaim to be sacred.

Institutions

National Council of Jewish Women
53 West 23rd Street
New York, NY 10010
(212) 645-4048

National Federation of Temple Sisterhoods
838 Fifth Avenue
New York, NY 10021
(212) 249-0100

Religious Action Center
2027 Massachusetts Avenue NW
Washington, DC 20036
(202) 387-2800

Religious Coalition for Abortion Rights
100 Maryland Avenue NE
Suite 307
Washington, DC 20002
(202) 543-7032

Homosexuality
A Reform Jewish Perspective

JOHN E. HIRSCH

Introduction

No one knows what makes a person homosexual. No one
chooses to be gay or lesbian; no one wakes up one morning and says, "Today I think I'll be a homosexual." Nor
can anyone turn a heterosexual into a homosexual (or
vice versa). Homosexuality is not what a person does but
who a person is. It is not a psychiatric or personality dis-
order; it is just another part of one's personality. Some
scientific studies are beginning to show that it may be a
genetic predisposition or a trait developed in utero.
Homosexuality exists in virtually every culture and society. It crosses all boundaries of race, religion, national
origin, and social and economic status. Homosexuality is,
quite simply, a human being's sexual orientation—a trait
responsible for the physical or sexual attraction of one
person for another of the same sex. This sexual orientation has been the cause of serious prejudice and untold
bigotry.

For millennia, gay and lesbian Jews have been stig-
matized, ostracized, and held in moral disdain. Reform
Judaism now recognizes this as a grievous wrong. Rabbi
Alexander Schindler, former president of the Union of
American Hebrew Congregations, called for "a grasp of
the heart," sensitivity, and acceptance of gay and lesbian

Jews as congregants, rabbis, cantors, educators, staff, and leaders, in accordance with the positions of the UAHC and the Central Conference of American Rabbis.

Traditional Jewish Position

A great deal has been written about Judaism's position on homosexuality. While it is true that there are prohibitions in the Torah against homosexual acts, in recent years some rabbis and scholars have contended that the Bible and, therefore, Judaism are not homophobic.

In the Bible there are only three references that apply directly to homosexuality: "Do not lie with a male as one lies with a woman: it is an abhorrence" (Leviticus 18:22). "If a man lies with a male as one lies with a woman, the two of them have done an abhorrent thing; they shall be put to death" (Leviticus 20:13). "No Israelite woman shall be a cult prostitute, nor shall any Israelite man be a cult prostitute" (Deuteronomy 23:18).

Each of these references clearly prohibits homosexual acts between men. (The Torah does not acknowledge homosexuality in women.) In "Gay and Lesbian Jews: An Innovative Jewish Legal Position," however, Rabbi Bradley S. Artson argues for Judaism's tolerance of homosexuality, contending that the Torah does not consider homosexual acts in the context of homosexual love. He contends that the Bible is concerned only with heterosexuals who engage in homosexual acts as an expression of idolatry or of power (i.e., of rape or of pleasure). The proscriptions in Leviticus, Artson argues, are directed at random homosexual acts between two men, some quite young, who are more than likely not homosexual. The reference in Deuteronomy equates prostitution with idolatry. In this context, the cultic homosexual act, like the cultic heterosexual act, is a form of idol worship that is strictly forbidden.[1]

The Bible then is not homophobic. The idea that two men or two women could love each other and live together in a committed relationship is something that the Bible does not discuss. The Torah does not prohibit homosexual love because it had no knowledge of homosexual love. The Torah only prohibits sexual acts that are coercive, morally degrading, or violent.

Rabbinic literature, too, contains no examples of homosexual love. Instead, the rabbinic writers condemned activity that treated someone as a sexual object or that was an expression of idolatry or oppression.

Artson concludes that a thorough review of Jewish texts fails to disclose opposition to homosexual orientation. On the contrary, the texts reveal that our sages were totally oblivious to even the remote possibility that people of the same gender could have a loving, caring, monogamous sexual relationship. Further, Artson claims that modern Judaism can certainly tolerate same-sex love:

> The morality of the sex act is not determined by gender.... Rather, human beings imbue acts with meaning and morality. The Torah and its traditions insist that sex, as with any other human striving, should be directed toward a greater sense of sacredness, in the service of human love and caring. [2]

The conclusion that Artson reaches is that we must see homosexual relations as legitimate. Tolerance of homosexual relations will not only encourage homosexuals to be more open about their orientation but may also prevent their becoming involved in destructive relationships just to mask their sexual identities. Tolerance will promote more stable homosexual relationships. Judaism must accept homosexuality as a halachically acceptable sexual orientation. There is nothing to be feared from this stance when there is much to be gained.

In light of modern science and contemporary thinking, the Reconstructionist and Reform movements have reevaluated *halachah* and proscriptions against homosexual love. In his State of the Union address to the Biennial Assembly of the Union of American Hebrew Congregations on November 4, 1989, Rabbi Schindler said:

> There must be a policy enunciated by which the many gay and lesbian Jews in our community can know that they are accepted on terms of visibility, not invisibility.... They must know that we place no limits on their communal or spiritual aspirations.... In all of this, I am working to make the Reform Jewish community a home: a place where loneliness and suffering and exile ends; a place that leaves it to God to validate relationships and demands of us only that these relationships be worthy in His eyes; a place where we can search, together, through the written Torah and the Torah of life, to find those affirmations for which we yearn.

Responding to this charge, Reform Judaism is working to remove stumbling blocks and "open the eyes of the blind" so that gay and lesbian Jews can enjoy all of the privileges and responsibilities of membership in Reform synagogues. The goal is enlightenment of non-gay and lesbian individuals and the full acceptance and smooth integration of gay and lesbian Jews into all congregations.

Reform Jewish History

For more than two decades, the Union of American Hebrew Congregations has forcefully addressed issues of discrimination against gays and lesbians. In 1977, at its Biennial in San Francisco, the UAHC General Assembly passed a resolution deploring discrimination against gay men and lesbians. At the General Assembly of the UAHC, held in Chicago in 1987, a historic resolution calling on member congregations throughout North America to accept gay men and lesbians into all aspects of congregational life was presented and overwhelmingly passed. The preamble to this resolution states, in part, the following:

> God calls upon us to love our neighbors as ourselves. The prophet Isaiah charges us further: "Let my house be called a house of prayer, for all people" (Isaiah 56:7). And, armed with other teachings of our faith, we Jews are asked to create a society based on righteousness, the goal being *tikkun olam*, the perfection of our world. Each of us, created in God's image, has a unique talent which can contribute to that high moral purpose;

and to exclude any Jew from the community of
Israel lessens our chances of achieving that goal....
Sexual orientation should not be a criterion for
membership of or participation in an activity of
any synagogue. Thus, all Jews should be welcome,
however they may define themselves.

The passage of these resolutions served as a prelude
to events at the 1989 Biennial in New Orleans. First, in
his presidential address, Rabbi Schindler called upon
congregations to implement the Chicago Biennial resolution. Second, a new resolution was passed that
strengthened the Chicago Biennial resolution, calling on
congregations to welcome as members gays and lesbians
who are single, in couples, or with families.

As a sign of its changing attitude toward the role of
gays and lesbians in Reform Judaism, the UAHC has
incorporated gay and lesbian Jewish issues in the work of
its Committee on the Jewish Family and its Task Force
on Youth Suicide Prevention. Gay and lesbian families
are now one of many configurations that make up the
new Jewish family. Some of the recommendations of the
UAHC Jewish Family Committee include the following:
welcoming all family structures into the synagogue community; building self-esteem in Jewish children; validat-
ing Jewishly the specific family unit of which a child is a
part; helping persons acknowledge and come to terms
with their sexual identities; educating the Jewish community to fully accept all Jews regardless of their sexual
orientation. In 1990 the Central Conference of
American Rabbis passed its own resolution that, while
affirming the status of the traditional heterosexual
model, made it possible for openly gay and lesbian

students to be ordained as rabbis. In 1991 the National Federation of Temple Sisterhoods and the National Association of Temple Educators both passed resolutions calling for an end to discrimination based on sexual orientation in congregational employment and congregational life.

Education

The importance of education about sexual orientation cannot be overstated. Education is the key to dispelling negative myths and stereotypes about gays and lesbians. (For example, gay men are not necessarily effeminate, and lesbians are not necessarily masculine.) Most gay and lesbian people look and act no differently from heterosexual people; a person's sexual orientation cannot be identified with or determined by outward appearances. One of the most hurtful and harmful stereotypes is the canard that gay men are child molesters. From law enforcement records, we know, in fact, that more than 90 percent of all sexual assaults are committed by heterosexual men against female children.

Finally, it is necessary to dispel the myth that homosexuals do not make good role models and should not be employed as teachers or rabbis. People can be good role models, regardless of sexual orientation, if they act in a moral and ethical way and are capable of forming positive relationships with one another. Since homosexuality is neither a matter of choice nor a learned trait, young people are in no danger of switching their natural sexual orientation.

Conclusion

Reform Judaism has set the course for the integration of gay and lesbian Jews into the synagogue. Reform Judaism is committed to the acceptance of all Jews within the community without regard to sexual orientation.

Bibliography

Artson, Bradley Shavit. "Gay and Lesbian Jews: An Innovative Jewish Legal Position." *Jewish Spectator*, Winter 1990, 6.

Balka, Christie, and Andy Rose, eds. *Twice Blessed: On Being Lesbian, Gay, and Jewish*. Boston: Beacon Press, 1989.

Gilman, Susan. "Gay and Lesbian Rabbis." *The Jewish Week*, 26 April–2 May 1991.

Goldman, Ari L. "Reform Conference Debates Allowing Homosexuals to Become Rabbis." *The New York Times*, 27 June 1989.

"Reform Judaism Votes to Accept Active Homosexuals in Rabbinate." *The New York Times*, 26 June 1990.

Hirsch, John E. "Don't Ghettoize Gays." *Reform Judaism*, Spring 1988, 14–15.

Kahn, Yoel. "Judaism and Homosexuality: The Traditional /Progressive Debate." *Journal of Homosexuality* 18, nos. 3 and 4 (1989–1990).

"The Kedushah of Homosexual Relationships." *CCAR Yearbook* 89 (1989).

"Rabbi and Gay: A Personal Perspective." *Reform Judaism*, Winter 1990, 8.

"Homosexuality." *Keeping Posted*. 32, no. 2, November 1986.

Marder, Janet. "Our Invisible Rabbis." *Reform Judaism*, Winter 1990, 4–7 and 9–12.

"Gay and Lesbian Jews' Resource Committee." New York: New York Federation of Reform Synagogues, 1991.

Plant, Richard. *The Pink Triangle: The Nazi War against Homosexuals*. New York: Henry Holt, 1986.

UAHC Task Force on Lesbian and Gay Inclusion. *Kulanu (All of Us)*. New York: UAHC Press, 1996.

Whitlock, Katherine. *Bridges of Respect*. Philadelphia: American Friends Service Committee, 1989.

Rape and Jewish Law

MELINDA PANKEN

The documentation and discussion of rape has a long history in Judaism, and with the passage of time the Jewish understanding of rape by rabbis and scholars has evolved and changed. Originally Jewish law viewed rape as an act of forced sexual passion. Today, with the growth of feminism and the modern disciplines of psychology and sociology having led the way, we now understand rape to be an act of violence and power.

In the *Tanach* (the books of the Torah, Prophets, and Writings), rape was portrayed as a non-consensual sexual act that could be perpetrated against either men or women. In Genesis 19:5, for example, we read that when three strangers visited Lot, the citizens of Sodom stormed his house, demanding of Lot that he deliver his male guests into their hand, "that we may be intimate with them." Later in Genesis 34, we watch with horror the rape of Jacob's daughter, Dinah, by Shechem. Finally there is the gruesome story in Judges 19 of the gang rape and murder of the Levite's concubine.

There are elements of violence and aggression in each depiction, but none of the stories focuses on the humiliation and violation of the rape victim. Instead, as in the stories of Dinah and the concubine, it is the men—the husbands, brothers, and fathers—who suffer the indignity that drives them to seek vengeance. These narrative accounts of rape in the *Tanach* give no voice to the women who have been violated.

This lack of emphasis on the degradation of the women probably explains in part the biblical legislative view of rape as an assault on a woman for which she and her father could be financially compensated:

> If a man is found lying with another man's wife, both of them—the man and the woman with whom he lay—shall die. Thus will you sweep out evil from Israel. In the case of a virgin who is engaged to a man—if a man comes upon her in town and lies with her, you shall take the two of them out to the gate of that town and stone them to death: the girl because she did not cry out for help in the town, and the man because he violated another man's wife. Thus you will sweep away evil from your midst. But if the man comes upon an engaged girl in the open country, and the man lies with her by force, only the man who lay with her shall die, but you shall do nothing to the girl. The girl did not incur the death penalty, for this case is like that of a man attacking another and murdering him. He came upon her in the open; though the engaged girl cried for help, there was no one to save her. If a man comes upon a virgin who is not engaged and he seizes her and they are

discovered, the man who lay with her shall pay the girls father fifty [shekels of] silver and she shall be his wife. Because he has violated her, he can never have the right to divorce her.

(Deuteronomy 22:22–29)

In this passage, the law attempts to establish several criteria for rape. If a married woman and a man engage in consensual sex, both are liable for the sexual sin of adultery. In the case of a betrothed virgin who is raped within a town, the act cannot be defined as rape if she does not call for help. (This situation also suggests an adulterous act on her part because her betrothal allows others to see her *as if* she were married to her betrothed.)

The only time a woman may not be punished is when she calls for help and receives no response. In essence, a sexual act is considered rape whenever the woman protests. Moreover if the girl is a virgin, her father may be compensated monetarily. This is because the act of rape prevents the father from receiving a bride price. In addition, the offender is required to marry her, since chances were slim that a woman who was no longer a virgin would be able to find a husband. Finally, the man who rapes a woman is not only required to marry her but loses all rights to divorce her. Strange as these last laws may seem, they were actually intended to protect the victim by assuring her a husband. Only after Maimonides' revision of talmudic law did a woman receive the right to choose whether or not to marry the man who raped her. The right to approve or disapprove of her wish to marry her rapist was also extended to her father.

In Nachmanides' commentary on the Torah, rape is defined by whether or not a woman has cried for help. If witnesses see a maiden lie with a man, warn them both to stop, and the maiden does not cry for help, it is not an act of rape:

> For normally any woman being raped cries out to the town for help to be saved.... And if they see her in the field when he holds her and lays with her she is considered raped and not liable. And the reason for "and she cried out" (Deut 22:27) is [to indicate that] it is possible that she cried out...for even if they did not hear her cry out she is not liable because she had no rescuers there. And the general rule is that if she had rescuers there, whether in town or in the countryside, she is liable, and if she has no rescuers, whether in the countryside or in town, she is not liable.
>
> (Nachmanides on Deuteronomy 22:23)[1]

For Nachmanides, a woman must protest the sexual act for it to be defined as rape. This interpretation is noteworthy for the amount of faith it places in a woman's capacity to decide whether or not she could have been saved by calling out. The effect of the interpretation is to grant the woman a greater say in establishing whether or not she has been the victim of rape.

The talmudic rabbis struggled with the definition of and the legal issues surrounding the act of rape. One of the more difficult problems they tried to solve was the reason for requiring financial compensation. Unlike the authors of the Torah, these sages did not link compensation to loss of the bride price. Instead they saw payment as a necessary response to the humiliation and pain suffered by the victim:

> *Mishnah*: The seducer pays three forms [of compensation] and the violator four. The seducer pays compensation for indignity and blemish and the [statutory] fines, while the violator pays an additional [form of compensation] for the pain.

> *Gemara*: [He pays for the] pain of what? The father of Samuel replied: For the pain [he has inflicted] when he thrust her upon the ground. Rabbi Zera demurred: Now then, if he has thrust her upon silk stuffs would he for similar reasons be exempt? And should you say that the law is so, indeed, was it not [it may be retorted] taught: Rabbi Simeon ben Judah stated in the name of Rabbi Simeon: A violator does not pay compensation for the pain [he has inflicted] because the woman would ultimately have suffered some pain from her husband, but they said to him: One who is forced to intercourse cannot be compared to one who acts willingly?

> (*Ketubot* 39)

The rabbis distinguish between the experience of one who is forced to engage in sex and one who participates willingly. They recognized that a virgin will experience physical pain the first time she has sexual intercourse, but they acknowledge that greater pain is involved when intercourse is not consensual. This is what they mean then by the pain of the indignity and the blemish, for a raped woman suffers deep psychological trauma. Later commentaries expand this notion by applying it to sexual relations between a husband and wife, arguing that no good comes of the forced sexual union of husband and wife, even if it is for the ostensible *mitzvah* of procreation. They thereby acknowledge the existence of marital rape and prohibit such an act.

Yet despite the implied sensitivity of the talmudic rabbis to the humiliation of the rape victim, they also believed that a woman might still derive enjoyment and pleasure from the sexual act itself:

> A woman once came to Rabbi Yohanan and said to him: "I have been raped." He said to her: "And didn't you enjoy it by the end?" She said to him: "And if a man dipped his finger in honey and stuck it in your mouth on Yom Kippur, is it not bad for you yet enjoyable by the end?" He accepted her.
>
> (Jerusalem Talmud, *Sotah* 4:4)

While it is evident that the rabbis had little understanding of female sexuality, they were astute enough to realize that pleasure resulting from rape does not negate its status as an immoral act.

Maimonides also picks up on this idea, expanding the protection granted to women:

The victim of duress is entirely exempt, both from flogging and from offering a sacrifice; needless to say, she is also exempt from the death penalty, as it is said "and to the maiden you shall do nothing" (Deuteronomy 22:26). This holds true only when the victim is a woman, since duress cannot apply to the man, for no erection is possible without his own intention.

A woman who is subjected to duress at the beginning of intercourse but finally acquiesces to it, is also entirely exempt; once a man has begun sexual intercourse with her under duress, she cannot but acquiesce, seeing the human impulse and nature compel her to ultimate assent.

(*Mishneh Torah, Issurei Biah* 1:9)

Maimonides is clear here that one who experiences sex under duress is exempt from any form of punishment.

What we see in Jewish law is a trend in refining the definition of rape and developing rules in order to protect women. Our understanding of rape today and the motivations behind rape reflect a greater knowledge of how human beings behave. But Jewish law makes it clear, as Rachel Biale argues, that a "woman does not need to be kicking and screaming from start to end in order for us to rule that she has been raped. Sex begun under duress and intimidation is, by definition, rape." [2]

Acquaintance Rape

JAMES D. SEWELL

Rape is one of the most feared personal crimes in today's society. For many women, especially in an urban environment or on a college campus, this fear manifests itself in the image of the hulking stranger, armed with a weapon, who materializes from the shadows. That fear further translates itself into a variety of methods of prevention: better locks in one's home, improved lighting around the residence, a sense of heightened awareness, and assertive, precautionary behavior.

Yet sadly, statistics on the subject indicate that rape is not most commonly a "stranger-on-stranger" crime. Instead, the typical rapist is someone known to the victim. In the campus community, that offender is too often an acquaintance or, worse, a date. Yet, regardless of the relationship of the offender, rape by stranger or acquaintance is still sexual violence.

Over the last several years, across the country, headlines have called to our attention the reports of date and acquaintance rape in our campus environment. In several cases, the victims are assaulted by groups of males in fraternity houses and other collective residences. In others, we have seen reports of innocent victims who unwittingly found themselves in situations where the rapist was able to coerce and control their behavior. A major study of 7,000 students at 35 colleges and universities across the country brought forth some startling statistics:

- 52 percent of the women surveyed have experienced some form of sexual victimization.

- One in every eight college women were the victims of rape.
- 47 percent of the rapes were by first-time or casual dates or by romantic acquaintances.
- Over one-third of the women raped did not discuss their experiences with anyone; more than 90 percent did not report the crime to the police.

From a law enforcement standpoint, the crime of date rape is difficult to prevent. The traditional methods of discouraging the stranger-assailant—locks, lighting, improved physical security—obviously cannot deter someone who is allowed into or belongs on the premises. In many cases, the assault in fact occurs on the assailant's turf. The critical question is, then, what steps can a collegiate woman take to reduce her chances of being the victim of a rape by someone she knows?

First, it is appropriate to dissect the typical situation which can result in rape in a social setting. Frequently, the assault occurs in the residence of either the assailant or the victim.

In many cases, it involves a couple who have only recently met and who are on the first, second, or third date. The rape typically occurs when a woman is alone with the man, and often when others are relatively close by. Far too often, alcohol and drugs are a significant factor in date rape; many victims indicate that they had too much to drink and, when they realized their situation, it was too late to avoid the crime. Many times, the rape begins with mutually allowed heavy petting and the man ignores or fails to understand the woman's protest of "no."

In many and probably most cases, the rape is spontaneous and few rapists carry the self-image that they are sex offenders and have done anything illegal. What thoughts allow the man to rationalize this behavior? Perhaps several can be identified. First, he may assume that the woman, in saying "no," really means "yes" and is only playing hard to get, and thus a part of her expected sexual role. He may assume she is a tease or that her reputation, which he often gathers from friends, says that she will go all the way; as a result, he may believe that sexual activity with anyone implies consent with all.

He may feel that if she pets, she'll do "it," and he may assume that sex is typical payment for a good evening of dinner, drinks, and dancing. He also may accept the traditional macho role: men should be aggressive and assert their sexual needs, women must be passive and subvert their feelings. Finally, there may be poor understanding, mixed messages, or failure on the part of both parties to communicate their social and sexual expectations.

With this awareness, what can men and women do to reduce their chances of being in a date rape situation? The following are some facts to know and suggestions to follow for everyone to better protect themselves. These were originally printed by the University of Michigan Sexual Assault Prevention and Awareness Center.

Men, it is never O.K. to force yourself on a woman, even if...

- you think she's been teasing and leading you on,
- she asked you out,

- you have heard that women say no but mean yes,
- you think it is "manly" to use force or coercion to get your way,
- or you think that she will expect some force or coercion.

Whenever a woman is forced to submit to unwanted sexual relations, it is rape—and not a successful seduction by a lover, friend, neighbor, acquaintance, or stranger. Therefore, you have an obligation to:

- Be aware of stereotypes that set you up into acting in forceful or coercive ways, such as "aggressive behavior is masculine." Don't get trapped by these roles.
- Be honest: communicate what you want honestly, assertively, and respectfully. That means speaking your needs and listening to the other person's needs.
- Remember—"no" means no.
- Be aware that "force" can be emotional coercion and intimidation as well as physical force.
- Realize that if a woman is unable to give consent (i.e., is drunk), it is still rape.
- Know that physical affection does not always have to lead to sex.
- Confront friends who you know have put women in uncomfortable sexual situations or have committed rape. Let them know how you feel.

Women, remember to:

- Keep your rights in any social situation. You have the right: to be concerned about yourself and not worry about taking care of others; to do only what you want to do; to say no.

- Be aware of your feelings and express them assertively.

- Say no when you mean no, say yes when you mean yes. Use eye contact and tone of voice to show you mean what you say.

- Put yourself above the rules of etiquette and social norms when you feel threatened by either a stranger or an acquaintance.

- Be willing to make a scene, if necessary, to get out of a troubling encounter.

- Trust your instincts: Be aware of specific situations in which you do not feel relaxed and in charge.

- Make decisions for yourself. Decide in advance what you will tolerate. Set limits and take steps to cut off interactions that exceed them.

- Be aware of female stereotypes that prevent you from expressing yourself, such as "anger is unfeminine" or "being passive is feminine." Don't allow yourself to be trapped by them.

- Be aware of what is going on around you.

- Have your own transportation in dating situations, either your own car or an arrangement with a friend. Otherwise, be sure to carry enough money for a phone call and a cab.

- Support your friends—don't pressure them when they are unsure about a situation. If a friend asks you to leave with her from a party because she is uncomfortable, help her out.

- Stand up for yourself.

Our role is to change the culture of violence and aggression which has allowed date and acquaintance rape to continue to exist at our institutions of higher education. To effectively confront this problem, it is our responsibility as campus leaders to:

- Develop programs on sexual responsibility and acquaintance rape.
- Exert a leadership role in developing and implementing a campus curriculum on date rape, sexual responsibility, and healthy sexual attitudes for women and men.
- Demand and support serious consequences for campus citizens who engage in practices which result in or encourage date rape.

Sexual violence and date rape are realities on our college campuses. Often, because the victim blames herself for being in the situation and believes that she did not say "no" clearly, the effects of rape by an acquaintance are often more emotionally damaging than one committed by a stranger.

The elimination of this crime from our halls of learning requires a commitment from and action by both women and men, and mandates both sexes to expect and receive mutual respect, sexual control, and social responsibility.

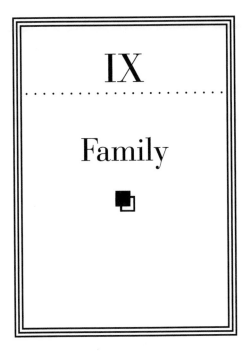

IX

Family

The Elders Who Stand
at the Gates of the City

GERARD W. KAYE

North American society has created a way to
separate children from their parents—it's called college.
Going to college is not like going to summer camp for a
short session and then for a longer session with the passing of each year. Instead, attending college is so radical a
separation between parent and child that the child who
goes must be prepared to take on many new personal
responsibilities overnight. Yesterday you lived at home;
today you are (more or less) on your own. No one will tell
you to pick up your shirt, get in on time, be careful cross-
ing the street, or remind you to do your homework. It's
up to you to do all these things.

Psychologically speaking, the process of separation is
one of the culminating acts of maturation. Separation is
a natural stage that everybody goes through at one time
or another. Regrettably, there is only one moment when
this takes place, and it doesn't allow for a planned
arrangement. On the day that you arrive on campus,
your parents experience tremendous feelings of conflict.
They are anxious for you to take up this next part of your
life with as much dispatch as possible. But they also don't
want to leave you, their "baby," alone in this strange land.

You, on the other hand, are as anxious as possible to
enter and discover what this new and strange world has
to offer. At the same time, you don't want to appear as if
you are shoving your folks into the car to head back
home to Schenectady. These are the moments that cause

the type of conflicts that grow out of, on the one hand, the absence of companions and a familiar environment and, on the other, the need to set your psychological kite flying. Some students spend their first night on campus roaming the halls enjoying the sweet taste of freedom, while others are found sobbing uncontrollably in their darkened dorm room. Soon, the separation sets in, and life resumes a kind of routine commanded by classes and exams.

Not many hours pass before Mom calls to find out how things are going. You breathe a sigh of relief to hear her voice at the same time that you boldly inform her and Dad that you can take care of yourself. As school life continues, however, you soon discover how everyone is getting the same phone calls while cavalierly announcing how insecure parents are.

You happily realize that you're just like the other students, and this comforts you—that is, until the High Holy Days intrude shortly after classes have begun. For with the arrival of the High Holy Days, you also recognize that you are not exactly the same as other students. You may use these days as an opportunity to sneak home for a day of required or desired family time or use them as an opening for exploring the Jewish community on campus. Whatever your response is, it is at this time that you remember that you are Jewish and that your mother and father sent you not just to receive an education but to develop spiritually.

"If a child desires a favor from the townsfolk, and knows that it will be granted for his parents' sake, even though the child could also get it of his own account, nevertheless, the child should not say: 'Do it for me,' but rather: 'Do it for my parents in order to attribute favor to the regard that people have for the parents' " (*Shulchan Aruch*). Jewish tradition here tries to define more clearly the commandment of "honor your father and your mother" for the child who no longer lives with his or her parents. The question you might want to ask today is how can you honor your parents while you are on campus and they are at home. Some actions you might consider are quite simple and painless.

First, parents want to know that you are eating regularly, still alive, and not doing many of the things that they did when they were students. You will quickly discover that they call with all sorts of oblique questions, such as "So how is your friend Beth doing? Is she eating regularly and getting any sleep (alone)?" In order to understand their sudden interest in Beth's well-being, just substitute your name for hers and you can gently smile while you answer. "Gee, mom and dad, it's interesting that you ask. She's really doing O.K., even though campus food is never as good as yours, mom. I know that she does go to class all the time because I see her there every day." Get it? Just another way to honor your parents. Try to answer the questions they didn't ask.

And remember not to call your campus quarters "home" too often—your mother and father may get hurt as they think fondly about the days when you used to mess up your old room with regularity. Don't rub your absence into their faces. Honor your mother and your father.

Parents are not exempt from their responsibility either, however. As it is written in the *Shulchan Aruch*, "a parent is forbidden to place a burdensome yoke upon the children; [a parent] must not be too exacting in demanding honor from them so that the parent may not cause them to stumble into sin. A parent should rather overlook their shortcomings and forgive them."

New "families" will emerge for you on campus. This will include the new friends you make as well as old acquaintances who had moved away in third grade only to reappear on your campus. In addition, you will form important relationships with those faculty who genuinely care about their students. All of these relationships offer powerful forms of support. Forming new friendships is a risky business because new relationships evolve out of unusual circumstances or awkward situations—those times when you can't find anyone to help you with your statistics homework except for that nerd you wouldn't talk to last week. Just remember, although you should take advantage of people's willingness to help, that doesn't mean you have to move in with them.

Jewish life on campus is varied. Explore it for yourself before you automatically assume that every Hillel is boring and every fraternity is cool. Both may seem true, at first. But a little more exploration may reveal that both of them offer something, even if it is nothing more than the bulletin board notices. Looking for a job on the Greek house board is less likely to be as productive as looking at one in the Hillel house. More than that, Hillel (and similar places) will offer a group of people who have some serious interest in their Judaism. Many campuses even have Reform chavurot, which exist as a part of KESHER—the North American network of Reform Jews on campus. This doesn't mean that people like you won't gather in other places—it only means that the odds increase under a Jewish or Reform Jewish roof.

Adults in a campus community often wear a strange demeanor—it's hard to tell how to respond to the

Passover seder invitation or the break-the-fast at the local temple president's home. Shabbat dinner invitations at the home of friends of your father's can actually be pleasant as long as they don't behave like surrogate parents. Remember, you may not only get a decent meal but meet interesting, pleasant, and helpful adults. Campus faculty are often willing to engage you in their family's life as well, particularly if you are majoring in microbiology and they teach architecture. (This avoids any potential conflict of interest.)

Don't forget that you are as valuable a resource to the local synagogue school as it is to you. Here you can feel a sense of home as often as you want and to whatever degree you wish. Jobs, services, Shabbat, and new friends can all provide an anchor at a time when sometimes you feel like you are floundering.

Finally, your college years do have one more agenda in store—you will probably meet your future spouse there.

Honor your father and your mother.

Now perhaps I should explain what the title of this essay means. It's something of a psychology lesson. Deuteronomy 21:18 informs parents that if they have a rebellious child, they should take the youngster to the gates of the city where the elders stand. There the elders stone the child to death. Honor your father and your mother so that your days may be long upon the earth.

Just in case your were wondering, however, you should know that Jewish law outlined just enough circumstances so this law could never be fulfilled. No child was ever really stoned to death; the law was, however, a powerful motivator. Imagine what the effect must have been when parents took their rebellious child for a walk and said, "See those old guys over there? Did you notice the pile of rocks next to them? You might want to read this particular line in the Torah about honoring your mother and father. Now, about staying out all night and not doing your homework."

The Family
What It Is and How It Works

SANFORD SELTZER

No institution has undergone as much change or has been the subject of more controversy than the American family. Industrialization and urbanization, the technological and sexual revolutions, and the emphasis upon individual choice are only some of the powerful factors contributing to the transformation of the family. Today, it is a far cry from the traditional image depicted in textbooks, on motion picture screens, and in television sitcoms.

The Jewish family has not escaped these sociological realities. It, too, has undergone significant restructuring and is now the topic of much debate. Genuine concerns have been voiced regarding its viability and its capacity to fulfill its historic role. Judaism portrayed the home as a *mikdash ma'at*—a small sanctuary. Its religious importance was reflected in the array of home observances linked to the festival cycle of the Jewish year, with specific responsibilities apportioned to all family members according to age and gender.

By the end of the rabbinic period of Jewish history, the family had been clearly defined. Marriage was essential. Early marriage was encouraged as a result of limited life expectancy and as a means of controlling sexuality. Mothering and the care of the household were a woman's primary obligations. Her virtue would be recounted by her husband each Friday evening as he read the passage from the Book of Proverbs (31:10–31) describing her as "a woman of valor who...eateth not of the bread of idleness," and "who looketh well to the ways of her household."

Since children were the only reliable safeguard of Jewish continuity, fulfilling the biblical injunction to "be fruitful and multiply" was incumbent upon every married couple. The high rate of infant mortality and the constant threats of persecution, exile, and even death underscored the imperative to bear as many children as possible.

Although the existence of an entire tractate of the Talmud dealing with divorce (*Gittin*) would indicate that its occurrence was not uncommon, the frequency of divorce is difficult to measure. Women were at the mercy of their husbands in securing a bill of divorcement (*get*). The rabbinic observation that a recalcitrant husband should be beaten until he agreed to give his wife a divorce is a telling commentary.

Intermarriage was not tolerated and was seen as a constant threat to the survival of the Jewish community. Jewish law deemed such unions, when they occurred, as invalid. They came under the halachic category of *ein kiddushin tofsin*—an un-religious marriage—and were treated accordingly.

Although it is difficult to believe that there were not gays and lesbians among the ancient Israelites who came out of Egypt, stood at Sinai, and entered Canaan, homosexuality was explicitly forbidden. The aversion to homosexuality is quite understandable. It grew out of a number of factors, including an ignorance of genetic and psychological factors affecting sexuality, the necessity of insuring the birth of children, and the ongoing struggle against the intrusion of foreign customs and practices that could undermine what the rabbis had determined to be normative and appropriate. It is, therefore, important to acknowledge that the so-called traditional Jewish family of the past was no less influenced by a host of sociological, economic, and cultural circumstances than its contemporary counterpart.

However sweeping the impact of modernity upon the Jewish family, the evidence appears to confirm that marriage and children are important for American Jews, and the family unit is central to religious expression. Jews marry and remarry in record numbers. One finds few anti-marriage advocates among Jews.

Despite the ready availability of abortion, at least for the present (Reform Judaism has been outspokenly pro-choice), easy access to birth control devices, and the emphasis upon sexual pleasure as an end in itself, the Jewish family, although smaller in size, is still thriving. Jewish parents are demanding day care under Jewish auspices, a growing need which the Reform movement has accepted by calling upon its congregations to provide day care on behalf of its constituency. The high rate of intermarriage among Jews is a great concern. The

Reform movement's Commission on Reform Jewish Outreach has encouraged non-Jewish spouses to convert to Judaism and couples in mixed marriages to affiliate with synagogues and enroll their children in religious schools.

Despite the lack of solid statistics, a growing number of Jewish men and women have openly declared that they are gay and lesbian. Reform Judaism has welcomed gay and lesbian congregations and has fought for gay rights. Gay and lesbian couples are now asking that rabbis sanctify their relationship in an appropriate Jewish ceremony, a request that for the most part has gone unheeded.

The advent of new reproductive technologies, as well as opportunities for adoption and foster parenting, will enable gay and lesbian couples to parent Jewish children should they desire to do so. Another unprecedented phenomenon is the growing number of adopted children whose origins are non-Caucasian. Their presence signifies the emergence of a multiethnic, multiracial Jewish community in the coming years. Although the divorce rate among Jews continues to be somewhat lower than that among other religious groups, it is formidable enough to warrant greater attention to the needs and concerns of single parent and blended families. The same holds true for the increasing population of older Jewish men and women, who will play an unprecedented role in twenty-first century American Jewish family life and in setting the institutional priorities of the Jewish community. These individuals can no longer be neglected, ignored, or stereotyped.

In the twenty-first century it will no longer be possible to speak of the "Jewish family" but rather of Jewish families. Perhaps the Jewish family was always a myth, but an abiding impression has prevailed. Whatever the family configuration, the Jewish home of tomorrow can still be a small sanctuary devoted to the celebration of Jewish life and the transmission of the Jewish heritage.

Bibliography

Ackelsburg, Martha. "Family Or Community?" *Sh'ma*, 20 March 1987.

Blankenhorn, David, Steven Bayme, and Jean Bethke Elshtain, eds. *Rebuilding the Nest: A New Commitment to the American Family*. Milwaukee: Family Service America, 1991.

Cohen, Steven. *American Modernity and Jewish Identity*. New York: Tavistock Publishers, 1983.

Fishman, Sylvia Barack. "The Changing American Jewish Family in the 80's." *Contemporary Jewry* 9, no. 2 (1988).

Glicksman, Allan. *The New Jewish Elderly. A Literature Review*. New York: American Jewish Committee, 1990.

Handelman, Susan. "Family, A Religiously Mandated Ideal." *Sh'ma*, 20 March 1987.

Thorne, Barrie, and Marilyn Yalom, eds. *Rethinking the Family*. Boston: Northeastern University Press, 1992.

Whitehead, Barbara Dafoe. "Dan Quayle Was Right." *The Atlantic Monthly*, April 1993, 47–84.

We're in Love, But...
Intermarriage and the
Reform Movement Today

SHARON FORMAN

My mother kissed me as we stood outside my dormitory. She and my father were about to leave after dropping me off for my first year at college. "You always liked those gothic fairy tales where people lived in high, towering castles," laughed my father as he gazed up the eighty-nine twisting steps to my room on the top floor. "Just don't fall in love with that lovely boy who helped us carry all of your things upstairs," they warned. "He's probably not Jewish."

Thus began my four years of college. I was encouraged to study with non-Jews, live with them, even be their best friends. Whatever I did, however, I had to guard against falling in love with them. Love could lead to marriage, and marriage to someone who did not share my Jewish background, my memories of hunting for the *afikoman* at family seders, my desire to hear the blasts of the *shofar* on Rosh Hashanah. Embedded in my parents' warning to me was their fear that marriage to a non-Jew could lead to my dismissing my 4,000-year old heritage altogether, an abandonment of a faith and a civilization. The kind young man who helped me carry my bags was a potential threat to my Jewish identity. If I married him, the Jewish identity of my future children might also be at risk.

Although I have attempted to avoid the issue of inter-marriage (by trying to restrict my dating to Jews only—a difficult and sometimes heartbreaking commitment), many of my Jewish friends are now confronting the issue of intermarriage very seriously (a difficult and heart-breaking task). They care about their Judaism and love their non-Jewish partners. How can they live with both of these potentially conflicting loves? How can they be part of the Jewish community if their spouses are not Jewish? What will happen to their children? Can they lead rich, Jewish lives without the support of a Jewish spouse? Have they betrayed Judaism by marrying some-one they truly love who does not happen to be Jewish?

As far back as biblical times, Hebrew parents (they did not refer to themselves as "Jews" at that time) wor-ried about their children leaving the tribe for the alien tribes that did not worship one God. Even Moses did not marry a Hebrew woman. Tzipporah, Moses' wife, joined the Hebrew tribe, however, and even performed the circumcision for her infant son. It seems that there was a measure of acceptance for a non-Hebrew to be affiliat-ed with the Hebrew tribe.

While Joseph worked in Pharaoh's court, he married an Egyptian woman, Osnat, who was the daughter of a priest. In spite of their mother's non-Hebrew lineage, Manasseh and Ephraim were accepted into the commu-nity of the Hebrews. On his deathbed, Joseph's father, Jacob, met his half-Egyptian grandchildren, blessed them, and formally adopted them into the family: "Now, your two sons, who were born to you in the land of Egypt before I came to you in Egypt, shall be mine; Ephraim and Manasseh shall be mine no less than Reuben and Simeon" (Genesis 48:5).

To this day, fathers in traditional Jewish families bless their sons on the Sabbath with Jacob's benediction: "May God make you like Ephraim and Manasseh." Thus, in spite of Joseph's intermarriage, his children were welcomed and blessed as full members of the Hebrew tribe.

The Torah, however, also offers some harsher attitudes toward the dangers of intermarriage. In the Book of Deuteronomy, there appears an edict that clearly opposes marriage to those from other groups: "You shall not intermarry with them: do not give your daughters to their sons or take their daughters for your sons. For they will turn your children away from Me to worship other gods, and the Lord's anger will blaze forth against you and He will promptly wipe you out" (Deuteronomy 7:3–4). Here the biblical author warns of the threat to the tribes' survival and to their special relationship to God should members marry outside of their group.

Ideology and human relationships struggle in a painful contest. In order for Judaism to survive, to be a meaningful way of life for its followers, Jews must exist. Yet, when two people love each other so much that they wish to spend their entire lives together, they may be willing to compromise on the issue of religion. Our ancestors dealt with this challenge either by accepting non-Hebrew partners into the tribe and adopting them as Hebrews or by forbidding such unions altogether.

In North America today, we live in an open society. Our "tribal" leaders do not dictate whom we marry. We are free to make these kinds of choices for ourselves.

According to recent statistics, approximately half of "born Jews" who married chose non-Jewish spouses in the last few years. The non-Jewish partner officially converted to Judaism in about 5 percent of these marriages. Since 1985, twice as many interfaith couples have been formed as Jewish couples. Studies indicate that 28 percent of children in mixed marriages are being raised as Jews.

Intermarriage is clearly a reality of contemporary Jewish life, and the Reform movement is working to confront the challenges it presents. Reform Judaism's approach to intermarriage reflects its commitment to creating a vibrant Jewish life while meeting the challenges of modernity. In 1978, the president of the Union of American Hebrew Congregations, Rabbi Alexander Schindler, called for the development of an Outreach program to respond to the needs of individuals converting to Judaism (Jews-by-Choice), couples in intermarriages, and those people interested in learning about Judaism.

The Reform Movement's official policy on outreach encourages welcoming and integrating new Jews-by-Choice into the Jewish community; welcoming intermarried couples; encouraging them to identify and raise their children as Jews; and establishing education programs so that people can learn more about Judaism. There is a Commission on Reform Jewish Outreach as well as outreach coordinators in every North American region. On the national, regional, and local temple levels, they work with couples, so that they and their children can have meaningful Jewish lives.

Reform temples offer "Introduction to Judaism" courses, which explore Jewish concepts of theology, holidays, life-cycle events, and history for those individuals considering Judaism, interfaith couples, and "born Jews." In addition, they sponsor support groups for interfaith couples and workshops focusing on Jewish traditions. The Reform movement has created a "Times and Seasons" program, an eight-week discussion group for interfaith couples, that encourages communication about religious identity, holiday celebrations, and the religious upbringing of children.

Rather than judging harshly or shunning intermarried couples, the Reform movement strives to welcome sincere and interested individuals into the Jewish community. As the boundaries between different religious and cultural groups in our society continue to collapse, retaining our unique heritage becomes even more challenging. It is the hope of the Reform movement that Jews will continue to learn about their tradition, to find deep meaning in their modern response to Judaism, and to encourage those people they love to share in the beauty of Jewish life.

Bibliography

Cowan, Paul, and Rachel Cowan. *Mixed Blessings: Marriage Between Jews and Christians.* Garden City, NY: Doubleday, 1987.

Einstein, Stephen J., and Lydia Kukoff. *Every Person's Guide to Judaism.* New York: UAHC Press, 1989.

Kukoff, Lydia. *Choosing Judaism.* New York: UAHC Press, 1981.

Petsonk, Judy, and Jim Remsen. *The Intermarriage Handbook: A Guide for Jews and Christians.* New York: Arbor House/ William Morrow, 1988.

UAHC-CCAR Commission on Reform Jewish Outreach. *Reaching Adolescents: Interdating, Intermarriage and Jewish Identity Development.* New York: UAHC Press, 1990.

A Jewish View of Divorce

ROLAND B. GITTELSOHN

Despite the high ideals of Judaism and the best efforts of individual husbands and wives, not every marriage has succeeded—either in the past or in our own time. Some religions are unalterably opposed to divorce. They decree that marriage is a permanent covenant which must never be broken. No matter how unhappy two people may be in their marriage, it must be maintained. In certain faiths divorce is prohibited; in others, a couple may be divorced but neither may subsequently marry again.

Judaism agrees that marriage is a sacred enterprise, one into which we should not enter lightly with the idea that it can be easily dissolved. The Talmud stipulates that "a man should not marry a woman with the thought in mind that he may divorce her."

It is clear, then, that in Judaism marriage has always been deemed a permanent, sacred bond, not to be disturbed or upset for slim cause. Yet our tradition does not prohibit divorce. It recognizes that even more tragic than the separation of husband and wife is their living a life of pretense and deceit. Often couples who have reached the end of the road remain together nonetheless in order to spare their children the consequences of a divorce. Now Judaism is aware of how tragic such consequences can be: children need a unified home, with discipline and love from both parents, to maximize their chance for wholesome development.

As difficult as divorce may be, a home which is intact

physically while broken spiritually, a home which is maintained though husband and wife are no longer in love with each other, perhaps have even come to hate each other, can harm children even more drastically than divorce. Judaism, understanding this, has provided the conditions under which two people whose marriage has failed may seek a separation.

They are first described in the Bible: "A man takes a wife and possesses her. She fails to please him because he finds something obnoxious about her, and he writes her a bill of divorcement, hands it to her, and sends her away from his house" (Deuteronomy 24:1). The first thing that will strike you in these words is that they give the privilege of divorce only to the husband. A complicated structure of talmudic law based on this biblical passage shows the same tendency; no direct right of divorce is provided for the wife. The rabbis seem to have been aware of this inequity. Therefore they provided that, in certain circumstances, a wife could petition the court to ask her husband for a divorce, and, if right was on her side and he refused, the court was authorized to pressure him until it obtained his assent. Maimonides expressed this principle of Jewish law as follows, "If a woman says, 'My husband is distasteful to me, I cannot live with him,' the court compels the husband to divorce her, because a wife is not a captive" (*Yad: Ishut*, 14:8). So the possibilities for a woman to obtain a divorce were not quite so one-sided as they first appear.

Grounds for Divorce

In Jewish law a woman was entitled to a divorce if her husband refused to have sexual intercourse with her, if he contracted a loathsome disease which she was unable to endure, if his occupation caused an odor about his person which she could not stand, if he treated her cruelly, prohibited her from visiting her parents, changed his religion, or was notoriously immoral.

A husband could obtain a divorce if his wife was guilty of adultery, insulted him or his father in his presence, was morally indecent in public, disregarded the ritual laws pertaining to women, or refused to have sexual intercourse with him. If husband and wife agreed mutually that they did not wish to remain married any longer, no further justification was needed; the court was compelled to grant their request. In all cases, however, the rights of the wife to adequate support, stipulated in the *ketubah* (marriage contract) which was read during the wedding ceremony, had to be respected.

In Orthodox and Conservative Judaism it is necessary for a couple to obtain a religious as well as a civil divorce. The religious divorce, called a *get*, is issued by a rabbi or rabbinical court. In Reform Judaism the civil divorce is considered sufficient.

Only as a Last Resort

Judaism accepts divorce, but only as a last resort. Every possible effort must first be made to correct whatever may be faulty in a marriage, in the hope that it can be preserved. Indeed, reconciling a quarreling couple is considered a great virtue. The story is told of Rabbi Meir, who lectured to the public each Friday evening. A certain woman attended these lectures regularly. Her husband, who was not interested in them himself, objected to the fact that she returned home later than he wished. Finally he banished her from the house in a temper and said she could not return until she had spat in Rabbi Meir's eye. She spent the week with a neighbor and returned the following Friday to hear the rabbi's lecture again. In the meantime, the rabbi had heard of her husband's unreasonable demand. He called the woman to him before the assembled audience and said: "My eye gives me pain. Spit into it and it will be relieved." It took considerable persuasion before the woman was willing to comply but she finally did and her husband, when he heard of it, took her back again. We are not told whether she attended subsequent lectures, or if she did, how her husband reacted. The point of the story is clear: a great rabbi estimated his own dignity and position to be less important than the sacrifice of them to repair a broken marriage (*Yevamot* 37). We need not approve the behavior of a husband who obviously tried to dominate his wife's interests and activities.

Weighing Divorce

In short, Judaism avoids both extremes when it comes to divorce. It does not view the rapid rise in divorce rates as an unmitigated evil. To the degree that mistakes are corrected, and prolonged tension and anger averted, easier divorce is laudable. Unfortunately, however, too hasty a resort to divorce prevents some couples from working toward success in their marriages. Few marriages are immediately and automatically successful; more require effort, adjustment, and work. When a quick escape from problems is substituted for a sustained attempt to resolve them, much potential happiness can be lost.

Marriage is a sacred commitment, not a transient strategy of convenience. It ought not be dissolved until every reasonable effort has been made to fulfill its promise. And when divorce becomes inevitable, each partner must accurately assess the reasons for failure as well as his or her own culpability. To detour such honest evaluation or to thrust the entire blame on one's partner is to risk that the same or a similar mistake will be repeated.

"You Shall Rise Before the Aged and Show Deference to the Old"

RUSSELL SILVERMAN

Recent demographic studies place the Jewish population of North America between 5,500,000 and 6,000,000. Of that population, nearly 17 percent, or approximately 1,000,000 Jews, are 65 years old or older. With the baby boom generation less than two decades away from swelling that part of the population, Reform Judaism must turn its attention to this rapidly increasing segment of American Jewry.

The rapid growth of Reform Judaism has been led by these same elderly. They have established hundreds of new congregations across North America, helping to build synagogues and enhance the quality of life within those congregations. They have also established programs that have served their successors well. Now it is up to those successors—that is, ourselves—to provide programs that are appropriate to the needs of their elderly predecessors.

Myths and Misunderstandings

Our understanding of the "elderly" is fraught with myths and misconceptions. First among the most common myths is the notion that a large proportion of the elderly live in some type of institution. The second misconception is that most elderly are interested in only those ideas and concepts that come from and are representative of "the good old days" and not society today. The third myth is that most elderly suffer from Alzheimer's disease or some form of senility and are all too often prone to forget times, dates, and places. The fourth is that most elderly are poor. The fifth and last is that the elderly are not interested in the same programs and services that concern the non-elderly.

The truth is very different from these myths. A relatively small proportion of the elderly population is in an institution at any time. Demographers estimate that the number is approximately 7 percent. That means that 93 percent of the elderly Jewish population is able to participate in the same activities of life as are available to everyone else.

The elderly also have a wealth of knowledge borne out of trial and error—mistakes made during their lifetimes. Too often we fail to listen and be thankful for the advice and counsel of the elderly, who know the obstacles before us. Shouldn't we glean the wisdom that the elderly have? It might make our own lives easier.

Talmudic scholars addressed the third myth—diminution of the thought process—in two ways. In Bava Kama, it says, "People are accustomed to say: when we were young, we were considered adults in wisdom; now that we are old, we are considered as youths" (*Seder Nezikin, Bava Kama* 92b). In *Kinnim*, it says, "The unlearned lose the power of clear thinking as they grow old, but scholars gain in it as their years advance" (*Seder Kodashim, Kinnim* Chap. 3).

The death of some brain cells is part of the normal aging process. This process begins at a very early age. Who among us has not searched for a word only to find it not there when we wanted to recall and use it? Who among us has not seen a face which looked familiar only to forget the name associated with it? Loss of memory or forgetfulness is normal. The elderly simply have more years of memories and learning, which have replaced certain memories they may not, at a moment's notice, recall. This is not evidence of Alzheimer's or any related disease. Rather, it is a normal process of aging that does not lessen the acuity of one's mind.

While it is true that many elderly do live on pension and retirement incomes that are significantly smaller than their previous earnings, many elderly own their own homes, free and clear of any mortgage. They do not have children to put through college. They do not have many of the debts that younger people have.

The fifth myth is no truer than the previous four. The elderly need the same level of programming that congregations provide to their younger congregants. While the elderly are not in need of religious school, preschool, or camp programming, they do need social programming, social action programming, ritual involvement, and other activities within the synagogue. Our challenge is to provide those programs and services that meet the needs of the elderly while we continue to involve them in the other phases of synagogue programming. College students should include and utilize the elderly as valuable resources whenever possible.

A Programmatic Response

As perceived by the leadership of the Reform movement, the elderly's specific needs, desires, and issues center around three areas: involvement in service to the synagogue community and the general community at large; health care costs and services; and bioethical questions concerning health care issues and issues of death and dying.

Involvement. We believe that the elderly want to participate in programs that serve those in need, both within the synagogue family and in the general community. Many synagogues have developed extensive programs that serve the homeless and the hungry. The programs for our "Caring Community" are ideal vehicles for our elderly. The retired elderly have the time these programs require. Additionally, many programs created within the framework of the Caring Community are direct services to the elderly shut-ins and needy. A program that encourages elderly to help elderly is ideal for a congregation.

Health Care. We are all concerned with the rising cost of health care. While only 7 percent of the elderly at any point in time are in institutions, estimates are that one in four will be in a rehabilitation or long-term health care facility during their lifetime. Medicare pays for only part of the cost of care, and only under very strict conditions. All too frequently, the elderly facing institutionalization have deep concerns that their savings will be used up to pay for long-term care either for their spouse or themselves. Their dream may have been to save enough money so that their children may inherit something from them. Yet, long-term care can rapidly reduce whatever savings they have. We need to discuss appropriate alternatives to institutionalization or ways to reduce the financial impact of such care. We need to educate the elderly about available options and alternatives before they are confronted with these health care decisions.

Bioethical Decisions. How can I permit my spouse to continue to suffer? What can I do to avoid being kept alive as a vegetable? Who can act as a health care surrogate? What is a living will? What are my legal rights in deciding how I am cared for? Should the feeding tube be pulled or the ventilator disconnected?

As modern medicine stretches the boundaries of life beyond what was once thought possible, we are confronted with these dilemmas of life and death. The Reform movement needs to respond with material that will assist congregations, rabbis, and lay professionals in understanding the issues, framing Jewish responses to the difficult questions, and assisting those who must make decisions.

The Reform Response

The Reform movement is becoming more active in issues affecting the elderly. The formation of the

National Committee on Service to Older Adults is one response to these issues. Plans to enhance the four volumes of programs involving ideas for the Caring Community are already underway. The bioethics subcommittee has produced several case studies, as well as a document titled *A Time To Prepare* that provides guidance to those who wish to deal with living wills and health care surrogate appointments. The bioethics subcommittee will be producing additional documents in these areas. A third subcommittee will begin to prepare and distribute literature on health care issues.

National meetings will be conducted to energize the committee's work. At these meetings, facilitators will receive training, so that they can return to their communities and assist others in dealing with issues concerning the elderly. These facilitators will receive training in bioethical issues, health care issues, and an overview of Caring Community ideas. The goal of the training program is to provide certification for facilitators in the vital issues and responses in the three areas of bioethics, caring community, and health care. It is envisioned that these facilitators will enable the work of the committee to be broadened into individual communities and synagogues much faster, and with appropriate lay support, than if we attempted to work strictly through a national committee system and distribution of literature.

Ultimately, our society will be judged not on its politics, its GNP, or other signs of wealth but on how it treated its elderly. The Torah teaches us that we should respect our elders and treat them properly or else fear the retribution of God: "You shall rise before the aged and show deference to the old; you shall fear your God: I am the Lord" (Leviticus 19:32). Or, as Rabbi Joshua ben Levi said: "Honor and respect the aged and saintly, whose physical powers are broken, equally with the young and vigorous one; for the broken Tablets of Stone no less than the whole ones had a place in the Ark of the Covenant."

What Does Judaism Say about Death and Dying?

BERNARD M. ZLOTOWITZ

When confronted by emotionally traumatizing events, even the most rational people turn to traditional patterns of behavior for support. This is especially true of our response to death and dying. What follows is a discussion of traditional Jewish customs and beliefs surrounding death and dying. In its adherence to the principles of personal freedom and choice, Reform Judaism follows a modernist liberal approach to the full range of customs and beliefs. According to Reform Judaism, Reform Jews may practice whatever customs they deem meaningful. No practices are viewed by Reform as either authoritative or required.

The overarching principle that guides the Jewish view of death and dying is the dignity and sanctity of human life. The traditional view is that this world is a *prozdor*, a temporary corridor, on the path to eternal life. While

Judaism does not view the afterlife as the goal of living or as the driving force behind one's value system in this life, rabbinic literature abounds with speculation about the afterlife. It should be noted that within Judaism there is no one halachic view of "the world to come" (*haolam haba*). There is only some consensus and much speculation.

The basic principle is that one must not do anything outside of the natural process to hasten death or prolong life. Thus, suicide is treated in Judaism as a sin because it violates God's laws protecting the sanctity of life. Judaism has always affirmed that life is sacred and suicide abhorrent except under special circumstances, such as martyrdom, when the act is deemed not only permissible but at times appropriate.

But what about people who are very sick and suffering from excruciating pain? May they take their own lives (or have someone else do it) to end their suffering? In other words, is euthanasia permissible?

It is a violation of Jewish law tantamount to murder if done actively (i.e., if a pill is taken or a fatal injection is given). However, if it takes the form of a passive act, then there is no prohibition. Moses Isserles (a sixteenth-century rabbi) defined passive euthanasia as follows: "If there is anything which causes a hindrance to the departure of the soul, as for example the presence near the patient's house of a knocking noise, such as wood-chopping, or if there is salt on the patient's tongue, and these hinder the soul's departure, it is permissible to remove them from there because there is no act involved in this at all but only the removal of the impediment" (*Shulchan Aruch, Yoreh De'ah* 339:1).

Thus, the removal of any mechanical instruments and thus allowing the person to die in peace and dignity would be permitted because it is equivalent to removing salt from the patient's tongue. The rabbis teach that the body, although it is made of dust, nevertheless is holy. When a person dies, special attention is required for its care including ritual washing (*tahara*), giving it the respect it deserves. In fact, the committee that prepares the body for burial is known as the *chevrah kadisha*, literally, the "holy society," or Jewish communal burial society.

The Funeral

The funeral is generally conducted in two parts: The first takes place at a funeral chapel or in a synagogue (the former is far more frequent). Prior to the funeral service, *keriah*—"tearing"—takes place. That is, a ribbon attached to the lapel or a dress on the left side over the heart (if it is a parent) or on the right side (if it is a spouse, sibling, son, or daughter) is torn, symbolizing the tearing away of a family member and the grief the mourner is experiencing. Following this ceremony, the family enters the chapel and the rabbi conducts the funeral service by reading psalms, delivering a eulogy, and offering a prayer known as *El Male Rachamim*—O God Full of Compassion—an appeal to God to care for the soul of the deceased. Second, at the cemetery the body is interred in the earth or in a vault (mausoleum). In Reform Judaism, burial is the normative Jewish practice. After the body is lowered in the grave, the family and friends sometimes shovel dirt over the casket. Other times, the casket is left level with the ground and covered with a green grass-like mat, or, on rare occasions, with flowers. The rabbi then offers prayers committing the body to the earth and the soul to God. In traditional

Judaism, a prayer is offered expressing the faith that the body will be resurrected in messianic times. The service is concluded with the saying of the *Kaddish*. A special *Kaddish* is recited in traditional Judaism.

Mourning

After the funeral, traditional Jews wash their hands ritualistically before entering their home. This serves as a reminder that their contact with the dead rendered them ritually unclean; therefore, they must cleanse themselves symbolically. Then they eat a meal prepared for them by their neighbors, beginning with a hard-boiled egg to symbolize that life goes on. They then sit *shivah* (literally, "seven") for seven days on a low bench. (The reason *shivah* continues for a week is because the first seven days are considered the most intense period of feeling the loss of a loved one.) After a person's death, all the mirrors in the home are covered over and all the water in pans and dishes and pots are spilled out, a custom that dates back to medieval times when people usually died in their homes. The belief was that as the body was being carried out, the soul, hovering over the body, would leave with it. But if the soul saw its reflection in the mirror or water, it would notice that the body was leaving horizontally rather than vertically. The abnormality would cause the soul to panic and refuse to leave, remaining behind and haunting the house. During the week of *shivah*, the mourners do not wear clothing made of leather, especially shoes, because that is a luxury and brings pleasure. Showering, bathing, shaving, changing clothes, listening to music, or watching television is prohibited for the same reason. A seven-day candle is lit, and morning and evening services are conducted with a *minyan* in the home of the mourners, for they are not permitted to leave the premises during the *shivah*, except on the Sabbath.

Children of the deceased continue their mourning for 30 days, known as *sheloshim* ("thirty"), but on a diminished scale. They still wear the torn ribbon, do not shave or listen to music or watch television, but may bathe and shower. The children's mourning period lasts a full year. After the *sheloshim*, they no longer wear the torn ribbon but are still forbidden to hear music, watch television, or attend any joyous occasion. They continue to recite *Kaddish* for eleven months.

In Reform Judaism, the tearing of the ribbon prior to the funeral is optional, as is washing the hands before entering the house after the interment. The *shivah* period is also optional, as are wearing clothes without leather or sitting on *shivah* benches. Nevertheless, most Reform Jews choose to sit *shivah* at least three days. Like traditional Jews, Reform Jews light a candle that will burn for seven days and a service is held in the mourners' home. A *minyan* is not necessary, but if the mourners wish one, men and women are counted into the *minyan*. Covering the mirrors is optional. No distinction is made between *shivah* and the *sheloshim*. Reform Jews are permitted to listen to music, watch television, and participate in *simchot* ("joyous occasions"). They say *Kaddish* for a full year, at least once a week at Sabbath services.

The Kaddish

The *Kaddish* has a powerful pull on the Jew. Among traditional Jews, it is believed that it has the power of redeeming the soul from the suffering of hell. It is recited for eleven months during the first year of a parent's death, and each year on the anniversary of the death of the loved one (*yahrzeit*). Originally, the *Kaddish* (literally, "holy") had no connection with death. Written in Aramaic (a sister language to Hebrew), except for the last verse ("The One who makes peace"), which is written in Hebrew, the *Kaddish* is a doxology (a prayer of praise to God). No mention is made of death or dying. In ancient times (and still today) it was recited at the close of congregational prayers, after the scriptural lesson, and at the conclusion of every study session in the *Bet Hamidrash* and the synagogue. At the end of each discourse, the recitation of the *Kaddish* lifted the spirits of the assembly, raising its hopes of the Messiah's coming.

In time, the *Kaddish* became associated with the death of a scholar and was recited at the end of the *shivah* period (*Soferim* 19:12). Later, out of concern for the feelings of others, it was recited after every Jewish burial (Nachmanides, *Torat Haadam*, p. 50). Among the Orthodox, only male children say *Kaddish*, and they do so for eleven months.

The eleven-month period is based on the belief that a person can be sentenced to *Gehenna*—hell—for a maximum of twelve months. However, children cannot conceive of their parents being so sinful that they would get the maximum sentence. Therefore, it became the custom that *Kaddish* be recited for eleven months to alleviate the pain of the soul in *Gehenna*.

Recognizing the powerful pull of the *Kaddish*, Reform Judaism added a paragraph referring exclusively to the dead to its 1940 Union Prayer Book. However, this paragraph was deleted when the liturgy was revised with the publication of *Gates of Prayer*. Furthermore, in many Reform congregations, the whole congregation joins the mourners in saying *Kaddish* because not only is there a loss for the mourning family but for all Israel. The congregation, therefore, joins in reciting *Kaddish* to show solidarity with the mourners.

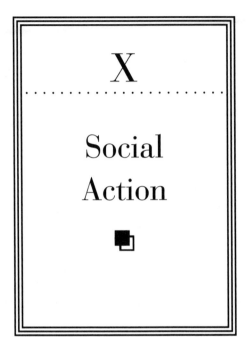

X

Social Action

Mandate for Social Justice

DAVID SAPERSTEIN

Jews have a historic mandate to be advocates for social justice. It is almost as though this mandate is part of the Jewish genetic makeup.

Based on the *Aggadah*, our tradition creates a vision of humanity, God, and the universe that leads us to believe there are certain eternal and universal values. Most of them are familiar to us, but let us put them in a political context.

- The belief that we are all made in the divine image of God and, as such, are endowed with infinite value is the fundamental concept of human rights that animates democracy today.

- The belief in the fundamental equality of all people, derived from those aggadic stories that say we were all descended from one couple, and that Adam was made from the dust of the four corners of the earth, provided concepts indispensable to our modern notion of human rights and liberty. None of us, therefore, can claim that our parents had greater *yichus* ("noble" ancestry) than did other parents. We are all children of God, all descended from the same source.

- The concept that property is held in a relationship of trust with God is expressed in the verse "The earth is the Eternal's and the fullness thereof." We believe in private ownership, but the obligation to share God's wealth with those of God's children

386 / Where We Stand

who are less fortunate is a central focus of Judaism's social legislation. In addition, as with any trust, we are responsible to protect the "corpus" of that trust. It is no surprise, therefore, that the Bible contains some of the earliest legislation protecting the environment.

- The belief that human beings can improve themselves and can create a better world is one of the fundamental distinctions between Judaism and Christianity. Normative Christianity argued that there were limits upon the ability of human beings both individually and collectively to improve their world, that the messianic age and the Messiah would only come after the destruction of the world and would mark the end of history as we know it. Maimonides, on the other hand, argued that the messianic age would grow out of history, that we would create the messianic world through the work of our own hands, and that the coming of the Messiah to rule over the messianic age would be the sign that we had finally achieved that world of which our tradition has always dreamed.

We believe that we can create a better world and that we are an integral part of *tikkun olam*, creating a better world.

Our tradition tells us that when God created the universe, one part of creation was left undone. That part was social justice. God then gave us something that was given to nothing else in creation—wisdom: the ability to understand the difference between right and wrong, good and evil, blessing and curse. It is as if God said, "Here's the blueprint—the Torah. Here is the world that should be built, but now you must build it." By allowing us to be partners with God in the fulfillment of creation, God ennobled humanity, raising us above mere existence by infusing our lives with a sense of destiny and purpose.

Closely appended to this notion is the belief in free will, without which democracy would not exist. This belief was held by a minority in the history of Western civilization. Ancient Greeks tell us of Fates that played games with human destiny: From the concept of original sin in Catholicism to predestination in Calvinism, Christianity sets limits on human freedom. Against those notions (which resonate even to our own time in certain psychological schools of thought) is juxtaposed a clarion vision of the human condition, a vision of being able to determine our own destiny. "I have set before you this day, life and death. The blessing and the curse, good and evil." But God does not say, "I'm going to tell you how to choose." It is almost as though God is pleading with humanity, saying, "Look, I give to you that which I have given to nothing else in creation—the ability to understand the difference between right and wrong. But if My words and values are to exist here on earth, it will be because of the choices that you make. I can tell you what you should choose and why you should choose it, but ultimately the choice is yours. Therefore, choose life in order that you and your children after you might live."

It is an extraordinary adventure to be a Jew in a world that cherishes rather than rejects these values. Look at the United States. In the past generation, Jews have had untold legal, political, and social opportunities. An activist Supreme Court, which protected the basic human rights and opportunities of the minority from the tyranny of the majority, has allowed us to move to the center of political, economic, and cultural life in the

United States. Now we have seen the reshaping of that activist court. As a result, the Supreme Court is failing to maintain its role as the guarantor of our fundamental rights, and we must turn to Congress to fill those gaps.

As the bearers of a tradition that affirms the ideals of freedom, equality, and social responsibility as universal values, Jews must insist that government policies be tested by whether they further or impede these values of social justice.

No one can categorically state whether the views of the Republicans or Democrats are what God wants. God has not ordained monarchies or democracies. God has not ordained socialism or capitalism. God has not ordained food stamp programs. These are human inventions, and good, moral people can differ over whether Judaism's universal values are impeded or fulfilled by these particular policies.

These different viewpoints should not dismay us. Indeed, every page of the Talmud is filled with both minority and majority opinions. Make no mistake about it, however. To be a Jew means to be involved in testing those values. To be a Jew means to speak out on these issues. To be a Jew means to be bound up with the struggle for social justice.

Jewish activism is needed more now than at any other point in human history. Technology has so reshaped the world that the consequences of our acts have unprecedented implications. The changes in technology mean that we are the first generation in human history that does not have the liberty to make mistakes and learn from them.

Will we find peaceful ways for nations to resolve their

differences, or will we blow up the world in a nuclear holocaust? Will we continue to contaminate our environment, or will we bequeath to our children God's beneficence and bounty enriched by our presence here? Will we use technology to enhance our freedoms or to diminish them? Will we use the technology of genetic engineering to build Hitler's master race or to cure birth defects?

We have choices. We can be the author of those decisions or we can be the audience; we can speak out or remain silent and in the vacuum of our silence hear voices, shrill and angry, that do not share our values and our dreams.

It is almost as though all of human history has been a test run for this moment, and this time it counts. In our time, we will finally decide.

Preserving the Environment
The Ultimate Havdalah

PETER E. KASDAN

In Genesis 1:31 the Torah describes God's reaction to the new universal reality: *Vayar Elohim et kol asher asah vehineh tov me'od*—"And God saw all that had been made and found it very good." The great rabbinic scholars of our tradition teach us that after creating each part of this new universal life force, God found each unique part of it "good." It was only after God had created human beings, at the very end of the sixth day of the creation process, that God was moved to find the total creation "very good."

I sometimes think that human beings believe the words "very good," uttered at that special moment in the creation process, hint at perfection—that is, our perfection! We like to call ourselves the highest form of life in the universe. This is a comforting and egocentric thought, one that permits us to view other life-forms as less important than we are and, therefore, expendable. We also believe that we, who are God's partners in the ongoing creation, are indestructible, while other, less complex life-forms are dying all around us from some inherent weakness in their natural composition.

But our tradition reminds us that this is not so. In fact, it teaches us that we are linked to each part of creation—from the simplest one-celled creatures that begin the food chain to the complex creatures we paternalistically think of as "almost human." There are many teachings within Jewish literature that deny our perfection. We are not perfect creatures; we can never become perfect creatures. We are finite and thus merely part of the creation. Taking a different approach, Edmond Fleg uses a midrashic source to pen the piece below, which is now part of our prayer book *Shaarei Tefilah (Gates of Prayer)*:

> Then Isaac asked the Eternal: "Creator of the world, when You made the light, You said in Your Torah that it was good; when You made the expanse of heaven and earth, You said in Your

Torah that they were good; and of every herb You made and every beast, You said that they were good; but when You made us in Your Image, You did not say of us in Your Torah that humanity was good. Why, God?"

And God answered Isaac: "Because you I have not yet perfected; because through the study of the Torah you are to perfect yourselves and then to perfect the world. All other things are completed; they cannot grow. But humankind is not complete; you have yet to grow. Then will I call you good!"

(*Shaarei Tefilah*, pp. 667–68)

The final line of this teaching says it all: "Only then will I call you good!" It is interesting that here, at the very beginning of our involvement in and with creation, God does not refer to us as "very good" but only as "good," and even that adjective is to be used only when we, as a species, have overcome our inherent imperfection. We may like to think of ourselves in more lofty terms, but this midrashic teaching is a far more accurate description of who we are.

This notion of the total creation, which God calls "very good," I see as the first moment of separation—of *Havdalah*. God must have understood the uniqueness of that moment, too—why else the sudden change from "good" to "very good"? For me, Havdalah is one of the most beautiful of all Jewish rituals. It requires a sensitivity to my surroundings and an admission of my imperfections, yet it also holds out the possibility that I have the power to reach beyond myself and grasp the purity of that original moment of creation, even if only for a microsecond. *Havdalah* allows me to be at one with the universe; it challenges me to become an environmentalist.

Among the selections for *Havdalah* in our prayer book, there are some magnificent statements in this regard. We are taught the following about the symbol of wine:

> Wine gladdens the heart. In our gladness, we see beyond the ugliness and misery that stain our world. Our eyes open to unnoticed grace, blessings till now unseen, and the promise of goodness we can bring to flower.
>
> (*Shaarei Tefilah*, p. 639)

We are taught the following about the symbol of spices:

> [They] console us at the moment of [Shabbat's] passing.... And their bouquet will make us yearn...for the sweetness of rest and the fragrance of growing things; for the clean smell of rain-washed earth and the sad innocence of childhood; and for the dream of a world healed of pain, pure and wholesome as on that first Shabbat, when God, finding the handiwork good, rested from the work of creation.
>
> (*Shaarei Tefilah*, p. 639)

And about the symbol of fire, we learn the following:

> We have the power to create many different fires, some useful, others baneful. Let us be on guard never to let this gift of fire devour human life, sear cities and scorch fields, or foul the pure air of heaven, obscuring the very skies. Let the fire we kindle be holy: Let it bring light and warmth to all humanity.

> (*Shaarei Tefilah*, p. 640)

Our tradition is clear about our need to be conscious of our environment, to be environmentalists. In fact, the very concept of environmentalism is part of the original moment of creation as it unfolded during those first six days. God built it into the system; it is not a choice that we have to make. It is part of the challenge made to Adam and Eve: "Fill the earth and master it; and rule the fish of the sea, the birds of the sky, and all the living things that creep on earth" (Genesis 1:28). God did not say to them, or to us for that matter, "Do what you want with these lesser creatures; create new strains, destroy those creatures you consider unimportant, pollute the air and the sea and the land, create weapons of destruction to level the landscape, and make the earth a waste heap!" God said: "Make *Havdalah*! Separate yourselves from all that is unholy, from all that is destructive, and take care of My creation!" As it is explained in our prayer book, "We have learned: Say always, 'The world was created for my sake,' and never say, 'Of what concern is all of this to me?' Live as if all life depended on you. Do your share to add some improvement, to supply something that is missing, and to leave the world a little better for your stay in it" (*Shaarei Tefilah*, p. 681).

Reform Judaism has become a leader in the environmental movement. Our congregations have become increasingly involved in recycling and preserving the environment locally, nationally, and internationally; they have functioned as soup kitchens and have stocked food banks for the homeless and forgotten; they have created equal access for those who are physically handicapped; they have made their synagogue facilities into smoke-free zones.

But, although we have done much, there is much more yet to be done, especially on our college campuses. We need to mobilize the idealism of our movement's college population, an idealism in keeping with what students have learned in their home synagogues. So consider this a call to every Reform Jewish college student: Please consider making your dorms or apartment buildings, your fraternity and sorority houses, your Hillels and clubs smoke-free zones; passive smoke is as much a killer as cigarettes themselves! Please make your schools accessible to the handicapped. Ensure that there are recycling bins for cans, glass, and newspapers in the buildings on your campus. Turn the food that is wasted in your college dining rooms and eating clubs into a source of food for the hungry who stand outside your campus gates. Create a soup kitchen on your campus. And if there are homeless people in your college town community, why not provide them with a place to sleep in those sections of your Hillel's facilities that are unused most of the week. If you are bold enough, consider pressuring your college administration to open infrequently used but heated parts of the school to the homeless so they may have a safe, warm place to sleep at night.

These are only some of the actions you can take to

preserve our natural and human environment. True, even if we did all these things, we would still have a long way to go before we could consider our world properly repaired. But these calls to action are an important stepping-stone toward what we might be able to create in our world on our journey toward self-completion—a journey that began long ago, when the world was new and fresh and innocent.

All we need to do is to recall our Creator's message and allow ourselves to see beyond ourselves, to see the world as it was first seen on that fateful sixth day. If we allow the sweet wine, the fragrant spices, and the warm glow of the twisted candle's light to enter our being, they may provide us with a *Havdalah* that will renew our commitment to our world, a world that God has given to us as a precious gift.

Homelessness

RELIGIOUS ACTION CENTER

On any given night, some 750,000 Americans are homeless. Over the course of a year, between 1.3 and 2 million people will experience homelessness. Thousands more are on the brink of homelessness, paying more than half their income for shelter and often forced to choose between buying groceries and paying rent. For those who live on the street, illness, danger, and humiliation are part of their everyday lives. As the National Low Income Housing Coalition has noted:

> Being homeless means having no place to store things that connect you to your past; often it means losing contact with friends and family; it means uprooting your kids from school and having to endure the shame of what is still considered by many as personal failure. For some, being homeless means having to break up the family just to find lodging for the night, since many "family shelters" do not allow older boys to stay and many homeless children are placed with relatives or in foster care. Being homeless means enduring the routine indignities of living on the margins, the frustration of not being able to provide for those who love you, and the anonymity of government assistance.

Despite programs aimed at reducing homelessness and despite a massive outpouring of goodwill by synagogues, churches, and civic groups across the country, the ranks of the homeless are swelling each year. In 1991, there were 5.3 million low-income renter households, not counting the homeless, with "worst-case" housing problems—paying more than half their income for housing, living in seriously inadequate units, or both. Despite this, many cities are imposing harsher restrictions on homeless people to reduce their visibility or force them to relocate.

A Prophetic Response

The Reform Jewish community quickly responded to the problem of homelessness, calling on Reform congregations to assist in establishing shelters, to provide volunteer staff for these shelters on an ongoing basis, to offer the use of their own facilities to provide shelter, food and clothing, and to form interfaith coalitions aimed at pressuring the federal, state, and local governments to contribute their fair share to solving the problem. This response, which came in the form of a resolution adopted by the Union of American Hebrew Congregations in 1983, echoes the mandate of the biblical prophets to "share your bread with the hungry, and bring the homeless into your house" (Isaiah 58:7).

The prophets themselves were exhorting us to follow a long-standing tradition of hospitality among the Jewish people. According to one *midrash*, Abraham is judged to be greater than Job because while the latter "opened [his] doors to the roadside" (Job 31:32), Abraham left his tent to seek guests among the passersby (Genesis 18:1–8). More recent Jewish history, with its exiles and expulsions, is a powerful reminder of our special obligation to provide for those with no protection.

A Contemporary Commitment

While the prophets teach us that homelessness is a profound human tragedy, Jewish tradition leaves us with little in the way of solutions to the problem. Yet our moral consciousness must be transformed into social action if the homeless are to be housed. Several groups, including the Reform movement, have recognized that solutions to homelessness will need to move beyond providing emergency shelter to addressing the problem of homelessness at its roots.

In a 1989 resolution, the UAHC outlined a plan for contemporary commitment to the long-term solutions of increasing the stock of affordable housing and providing the means for homeless people to make the transition from shelters and the street to permanent homes. The resolution suggests concrete steps for ensuring that all people are able to secure decent, affordable housing. These include:

1. Calling upon the United States Congress to develop and fully fund a national housing policy.
2. Urging members of Reform congregations to educate themselves about low-income housing and homelessness issues and to become more involved with these issues in their local communities.
3. Encouraging continued provisions for emergency shelter and expansion of "the only long-range solution"—permanent affordable housing.
4. Supporting local community nonprofit development organizations focusing on low-income housing.

These four steps—advocacy, education, involvement, and support—are guidelines not only for Reform congregations but for all who are working to eliminate homelessness.

Bibliography

"The Closing Door: Economic Causes of Homeless-ness." Washington, DC: National Coalition for the Homeless, 1990.

Kozol, Jonathan. *Rachel and Her Children: Homeless Families in America*. New York: Crown Publishing Inc., 1988.

Sh'ma: A Journal of Jewish Responsibility. Vol. 22, no. 422 (special homelessness issue), 29 November, 1991.

Institutions

Children's Defense Fund
122 C Street NW
Washington, DC 20001

Homelessness Information Exchange
1830 Connecticut Avenue NW
4th floor
Washington, DC 20009

National Coalition for the Homeless
1621 Connecticut Avenue NW
Washington, DC 20009

Religious Action Center of Reform Judaism
2027 Massachusetts Avenue NW
Washington, DC 20036

Other Resources

The UAHC College Education Department, in connection with the Jewish Council on Urban Affairs (JCUA) in Chicago, has organized an Urban Mitzvah Corp. This week-long program brings together twenty college students from across the country to work with Habitat for Humanity, rehabbing affordable housing in the Chicago area. For more information, contact the UAHC Great Lakes Regional Office at 100 West Monroe, Suite 312, Chicago, IL 60603 (312) 782-1477 or the JCUA at 220 South State Street, Suite 1910, Chicago, IL 60604 (312) 663-0960.

Hunger

RELIGIOUS ACTION CENTER

Nothing is more fundamental to Judaism than the moral obligation to perform acts of *tzedakah*—acts of righteousness. As it is written in the Talmud, "Aiding the poor and feeding the hungry weighs as heavily as all the other commandments of the Torah" (*Bava Batra* 9a). Nor may we forget the biblical command "And if your brother grows poor, and he comes under your authority, then you shall uphold him; though he be a stranger or a settler shall he live with you" (Leviticus 25:35).

The rabbis observe that the statement "your brother shall live with you" means that it is our personal and communal duty to ensure that our fellow human beings do not die of starvation. Although the person may be a "stranger" or "an alien settler," he or she should be included in the term "your brother" and should be treated in a compassionate manner.

The rabbinic sages regarded such compassionate care of another as an act worthy of association with the Divinity itself:

> God says to Israel, "My children, whenever you give sustenance to the poor, I impute it to you as though you gave sustenance to Me," for it says, "Command the children of Israel…My bread for My sacrifices…shall you observe unto Me." Does then God eat and drink? No, but whenever you give food to the poor, God accounts it to you as if you gave food to God.
>
> (*Numbers Rabbah* 28:2)

The virtue of caring for the poor and hungry is depicted in Jewish tradition as one of the salient attributes of the founding father of Judaism, the patriarch Abraham. In a midrashic commentary that begins with the phrases "Let your house be open; let the poor be members of your household; let a person's house be open to the north and to the south, and to the east and to the west," the rabbis described Abraham's humanitarianism in the following way:

> He went out and wandered about, and when he found wayfarers, he brought them to his house, and he gave wheaten bread to him whose wont it was not to eat wheaten bread, and so with meat and wine. And not only this, but he built large inns on the roads and put food and drink within them, and all came and ate and drank and blessed God. Therefore, quiet of spirit was granted to him, and

> all that the mouth of man can ask for was found in
> his house.
>
> (*Avot de-Rabbi Natan* chapter 7)

Elsewhere the Talmud admonishes, "One who has no pity upon his fellow creatures is assuredly not of the seed of Abraham our father" (*Betzah* 32b).

In Jewish communities, from biblical times to the present, there was free and generous giving of alms to all who asked—even to deceivers!—and there was also systematic and careful relief through established institutions. Each Jewish community boasted of a *tamchui*— public kitchen—which provided the poor with two meals daily. There was also the *kupah*—alms box—for the disbursement of benevolent funds to provide the poor with three meals for the Sabbath (*Mishnah Peah* 8:7). Moreover, as Rabbi Marc Tanenbaum testified before the Ad-Hoc Senate Committee Hearings on World Hunger on December 18, 1974, additional care was given to the itinerant poor, who were provided with a loaf of bread that sufficed for two meals and were entitled to the cost of lodging.

The role of human beings in the biblical creation stories exemplifies our tradition of combating hunger. In Genesis 1:29, Adam was told that the products of the earth would provide him with food. God said, "See, I give you every seed-bearing plant that is upon all the earth and every tree that has seed-bearing fruit; they shall be yours for food." After Adam was placed in Eden, "the Eternal God formed out of the earth all the wild beasts and all the birds of the sky and brought them to the 'Adam' to see what he would call them" (Genesis

2:19). In Jewish tradition, this implied a responsibility to share food. This is evident in Leviticus and Deuteronomy, where we are told that one may not reap the corner of the field or gather the gleanings or fallen grapes, because "for the poor and the stranger you shall leave them; I am the Eternal your God" (Leviticus 19:10). The postbiblical Jewish tradition also sought many ways to alleviate hunger.

The *Mishnah* tractate *Peah* defines the importance and scope of the biblical laws that prohibit reaping the corners of the field or collecting fallen grapes. While there is a minimum one must leave, there is no maximum: One must not give less than one-sixtieth for *peah*—corner. And although there was no fixed limit (above one-sixtieth) for *peah*, the amount depended on the size of the field, the number of the poor, and the extent of one's generosity (*Mishnah Peah* 1:2). It was the need of the poor that determined how much one gives, and it was one's generosity that determined the quality of what one gives. The owner of the field was required to be available to supervise the cutting by the poor (*Mishnah Peah* 4:5). Unless one was really poor, one could not take help: "Anyone who possesses the means for two meals must not accept anything from the poor soup kitchen" (*Mishnah Peah* 8:7).

The point is not only that the tradition provided a means for sharing but that the sharing was a religious obligation. The recipient was entitled to aid as a matter of law and not simply as a result of goodwill.

The responsibility to share with the less fortunate is evident in the many midrashic statements that were made and in the practical steps that were taken to feed the hungry. In one story, a saint who gives a coin to a poor man during a famine—even though his wife was opposed to the donation—is rewarded with the knowledge of how to increase his crops (*Avot de-Rabbi Natan* chapter 3). The act of prolonging one's meal on the chance that a poor person may come for food is so praiseworthy that the table of a person who performs this act is compared to the altar of the ancient Temple (*Berachot* 55a).

Our forebears in the postbiblical period not only experienced poverty, they took steps to cope with it. Sharing was common throughout Jewish life, whether through the practice of gleaning or through the community poor box.

Hunger and poverty are not issues of the past. With the enactment of the new welfare law signed in 1996, hunger and poverty will undoubtedly increase. Of the $54 billion that the new law cuts from the welfare system over the next six years, $28 billion is to come from the food stamps program. Moreover, the new law bars legal immigrants from receiving food stamps until they naturalize, accounting for an estimated $4.7 billion of the cuts to the food stamps program. In another especially harsh provision, the bill limits single, childless individuals ages eighteen to fifty to three months of food stamps while unemployed during any three-year period. The widely respected Center on Budget and Policy Priorities has estimated that in an average week, one million poor, jobless individuals who are willing to work but cannot find a job will go hungry because of this provision.

The food stamps program, which is to be cut by approximately $28 billion over the next six years, ensures that those too poor to provide for themselves or their families will eat. How do we reconcile our traditional mandate that we care for those in need with changes in national law that will cause millions to go hungry?

Racism

JOEL E. SOFFIN

The stands are filled with excited fans who are sharing one of America's favorite pastimes, the World Series. The game is being played at Fulton County Stadium in Atlanta. The level of enthusiasm is very high; everyone feels the excitement in the air.

Then in an act of support and encouragement for their team, the Braves' fans start what has come to be known as the tomahawk chop. Holding foam rubber mock tomahawks and shouting a so-called Indian war chant, they move their arms forward and back.

It's all part of the fun, isn't it? As long as acts like these are done with a sense of humor, what's the harm?

This was the same reasoning used by Oldsmobile dealers in New York, New Jersey, and Connecticut a few years back to justify their Japan-bashing commercials. In an effort to boost car sales, they compared the average height of American men to that of Japanese. The concluding pitch for the purchase of a Cutlass Sierra went as follows: "That's why our car is built for our size families, not theirs."

Are these indeed cases of racism or is all fair in sports and business? Are such imitations and portrayals of nonwhite racial groups fitting for a society in which diversity should be welcomed and appreciated?

Although we may not be inclined to describe the two situations presented above as racist, they do appear to be close, which is why such activities can be so disturbing. Their racial tinge also explains our defensive reaction to them.

Does the fun we have imitating stereotyped Indian behavior or do the sales we make at the expense of Japanese physical characteristics justify such veiled racism? Does fun or business reduce the morally reprehensible nature of the tomahawk chop or Oldsmobile commercial to an acceptable level?

In his book *Race*, Studs Terkel quotes Myles Horton, who writes the following: "I think like a white person but try to understand how black people might think. Their way of doing things may be better than my way, can be worse than my way, but I can't take the position that my way is always right without being a racist. Racism involves believing that your own race is superior." [1] Terkel then relates an incident from his own life:

> As I stepped onto the bus one early morning, the driver, a young black man, said I was a dime short. I was positive I had deposited the proper fare. I did a slight turn...fished out another dime and dropped it into the box. My annoyance, trivial though the matter was, stayed with me for the rest of the trip. Oh, I understood the man, of course. I know the history of his people's bondage. It was

his turn—a show of power, if only in a small way. If that's how it is, that's how it is.

As I was about to disembark, I saw a dime on the floor. My dime. I held it up to him. "You were right." He was too busy driving to respond. In alighting, I waved: "Take it easy." "You, too," he replied. I've a hunch he'd been through something like this before. [2]

Assuming that we know and understand the feelings of others can be presumptuous and, at times, racist. Seeing members of other races as fulfilling our expectations surely falls within the realm of racism. Appropriating the history of other races as we see it can only lead to a racism that thrives on stereotypes, myths, and lies.

Yet, in the situations I described above, certainly no harm was intended, no offense was meant. Or was it? It is so easy to ask others to have a sense of humor when it is someone else's culture or past that has been insulted. But should it be so easy to forget what Hillel taught long ago, "Do not judge another until you are in his position"? (*Pirke Avot* 2:5)

As Tim Giago, editor-in-chief of the *Lakota Times*, has written, "Indians are people, not mascots." [3] Giago strongly resents schools, such as the University of Illinois, that have Indian mascots. The mascot of Illinois is Chief Illiniwek, whose image may be found on the school's toilet paper! And then there is the Seminole warrior of Florida State University who rides into the football field in full regalia to thrust a burning spear into the turf. [4]

Imagine how you would feel if the following article appeared in your paper:

"CHICAGO—The Chicago Jews defeated the Houston Astros 2-1 Friday in front of a stadium full of wild fans waving yarmulkes and singing 'Hava Nagila.'" [5]

Indian children know that headdresses are spiritual in nature. They know that their people don't wear war paint and thrust burning spears at sports events. When they see these images of their people, they surely must feel ashamed to see their heritage insulted. Not surprisingly, many Indians have tried to pass as non-Indians by rejecting their history and becoming identity-less Americans. Just ask Stephen Bentzlin, a Sioux Indian who lost his life in the Gulf War. Steve was never comfortable revealing his identity to his fellow soldiers. As his mother expressed it: "When Steve wasn't home, he didn't like to tell many people that he was Indian. Some people won't be your friend if they know." [6] Yet as sorry as we feel for Steve, we should be careful about looking down upon his decision. After all, how many Jews have known such feelings and such responses? How many Jews have tried to pass as non-Jews? Perhaps more than you may even suspect.

Tolerance and understanding of Native Americans are increasing. Some now empathize with their concerns about Columbus Day; some understand their need to remind us of the Indian culture that existed in America before 1492. Some schools, such as Dartmouth and Stanford, for example, have dropped the racially insulting Indian names once attached to their sports teams. As a result of this understanding and action, it is a little easier today to be an openly proud Indian.

Everyone has prejudices; everyone stereotypes members of other groups. As Jews, we know how uncomfortable it feels when others make assumptions about us— that all Jews are smart or rich. Yet how often do we Jews stereotype others? How often may we be found tomahawk chopping with Braves fans or wearing the offensive cartoon of the Cleveland Indians on a baseball cap, with no regard for the sensitivities of the groups being caricatured? How often do we see Asian students as joyless, black students as militant, Latino students as cliquish?

Jewish tradition responds to racism in clear and direct ways. In the Book of Genesis, we are told that human beings are created in the image of God. Each and every one of us is sacred and holy and precious. Each contains a spark of godliness that cannot be denied and is deserving of respect and dignity. Indeed, when he was asked to find the most basic teaching in all of Judaism, Ben Azzai quoted Genesis 5:1, saying, "This is the story of humanity: When God created us, God made us in God's own likeness" (*Sifra* 89b).

Indeed, from a *midrash* about how God created Adam, we learn that God took dust from the four corners of the earth in equal measure. Some of the dust was red, some black, some white, and some as yellow as sand. God then mixed these with water from all of the oceans to indicate that all the races should be included in the first human and none be counted as superior to any other.[7]

The rabbis knew how difficult it is to overcome racism, which is why Rabbi Akiva taught that the greatest principle of the Torah was to be found in Leviticus 19:18: "Love your neighbor as yourself." [8]

Rabbi Samson Raphael Hirsch, qualifying this command of Leviticus, explained that it is virtually impossible, given the different kinds of human personalities, for the love of humanity to be commanded. No one can love all the people one knows equally. There will always be an individual whom one just cannot stand.

Yet the *mitzvah* to love your neighbor as yourself tells us that, even so, we must be as concerned about those important qualities of life that relate to our neighbors— their happiness, their health, and well-being—as we are for ourselves. No matter how unsympathetic they may be as people, we must still be as pleased by their success and as saddened by their misfortune as if either were our own. People who strive to fulfill this *mitzvah* of love cannot be racist.

The Reform movement has made this standard of behavior into a principle of action. For decades we have passed resolutions and taken action on civil rights measures, demanding equality for all groups and individuals in our society. We have worked for the payment of reparations to those Japanese-Americans relocated in 1942. We have urged the end of all stereotyping of Native Americans and have supported programs to enhance their welfare.[9]

But the challenge of racism remains. To quote Peggy Terry, a Kentucky woman who quit school after the fifth grade, "I think you become an adult when you reach a point where you don't need anyone underneath you. When you can look at yourself and say: 'I'm okay the way I am.' "[10]

Judaism teaches us that as adults we are required to see the humanity in everyone we meet. It commands us to look beneath skin color to see godliness, beneath stereotype and prejudice to find value. It urges us not to let racism divide us.

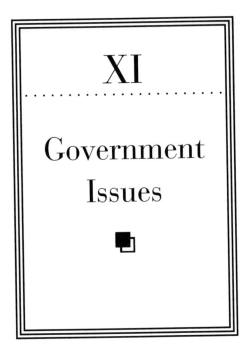

XI

Government
Issues

Separation of Church and State

RELIGIOUS ACTION CENTER

The First Amendment of the Constitution is the cornerstone of American religious freedom: "Congress shall make no law respecting an establishment of religion or prohibiting the free exercise thereof." This twin constitutional principle is the foundation on which respect for religious differences and the strength of organized religion in America have been built. Today, however, the traditional "wall of separation" between church and state is being threatened, creating the possibility of serious repercussions for the rights of America's religious minorities.

Separation of Church and State and the Supreme Court

The United States is the first country in the history of the world to build its society on the separation of church and state. Protected by the First Amendment and free from the coercive and potentially corrupt influence of the state, organized religion has prospered in America. The federal courts, particularly the Supreme Court, historically have had the responsibility to prevent majoritarian impulses from Congress and individual states from exercising control over religion and religious practice, enabling religious minorities to reach a status of full and equal membership in American society.

Since the early 1940s, the Supreme Court has sustained the "wall of separation" between organized religion and the state. In addition, the court has narrowed the power of government to regulate and impose sanctions for personal behavior related to religious observance. In case after case, the Supreme Court has struck down state-sponsored school prayer, Bible reading in public schools, the teaching of creationism, and other infringements of the First Amendment.

Religious Freedom and the Jewish Community

The Jewish community has been one of America's strongest advocates of the separation of church and state. Particularly in the twentieth century, as Jews have become stronger and more secure as a community, Jewish groups have fought to eliminate government subsidies for religious activity, stop religious symbols from being placed on public property, and prevent federal aid from being dispensed to parochial schools.

Biblical mandates and rabbinic rulings do not completely explain the Jewish community's strong commitment to religious freedom and the separation of church and state. Rather, historical experience demonstrates that the Jewish people have endured religious persecution at times when the state was controlled by a particular religion. The First Amendment made the United States the refuge of choice for Jews and others throughout the world when they were faced with persecution and oppression in countries without equivalent guarantees. American Jews have enjoyed the constitutionally guaranteed freedom to exercise religion and to organize communal lives under equal protection of the law. Therefore, the Jewish community has a deep stake in the preservation of the separation of church and state. As members of a religious minority whose history is dominated by oppression, we are especially sensitive to any effort to weaken the safeguards of pluralism and minority expression and are keenly aware of the dangers of a partnership between government and religion.

The Attack on Religious Freedom and the Separation of Church and State in the Courts

In 1990, the United States Supreme Court held in *Oregon Employment Division* v. *Smith* that the state of Oregon could deny unemployment compensation benefits to drug rehabilitation counselors who were fired for the sacramental use of peyote in Native American religious ceremonies. The Supreme Court's surprisingly sweeping decision nearly obliterated the protection of religious liberty guaranteed by the Constitution. The *Smith* decision disregarded the long-standing test for determining whether a governmental action unconstitutionally interferes with a religious practice. Prior to *Smith*, the Supreme Court's interpretation of the Free Exercise Clause of the First Amendment provided that a government law or practice that substantially burdened a person's religious practice was permissible only if the government could show that there was a "compelling governmental interest" in applying the law to an individual and that the particular burden on an individual's religious liberty was the least restrictive way for the government to pursue its "compelling interest."

The "compelling interest" test was widely considered a fair and effective means of balancing religious freedom and general applicability of laws. In ruling that the "compelling interest" test is a "luxury" that government is free to ignore, the *Smith* decision marked an abandonment of this well-respected standard and set a dangerous precedent for religious freedom.

In 1991, a bipartisan congressional coalition introduced the Religious Freedom Restoration Act (RFRA), legislation to restore protection for the free exercise of religion that was obliterated by the *Smith* decision. For over three years a diverse coalition of over sixty religious and civil liberties groups, spanning the political and ideological spectrum, fought for the passage of RFRA. In the fall of 1993, RFRA passed both the House and Senate and was signed into law by President Clinton. RFRA, simply but importantly, restores the two-part test that the Court discarded in *Smith*.

Recently, however, the constitutionality of RFRA has been under attack. The Supreme Court will be hearing a constitutional challenge to RFRA this term. [1] The case, *City of Boerne* v. *Flores*, involves a Texas town that rejected an application by a Catholic church requesting permission to expand. The town claimed that the church was part of a designated historic district. The local parish challenged the decision in court, arguing that the town's decision violated RFRA. While city officials held that RFRA was unconstitutional, parish officials argued that expansion was necessary for the church to survive. The town's challenge of RFRA was rejected by an appeals court and the Supreme Court agreed to hear the case in the 1996–1997 term. A broad-based coalition of religious organizations that fought for passage of RFRA hoped the

Supreme Court would clear up confusion over the law that has instigated the onslaught of frivolous cases.

In Congress

A school prayer constitutional amendment also poses a great threat to the separation of church and state, specifically the Establishment Clause. One of the great stories of the 104th Congress is the failure of the Religious Right and its allies to pass—or even vote out of committee—a constitutional amendment on school prayer or "religious equality." The Religious Right and its congressional allies in the 104th Congress came to Washington pledging that they would pursue passage of a school prayer amendment to the United States Constitution. Under the guise of "religious equality," this amendment would have changed the entire framework of the Constitution by altering the First Amendment for the first time in our nation's history.

In November 1995, House Judiciary Committee Chairman Henry Hyde (R-IL), Senate Judiciary Committee Chairman Orrin Hatch (R-UT), and Representative Ernest Istook (R-OK) introduced H.R. Res. 121, S.J. Res. 45, and H.J. Res. 127, respectively. Hyde and Hatch's amendments were virtually identical, focusing on governmental funding of religious activities and entities (e.g., sectarian schools, social services). Istook's proposed "religious equality" amendment, which had 100 cosponsors, included some of the same funding language found in the Hyde and Hatch versions and also specifically permitted "student-sponsored prayer in school."

In response to these amendments, Rabbi David

Saperstein, director of the Religious Action Center of Reform Judaism, and Brent Walker, director of the Baptist Joint Committee, testified before the Senate Judiciary Committee in November 1995, citing the lack of need for these proposed alterations of the First Amendment. Government involvement in religious activities is unnecessary because, according to Saperstein, "it is precisely that wall separating church and state that has kept government out of religion and has allowed religion to flourish with a diversity and strength in America unmatched anywhere in the Western world.... The idea of separating church and state...has, in fact, been America's single greatest contribution to the religious history of the world."

Speaker of the House Newt Gingrich (R-GA) and Ralph Reed, former executive director of the Christian Coalition, both had promised a House vote on a "religious equality" amendment by the end of the 104th Congress, conveniently planned to meet the printing deadline for the Christian Coalition's voter guides, which are sent to 100,000 churches in October in advance of Election Day.

However, the 104th Congress adjourned without any of these proposals being voted out of committee. In no small part, this was due to the outspoken opposition of the religious community. Organized by the Coalition to Preserve Religious Liberty, which the Religious Action Center of Reform Judaism cochairs, mainstream religious organizations were at the forefront of opposition efforts, making clear that politicians did not face a choice between people who value religion and those who do not.

In the summer of 1995, the Clinton administration

issued a directive to public schools on school prayer. The guidelines make it clear that the Constitution and current law protect a wide range of religious expression in public schools, while also prohibiting government-endorsed religious activities and entities. In his public remarks announcing the guidelines, President Clinton rejected the need for a constitutional amendment on school prayer or religious expression. The administration's show of commitment to preserving the separation of church and state is a remarkable victory for religious liberty.

The Jewish community maintains its deep respect for the conviction that the maintenance and furtherance of religion are the responsibility of the synagogue, the church, and the home, and not of any agency of government, including the public schools.

Bibliography

Boston, Robert. *Why the Religious Right Is Wrong: About Separation of Church and State*. New York: Prometheus Books, 1993.

Ivers, Gregg. *Lowering the Wall: Religion and the Supreme Court in the 1980s*. New York: The Anti-Defamation League, 1991.

Vorspan, Albert, and David Saperstein. *Tough Choices: Jewish Perspectives on Social* Justice. New York: UAHC Press, 1992.

Institutions

American Civil Liberties Union
132 West 43rd Street
New York, NY 10036
(212) 944-9800

American Jewish Congress
15 East 56th Street
New York, NY 10022
(212) 879-4500

People for the American Way
2000 M Street NW
Suite 400
Washington, DC 20036

Religious Action Center of Reform Judaism
2027 Massachusetts Avenue NW
Washington, DC 20036
(202) 387-2800

Capital Punishment

JUDEA B. MILLER

The Talmud records the following discussion:

The Sanhedrin that puts to death one person in seven years is called tyrannical. Rabbi Eleazar ben Azariah says, one person in *seventy* years. Rabbi Tarfon and Rabbi Akiva say, "If we had been in the Sanhedrin, no one would have ever been put to death." Rabban Simeon ben Gamliel says, "They would have [thereby] increased the shedders of blood in Israel."

(*Makkot* 1:10)

This discussion occurred at the same time that people were crowding circuses to see fellow human beings fight wild beasts to the death, watching gladiators engage in mortal combat in the Roman Collosseum, and attending public executions.

Jewish tradition agonized over executions. Procedural difficulties made it virtually impossible to carry out a trial involving the possibility of a death sentence. The fact that the rabbis disagreed on the ways an execution should be conducted makes one suspect that they probably never saw one carried out.

Today, however, people still refer to the Bible and religious tradition to justify capital punishment. It is remarkable how some who normally ignore other biblical laws insist on applying the biblical law of retribution: "life for life ... as he hath done so shall it be done to him: breach for breach, eye for eye, tooth for tooth" (Leviticus 24:18–20). They forget that the Bible also invoked the death penalty for Sabbath violators and adulterers. According to Deuteronomy, a child who is "stubborn and rebellious" may even be stoned to death. Fortunately, we no longer use this punishment. In fact, the Midrash suggests it was never used.

Biblical scholars even question how these punishments were conducted. Rabbinical commentaries point out that no two eyes are exactly alike. After all, who would compare their sight with that of a Picasso or a Chagall? Similarly, no two lives are exactly alike. As a result, the law of retribution was changed so that a monetary equivalent could be paid to compensate the victim or the victim's survivors. (Note that when Shakespeare wrote *The Merchant of Venice*, he was unaware of this change.) In *Bava Kama* 84a, there is a fascinating, sophisticated discussion of the application of these dire sentences.

Indeed, there were so many restrictions against carrying out the death penalty in ancient Israel and Judah that by the time of the destruction of the Second Temple by the Romans in 70 C.E., the death penalty had been rendered virtually unenforceable. As Rabbi Eleazar ben Azariah said, a court that had sentenced even one person to die in seventy years was regarded as a "tyrannical court."

Future generations may look back at our use of the death penalty with much the same revulsion that many of us now feel when we consider how capital punishment was used in the Middle Ages. At that time, the death penalty was carried out against blasphemers, witches, and pickpockets. The executions, however, failed to have their intended effect. It was not uncommon in England, when pickpocketing was a capital offense, for the very crowds watching the executions to have their pockets picked. The death penalty is no more of a deterrent today. Recognizing this fact, at least forty-five countries, including all the Western democracies except for one, have abolished the death penalty. The exception among the Western democracies is the United States, where the death penalty still exists in many states. Some courts in Texas and California have even debated whether executions should be shown on television. If the death penalty is a deterrent to crime, then executions *should* be public. Indeed, they should be shown on television during prime time. Schoolchildren should be taken to see them. For what good is a deterrent unless as many people as possible, especially the young, see it carried out? There is no lesson if it is done without spectators. If this sounds barbaric, it is only a logical extension of the argument that the death penalty is a deterrent to murder.

And yet, even if we allowed executions to be publicly witnessed, that would still not be a deterrent. This probably explains why there is no death penalty in England, where public hanging used to be common and still had little effect on crime. In the United States today, murderers have been executed, and we still feel no safer. Do we now walk the streets at night without fear? Convicted criminals have been executed and yet, as far as anyone can tell, the decrease in the assault and murder rate appears to have nothing to do with capital punishment. On the contrary, there is abundant evidence to indicate that capital punishment may encourage a climate of violence. The death penalty cheapens society's respect for human life and brutalizes the spirit of us all.

In addition to its lack of effectiveness as a deterrent, capital punishment creates other problems. In 1972 the U.S. Supreme Court acknowledged that the death penalty violated the principle of equal protection under the law since executions were carried out mainly against the poor—blacks, the uneducated, and, generally, the pariahs of society. That is why the Court had thrown out existing capital punishment laws. As former Supreme Court Justice William O. Douglas observed, "One searches our chronicles in vain for the execution of any member of the affluent strata of society." Because of the present conservative composition of the Supreme Court, it appears the death penalty has made and will continue to make a comeback.

We forget that the law is just a human instrument.

Human beings, even judges and juries, make mistakes. Because the legal system is administered by a vast number of people, it cannot avoid errors. This is why the taking of a life is so radically different from any other sort of punishment. An execution once carried out cannot be reversed.

A group of thirty-five experienced law enforcement officers, including a former New York City police commissioner and a former warden at San Quentin Prison, once described the death penalty as a deception that keeps us from dealing effectively with problems of law and order. In a public statement, they argued as follows: "As members of the law enforcement and criminal justice profession, we wish to express our strong opposition to the use of the death penalty, which amounts to a fraudulent hoax on the American people—pandering to our baser instincts, while perpetuating the myth that capital punishment is a cure-all for crime." Indeed, facts with regard to the matter may be summed up in a statement unanimously endorsed by every criminologist at the University of Florida: "We feel a professional and ethical obligation to report that there is no credible scientific research that supports the contention that the threat or use of the death penalty is or has been a deterrent to homicide."

Scientific research, in fact, suggests that the opposite may be true. A study of the 603 executions in New York State between 1907 and 1963 found, on average, two additional murders in the month following an execution and one additional murder in the second month. That murders increase following an execution is confirmed by studies conducted in other areas of the country as well.

The greater the publicity, the higher the number of postexecution murders.

But if these law enforcement professionals and criminologists do not believe the death penalty deters crime, why is it allowed to continue? One reason often heard is that capital punishment at least shows some sort of concern for the victim. The death penalty, however, in no way undoes the crime, nor does it benefit the victim. There is no evidence that it will even prevent another person from committing a similar crime. Capital punishment only adds to the violence of the original crime, because executions cheapen life. If we are ever to still violence, we must learn to cherish life.

The gallows, the electric chair, the guillotine, the gas chamber, the firing squad, and the lethal injection are not only instruments of death; like the cross used for crucifixion in the ancient Roman Empire, they are symbols of terror, cruelty, and irreverence for all life. If the death penalty does anything, it links our history of primitive savagery and medieval fanaticism to a modern totalitarianism. It stands for everything humanity must reject if it is to survive as a species.

So why is the death penalty being considered by our Congress and many state legislatures? Because more and more people are angry and frustrated by the siege mentality that has gripped our cities. It has been said that a conservative today is just a liberal who has been mugged. After experiencing crime, people tend to lash out in a mindless, irrational way. They call for the reintroduction of the death penalty. The temptation to reintroduce capital punishment, however, must be resisted. The crawl of humanity out of savagery has been long and difficult. We still have far to go. The angry call of the mob for blood must be resisted; otherwise, we will all revert back to savagery.

Addendum

In a moving passage from the *Mishnah Sanhedrin* 4:5, there is a description of the way a witness in a capital punishment case was interrogated:

How shall one impress witnesses in a criminal case with the gravity of their position? One takes them aside and charges them:

"Be certain that your testimony is no guess-work, no hearsay, not derived at secondhand, nor by reliance on the observation even of a trustworthy person. Remember, you must face a severe cross-examination. Know that a criminal case is by no means like a civil case. In the latter, he who has caused an injustice by his testimony can make monetary restitution, but in the former, the blood of the accused and his unborn offspring stain the perjurer forever. Thus, in the case of Cain, Scripture says, 'The voice of the bloods of your brother call to Me.' Observe that the text reads in the plural—not blood but bloods. For Abel's blood and that of his unborn seed were alike involved. It is for this reason that God created only one human in the beginning, a token to humanity that if one destroys one life, it is as though one had destroyed all humankind; whereas if one preserves one life, it is as though one had preserved all humankind."

Gun Control

ALBERT VORSPAN AND DAVID SAPERSTEIN

The statistics are staggering, mind-numbing. More than 15,000 Americans were murdered by firearms in 1994. Every two years more people are killed by handguns in the United States than the total number of Americans who were killed during the entire Vietnam conflict.

A study conducted by the Harvard School of Public Health in 1993 showed that 53 percent of adult Americans support a ban on the sale of handguns, and 81 percent of them support the registration of all handguns. Yet the wishes of the majority for a sensible control of firearm sales have been stymied by the formidable lobbying led by the National Rifle Association (NRA) and various gun manufacturers.

The proliferation of guns in the hands of Americans, abetted by easy access and availability, is considered to be a major cause of the soaring crime rate afflicting our country. Then why, in light of this harsh reality, has so little been done over the years to control the ownership of guns?

Rabbi Jerome K. Davidson, religious leader of Temple Beth El of Great Neck, New York, is one of many Americans who has grappled with this question. Rabbi Davidson not only spoke up from his pulpit; he also submitted his views to *The New York Times*, which published his letter (entitled "Trophies of Ineffective Gun Controls") on February 13, 1979. Although the letter was written more than a decade ago, it cogently sums up the issues that still arise whenever gun control is discussed.

> To the Editor: Brenda Spencer, a San Diego sixteen-year-old, last week momentarily diverted our attention from the big news made by strife in Iran and visitors from China. She did it by opening fire with a .22-caliber rifle in an elementary school, killing two and wounding nine, including children ranging in age from seven to twelve. "I don't like Mondays. This livens up the day. I just started shooting for the fun of it."
>
> There is no excuse whatsoever for a .22-caliber rifle, with five hundred rounds of ammunition, to have fallen into that girl's hands. She didn't steal it. It isn't a trophy someone brought home from the war. She received it for Christmas! Someone gave it to her as a present.

Such tragic occurrences are not rare. Who does not recall the college student who gunned down forty-five people, killing fourteen, from the top of a tower at the University of Texas? Have we already forgotten the mass killing in New Rochelle several years ago by an American Nazi whose apartment contained an entire arsenal? Have we pushed the ugly memory of the "Son of Sam" killings out of our minds? Or that of the Brooklyn high school student who murdered two fellow classmates in

the school's hallway? The TV evening news in most met-
ropolitan areas is replete with such tragedies, day
after day.

These shattering events reflect the unwillingness of
Americans to recognize the real danger that the private
possession of guns represents to our lives. There are over
70 million privately owned handguns in the United
States, approximately one gun for each adult and half
of the children in America. By the year 2003, firearm
fatalities are expected to become the leading cause of
injury-related deaths in the United States. But these
statistics are evidently not frightening enough to cause
the American people to overpower the National Rifle
Association and demand the enactment of effective
controls.

In Jewish tradition, the sanctity of human life is a primary value. In an increasingly impersonal and alienating
society, the dehumanizing of the human being and the
carelessness with which human life is taken stand in
direct violation of the affirmation of our tradition.

The Bible commands us, "Thou shalt not murder."
The Talmud teaches us that "he who takes one life it is as
though he has destroyed the universe and he who saves
one life it is as though he has saved the universe
(*Sanhedrin* 4:5).

The UAHC supports legislation to implement the
recommendation of the National Commission on the
Causes and Prevention of Violence to eliminate the manufacture, importation, transportation, advertising, sale,
transfer, and possession of handguns except for limited
instances such as the military, police, security guards,
and licensed and regulated pistol clubs.

430/ Where We Stand

The following background paper, prepared for the Commission on Social Action of Reform Judaism, helps clarify this issue.

Handgun Control Legislation

What are the arguments of the opponents of firearms control legislation?

1. They maintain that the right "to keep and bear arms," guaranteed in the Second Amendment to the Constitution, would be violated by such legislation.
2. They are afraid that gun control laws would hurt the responsible sportsperson who uses guns for hunting and marksmanship.
3. They claim that the legislation would not lower crime rates because criminals would still be able to obtain firearms illegally.

None of these arguments stands up to examination.

1. The Second Amendment states: "A well-regulated militia being necessary to the security of a free state, the right of the people to keep and bear arms shall not be infringed." This obviously was written in order to guarantee each state a militia, and the Supreme Court has stated many times, in upholding the constitutionality of gun control laws, that it does not apply to individual citizens bearing arms. In 1939, in *United States* v. *Miller*, the Court held

that "the Second Amendment applies only to those arms that have a reasonable relationship to the preservation of efficiency of a well-regulated militia." Furthermore, the Courts have established that rights given by the Constitution are not absolute and have recognized the government's power to limit such rights in the face of compelling interests of the general welfare and domestic tranquillity.

2. In nations with strict firearms laws, hunting still thrives. After the enactment of the laws controlling the purchase of guns in many states, the sale of hunting licenses increased. Legislative measures that would help prevent irresponsible individuals from owning firearms and set standards of competence for firearms usage should indeed increase the prestige, and certainly the safety, of gun sports.

    The purpose of gun control legislation is not to prevent legitimate ownership of firearms but to keep such arms from those who would misuse them. Furthermore, over the last few years, much gun control legislation has been aimed at stanching the proliferation of automatic weapons. While there are some who may "find satisfaction" in hunting deer with automatic weapons, the latter are hardly sporting weapons.

3. No one claims that gun control legislation is the neat and total solution to violence and crimes. But the fact is that it does cut down both the incidence of crimes in which guns are involved and the general rate of violent crimes. A comparison of our country with other nations is extremely revealing. In 1992, handguns killed 33 people in Great

Britain, 36 in Sweden, 97 in Switzerland, 128 in Canada, 60 in Japan, 13 in Australia, and 13,220 in the United States. Why is there such a discrepancy among these nations? One reason is that in France, Canada, Great Britain, and Japan, there is a virtual ban on the private ownership of handguns and assault weapons.

The Bureau of Alcohol, Tobacco and Firearms (ATF) reports that there were over 211,000,000 privately owned firearms in the United States in 1991. Every day newspapers are filled with tragic stories about people killed by others who should not have been allowed to own a gun. Each year brings horrifying stories of political assassinations that threaten the foundations of the American system of government. The situation deteriorates and the rate of gun crimes increases as a small minority mobilized by the National Rifle Association blocks legislative action to curtail the purchase of guns.

The results affront the conscience of all. To delay action further would be unpardonable. What Rabbi Davidson could only have imagined in 1979—that the American public would stand up to the powerful NRA lobby—finally took place in the early 1990s. The NRA's opposition to legislation barring so-called "cop killer" bullets actually cost them the support of law enforcement agencies. The NRA's opposition to legislation banning even assault weapons elicited a severe backlash in public opinion.

The climax came when the United States Congress voted on the Brady Bill, which established a national five-day waiting period for handgun ownership. In 1991, both houses of the Congress approved the Brady Bill, handing the gun lobby a major defeat, although it was able to block enactment of the law until February 1994.

The history of the Brady Bill illustrates the tragedy of our failure to enact gun control legislation earlier. On March 30, 1981, when John Hinckley, Jr., attempted to assassinate President Ronald Reagan, he shot and forever changed the life of the president's press secretary, James Brady.

Today, Mr. Brady is permanently brain-damaged and partially paralyzed—doctors say that he will never walk again. Since the shooting, his wife, Sarah, has courageously led the fight for legislation named after her husband, which would impose a national five-day waiting period before the purchase of a handgun is approved. The intent is to give people who seek to buy a gun in a moment of anger time to cool off, as well as to provide time for gun shop proprietors to check if the prospective purchaser has a criminal record or is mentally ill.

After former President Ronald Reagan reversed his oft-repeated position against gun control and declared his support of the Brady Bill, the measure was enacted into law and, despite initial threats to veto it, signed by President Bush.

In recognition of the Bradys' leadership in support of this legislation and their ability to overcome personal adversity to mobilize the public conscience, the UAHC bestowed upon Jim and Sarah Brady the Maurice N. Eisendrath Bearer of Light Award at the 1991 Biennial in Baltimore, Maryland. This award is the UAHC's highest honor.

Yet despite the victory of the Brady Bill, there has been little change in the Congress's position on gun control: The 104th Congress has been called one of the most anti-gun-control congresses in years.

This was proven when the House voted to repeal the 1994 ban on the manufacture, transfer, and possession of semiautomatic assault weapons and ammunition magazines that hold more than ten rounds. This attempt was made despite studies that show 76 percent of the American people are in favor of the ban and only 19 percent endorse a repeal. Although the repeal went no further than the House, it clearly indicates the attitude of the Congress.

It remains to be seen how the 105th Congress will vote on gun-control-related issues. However, because the newly elected Senate is more conservative and the House is only slightly more moderate, it is unlikely that any major gun control legislation will be passed by the 105th Congress.

Bioethics

RICHARD F. ADDRESS

Few areas of contemporary life are as exciting and dynamic as that of medical technology. Yet even as we watch with excitement scientists making discovery after discovery, we cannot help but grow worried by how these medical advances will affect our ethics. The question is, How does Judaism help us cope with these new realities?

The relationship between Judaism and medicine has a long history. (Indeed, perhaps the most eminent of all medieval scholars, Moses Maimonides, was himself a practicing physician in Egypt.) Jews have always sought guidance from their sacred texts, especially in matters of medicine and health. In large part, this was the direct consequence of the Jewish struggle to develop a rationale for interfering in God's creation. Jewish tradition wrestles with the idea that if everything stems from God, what mandate do we as Jews have to change the course of an illness, to fly in the face of Providence?

There are several texts in our tradition that, according to postbiblical interpretations, justify our intrusion into what some see as the divine plan. Passages such as Exodus 15:26 and Exodus 21:19 have long been used as mandates for individuals to heal. According to Leviticus 19, for example, the command not to "stand idly by the blood of one's brother" has generally been interpreted to mean that we have an obligation to heal the sick. This passage also explains why in talmudic times it was thought that a physician who refused to treat a patient was no different from one responsible for spilling the blood of that patient. Likewise, the tradition cautions us that in order to be healed, we are not to live in an area without access to some form of health care.

Maimonides is generally credited with transforming the job of healing into a mandate or obligation. This is at least how Maimonides interpreted the last part of the passage of Deuteronomy 22:2, although the context of the verse actually deals with lost property. If a person is ill, reasons Maimonides, he has lost his health; thus it is mandatory to assist that person in the healing process for "thou shalt restore [his health] to him."

Just from reviewing the above passages, as well as other texts and opinions not looked at here, we see a distinctly Jewish medical ethic emerge. It is this ethic that serves as the foundation for discussing bioethical issues from a Jewish point of view. The central component of this ethic is our obligation to recognize the dignity and sanctity of life and our obligation to preserve it so that it retains that dignity and sanctity. Only after this component is understood, can we address the difficult problems raised by genetic mapping and screening, surrogate parenthood, fetal surgery, fetal tissue use, abortion, experimental surgery and treatments, the allocation of resources, disclosure rules, health care costs, the artificial prolongation of life, and physician-assisted suicide.

To End a Life?

Time and space preclude discussing each issue in detail. But let's examine just one—the difficult decisions we must make concerning one who has reached his or her final hours. This is a hard enough issue to deal with without taking into account the Jewish point of view. So where does one start from within the Jewish tradition? Well, one place to begin is by examining responsa, a body of Jewish literature that serves as a living, vibrant, intellectual arena of discussion on issues like this one.

Responsa are a traditional form of Jewish literature that reflects, through a process of question and answer, how scholars apply tradition to contemporary concerns. In taking an overview of much of the responsa, we can see certain common concerns emerge. Just a cursory examination of our tradition, for example, reminds us how much Judaism emphasizes the fundamental dignity and sanctity of life. It thus stands to reason that this concept of dignity and sanctity should extend throughout the entire journey of our life, even until death. Our tradition underscores this fact by pointing out that we are created *betzelem Elohim*—in the image of God—and that we must, therefore, do all we can to maintain that image throughout our life's journey.

But this is also where the realities of medical technology challenge our concept of dignity and sanctity, as we are called upon to make decisions about care and treatment that raise questions about *tzelem Elohim*. Often a family finds itself in the difficult situation of having to recommend to a physician the extent, level, and possible withdrawal of treatment for a family member who is sick, injured, or possibly worse.

Recent responsa have begun to deal with these complex issues. Various guidelines have emerged, all of which are based on our tradition's fundamental belief in the dignity and sanctity of life. To us, all life is sacred, from its beginning to its end. Traditional texts have compared life to a flame, adding that nothing may be done to put out that flame. It is not a Jewish act to end a life before its time.

Yet we are often confronted with situations that aren't so simple. Technology has enhanced the state of limbo between life and death, and it is in that arena that we are often asked to play. Once again, the tradition is helpful. It introduces us to the concept of the *goses*—literally translated as "flickering out." We use the expression *goses* to indicate a person whose flame of life is flickering out and whose death is imminent (Jewish tradition suggests within three days), all aggressive medical treatment options having been exhausted. Often this is the scenario that presents itself after all available medical technologies have been used. An individual may be hooked up to a wide variety of life-sustaining machines; numerous therapies may have been already tried; in many worst-case situations, patients may be unconscious or comatose. The question is whether we are command- ed to continue the onslaught of technology and treat- ment once we find ourselves in this situation. The answer, according to Judaism, is no. When the end is clear, when the journey has been completed, when the flame is flickering out, we are under no obligation to continue suffering or pain, for that only reduces the dignity and sanctity of the life in question. Before one becomes a *goses*, everything may and, indeed, must be done to ensure a proper, dignified, and sanctified end of life. In our time, ongoing communication between family, patient, and health care provider has become fundamental for determining when this status begins. There are no set rules; there is no set standard. Each case must be judged on its own merits.

The Quality of Life

Quality of life is often a subject of heated debate in any discussion about end-of-life medical treatment. Within contemporary Jewish thought, differences of opinion have emerged about whether quality of life is a valid criterion in the decision-making process. A helpful phrase comes from a commentary written by Max Arzt on the High Holy Day prayer *Unetanah Tokef*. Arzt notes that the "quantity of life is in the hands of God, but the quality of life is in the hands of man." I have found this phrase to be particularly helpful.

Decisions regarding a person's quality of life are best left to that individual or to a properly appointed surrogate in case of the former's mental incompetence. The completion of the appropriate documents, preceded by honest discussion, can be among an individual's and family's most important acts. In 1985 a responsum entitled "The Quality of Life and Euthanasia" focused on several scenarios in which patients were in varying degrees of pain and control. After discussing the various contexts, the responsum helpfully concluded that "we should do our best to enhance the quality of life and to use whatever means modern science has placed at our disposal for this purpose. We need not invoke 'heroic' measures to prolong life, nor should we hesitate to alleviate pain, but we cannot utilize a 'low quality' of life as an excuse for hastening death." All life is wonderful and mysterious. The human situation, the family setting, and other factors must thus be carefully analyzed before a decision can be reached.

When a person becomes a *goses* and the ability to live free of immobilizing life-sustaining equipment (such as a respirator) is no longer possible, that is when the context of the person's quality of life becomes part of the decision to continue or withdraw aggressive types of treatment. If certain medical procedures are needed to bring about a possible cure or to alleviate a condition that will promise some form of independent life, then those procedures are to be done without hesitation. However, if those procedures are being used solely as a means to prolong a *goses* and are without therapeutic benefit— in other words, if they are "heroic" in the sense described in the above responsum—then we are under no obligation to use them. Indeed, we are even instructed that it is praiseworthy to remove from a *goses* that which impedes the natural departure of the soul from the body. In this way, the end of life is treated with dignity and sanctity. Many of our scholars from every branch of Judaism understand that when an individual becomes a *goses*, removal of artificial impediments to the natural dying process is permissible.

The humanity of our tradition calls upon each of us to remember that in making these decisions, it is helpful to keep in mind some basics. We are created in the image of God; thus we should view our existence as a manifestation of God's presence. In that sense, we are guided by a fundamental ethic—to preserve the dignity and sanctity of life. To ensure that we do so, we are aided in our decision-making process by a threefold approach that draws its strength from our own tradition.

First, there are the questions of context. What are the circumstances of the case? Is the person a *goses*? What is the medical scenario? What hope is there for recovery? What are the prospects for an independent life? What wishes have been expressed by the individual?

Second, given the context, what action should be taken based upon our understanding of the individual's wishes and Jewish tradition? Here, context will determine action, just as our tradition is clear in suggesting aggressive or passive therapies based upon whatever stage a person is in.

Third, in what way does the context determine the actions to be taken so that the fundamental dignity and sanctity of life is assured? By asking these questions about context, action, and value, we ensure that individuals will continue to be treated as *tzelem Elohim*, no matter where they are on their life's journey.

Speaking in 1989 at a bioethics seminar on termination of treatment, Rabbi Bernard Zlotowitz summarized his talk in the following manner:

> Jewish tradition affirms the sanctity of life. Thus even when there is no hope for the patient and death is certain, one should not hasten his death. At the same time, however, one should not prolong his death throes. Instead, one should permit him to die in peace. There is a delicate balance in any decision to terminate treatment, which is why it should always be done in consultation with the family, the rabbi, and the physician, and the patient, if possible.

We must never forget that while our allotted time on this earth is in the hands of God, the way in which we live our lives rests within our power. Our tradition offers—indeed, mandates—that we make choices about how we live our lives as we journey from birth to death. These decisions are holy acts, for they can tell us in many ways who we are, how we wish to be remembered, and how we understand the ultimate mystery, power, and passion of life itself.

Can a Jew Be a
Conscientious Objector?

PHILIP J. BENTLEY

Can a Jew base his or her status as a conscientious objector on Jewish grounds? The Jewish Peace Fellowship, an organization founded to support Jewish conscientious objectors, asked this question of Reform, Conservative, and Orthodox rabbinic organizations during World War II. All three organizations passed resolutions stating that a Jew could base a claim to being a conscientious objector to war on the basis of Jewish tradition. While few rabbis and scholars would say that such a position is characteristic of mainstream Judaism, few would deny that such a position is a legitimate one for a Jew.

What Does Jewish Law
Have to Say about War?

War is accepted as a reality in the Torah, Talmud, and other legal sources; it is, however, carefully defined in such a way that it is to be limited as much as possible.

Jewish law speaks of three categories of war. The first is *milchemet mitzvah*—the war commanded by God. Only two wars fall into this category: the original conquest of Israel by Joshua and the war to exterminate the evil nation of Amalek (Deuteronomy 25:17–19). Both of these wars were one-time events that took place in the

ancient past. The second category is *milchemet hovah*—
the required war. This category is intended for situations
during which one's nation is under attack (or the immediate threat of attack). Everyone is expected to participate in such a war. The third category is *milchemet
reshut*—the optional war. All other wars are included in
this category, which Jewish tradition defines as a war
waged at the discretion of the government. The ruler,
however, must consult with the council or legislature to
gain approval to wage war. There are several groups
exempted from serving in optional wars, including the
newly married, those who have just built or acquired a
house or vineyard, and those who are "disheartened"
(Deuteronomy 20:5–9). Although there has been much
discussion of who else may be exempt from serving in an
optional war, Judaism does include those who refuse to
serve in such wars by reason of conscience.

There are also many laws that restrict how a war may
be fought. No war in any of these categories may be
fought unless there is first an attempt to make peace
(Deuteronomy 20:10). Nor may anyone in a city under
attack be forced into the war. Even a siege, according to
Maimonides, was to be from "three sides only," meaning
that those who wanted to leave could do so (*Mishneh
Torah*, "Kings and Wars," 7:7). Moreover, following
Deuteronomy 20:19–20, human beings are forbidden by
Jewish law to destroy trees or other natural resources in
a war zone. (This passage from Deuteronomy became
the basis of the Jewish environmental law known as *Bal
Tashchit*, the prohibition against waste and destruction
even during war.) In the twentieth century, the prestate
Jewish self-defense units and the Israel Defense Forces
(IDF) follow a principle called *tohar haneshek*—purity

of arms. This principle states that Israeli soldiers may only use their firearms to defend themselves; they can never use those arms to oppress or loot an enemy.

Some who deny that a Jew can be a conscientious objector point out that the Talmud teaches, "If someone pursues you in order to kill you, turn and kill him first" (*Sanhedrin* 10). But what the Talmud actually teaches is more complex than that. Imagine that someone is pursuing you in order to kill you and you can stop that person without killing him. The Talmud teaches us that if you do kill him, you have committed murder (*Sanhedrin* 7a). Judaism clearly teaches us to restrict violence as much as possible.

Jewish Ethics Calls Peace
the Highest Ideal

Although the word *shalom* means peace, it does not simply refer to the absence of war. *Shalom* comes from a Hebrew word meaning "complete" or "perfect." It is a word that implies well-being and the world as it ought to be.

Peacemaking is actually a *mitzvah*. We are told to "seek peace and pursue it" (Psalms 34:15). While other *mitzvot* are largely to be performed or observed when the occasion arises, we are actually commanded to seek opportunities to make peace both where we are and elsewhere (*Leviticus Rabbah, Tzav*, IX, 9).

The Talmud teaches us to regard the fact that only one *adam*—man or human being—was originally created as a way of saying that every single human being is an entire world (*Mishnah Sanhedrin* 4:5). Whoever, therefore, destroys a single life destroys an entire world. Obviously such an idea, if taken seriously, makes warfare the most immoral enterprise imaginable.

We are also taught to refuse illegal or immoral orders. The story is told of a man who went to a great rabbi and said, "The authorities in my town have ordered me to kill someone and if I do not, they will kill me." The rabbi answered, "Let him slay you rather than you commit murder; who knows that your blood is redder? Perhaps his blood is redder!" (*Sanhedrin* 74a). Thus it seems that there is at least one stream of Judaism that regards it as better to be the victim than the murderer.

There are a great many sayings and teachings in Jewish tradition that elevate the value of peace and peacemaking over conflict and war. The most famous is from the Book of Isaiah: "The day shall come when they shall beat their swords into plowshares and their spears into pruning-hooks. Nation shall not lift up sword against nation, nor shall they train for war anymore" (*Isaiah* 2:2, 4). But there is also the teaching of Hillel: "Be of the disciples of Aaron, loving peace and pursuing peace" (*Pirke Avot* 1:12).

Where Does the Reform Movement Stand?

Without a doubt, the overwhelming sentiment in our movement is toward peace and peacemaking. A collection of UAHC social action resolutions (also called *Where We Stand*) contains a number of statements that urge us to continue the work of making peace, from a resolution supporting Woodrow Wilson's 1915 "Expressed Desire for Peace" to those calling for an end to the arms race. The UAHC resolution passed in

December of 1991 to support the war against Iraq was a unique exception to this general trend. Otherwise, when faced with the prospect of war, the Reform movement will always urge the exhaustion of all avenues for peaceful resolution before the use of military force.

For some, such a stand raises the question of being a conscientious objector in Israel. While there is a peace movement in Israel, there are few conscientious objectors. There are some members of the peace movement, however, who do refuse to participate in certain military activities. These individuals follow Jewish tradition no less than those who serve by asking what is the right thing to do in war. Peace activists in Israel today assert that they already know the risks of war and would rather pursue the risks of peacemaking. There are even Israelis who in their pursuit of peace have served time in jail.

This is why the Gulf War raised a powerful question. What would you do in the face of an evil dictator capable of causing great harm? Several years after the war, it has become increasingly obvious that corporate profits and shortsighted diplomatic policies allowed Saddam Hussein to gain the type of power he should never have had in the first place. It is also clear that going to war accomplished very little, despite our overwhelming "victory." Even a war considered to have been decisively won does not accomplish what it sought to achieve. This perhaps best explains why the peacemaker pursues other methods.

Endnotes

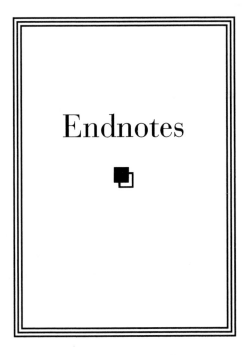

Endnotes

A Reform View of Jewish Law / ARON HIRT-MANHEIMER

1. This article was based on Dr. Solomon B. Freehof's writings.
   Dr. Freehof pioneered the introduction of responsa literature
   to the English-reading American Jewish public in *The
   Responsa Literature* (Philadelphia: Jewish Publication
   Society, 1955) and *A Treasury of Responsa* (Philadelphia:
   Jewish Publication Society, 1963). He later involved himself
   in the practical work of answering questions sent to him both
   as chairman of the CCAR Responsa Committee and in his
   capacity as a rabbi. He was Rabbi Emeritus of Temple Rodef
   Shalom in Pittsburgh. He has published six volumes of
   Reform responsa, each with an introduction that analyzes the
   changing Reform view of *halachah*.

Are Jews the Chosen People? / GARY ZOLA

1. Mordecai Kaplan, *Judaism as Civilization*, rev. ed.
   (Philadelphia: Jewish Publication Society, 1981), 43.
2. Leo Baeck, *This People Israel: The Meaning of Jewish
   Existence*, trans. Albert Friedlander (New York: Holt,
   Rinehart & Winston, 1964), 402.

God without Pronouns / DEBBIE FLIEGELMAN

1. Rita M. Gross, "Steps toward Feminine Imagery of Deity
   in Jewish Theology," in *On Being a Jewish Feminist*, ed.
   Susannah Heschel (New York: Schocken Books, 1983), 235.
2. Judith Plaskow, *Standing Again at Sinai: Judaism from a
   Feminist Perspective* (San Francisco: Harper & Row, 1990),
   144.
3. Gross, 236.
4. Elaine Pagels, "What Became of God the Mother?" in
   Womanspirit Rising: A Feminist Reader in Religion,
   ed. Carol P. Christ and Judith Plaskow (San Francisco:
   Harper & Row, 1979), 107.
5. Plaskow, 123.
6. Ibid., 125.

7. Ibid., 128.
8. Ibid., 127.
9. Ibid., 160.
10. Gross, 235.

How We Celebrate / SIMEON J. MASLIN

1. *Gates of the Seasons*, 17–33.
2. Ibid., 37–46.
3. Ibid., 48–66.
4. Ibid., 59–63, 79–84.
5. Ibid., 59–63, 80–81, 84–85.
6. Ibid., 89–93.
7. Ibid., 94–97.
8. Ibid., 65–74.
9. Ibid., 75–78.

Tradition's Table: Reform Mitzvah / LAWRENCE KUSHNER

1. *Sefer HaParshiyot: Parshat Terumah* (Aleph Publishers: Jerusalem, 1965), 128.

Jerusalem and the Jews / CHAIM RAPHAEL

1. Service International de Documentation Judeo-Christian, vol. IV, no. 2, 1971.

Grades Are a Means,
Knowledge Is an End / HENRY F. SKIRBALL

1. *Ides* is from the Greek suffix indicating "of" or "son of." Rambam is the acronym for Rav Moshe ben Maimon.
2. *Pirke Avot* is the ninth tractate, or treatise, in the order titled "Damages" of the *Mishnah*. The contents are ascribed to about 60 sages who lived during the period 300 B.C.E. to 200 C.E. Since this compendium is the traditional subject of Shabbat afternoon study between Pesach and Shavuot, it is found in most prayer books that include prayers for Shabbat.
3. In Judaism, this is reserved for God. "Do God's will as if it were your will so that God may carry out your will as if it were God's will. Nullify your will before God's will that God may annul the will of others before your will" (*Pirke Avot* 2:4).
4. Includes weekends, vacations, holidays, retirement, etc.

Denying the Holocaust

1. For example, Revilo P. Oliver is a retired University of Illinois Classics teacher; Robert Faurisson earned a Ph.D. in Literature from the University of Lyon; Arthur Butz is an engineer at Northwestern.

2. Israel Gutman, editor-in-chief, *Encyclopedia of the Holocaust*, vol. 2 (New York: Macmillan Library Reference, 1990), 788.

3. Raul Hilberg, *The Destruction of the European Jews*, rev. ed. (New York, Holmes & Meier Publishers, 1985), 263.

4. See Lucy Dawidowicz, *The War against the Jews, 1933–1945* (New York: Bantam Books, 1975), 150–166.

5. Gutman, 2: 489.

6. Ibid., 489.

7. Ibid., 490.

8. See *Holocaust* (Jerusalem: Keter Books, 1974), 104.

9. Gutman, 2: 657.

10. Ibid., 492.

11. Ronnie Dugger, *The Texas Observer*, August 1992, 48.

12. Gutman, 2: 641–642.

13. Gutman 4: 1593.

14. Dugger, 48.

15. *Holocaust*, 105–106.

16. Gutman, 2: 453.

17. Martin Gilbert, *The Holocaust: A History of the Jews of Europe during the Second World War* (New York: Holt, Rinehart & Winston, 1985), 219.

18. Hilberg, 873–76.

19. Gutman, 2: 541–544.

20. *Holocaust*, 86.

21. Ibid., 87.

22. Dawidowicz, 437.

23. Hilberg, 1223.

Cults / STEVEN HASSAN, RACHEL ANDRES, AND JAMES R. LANE

1. The above portion of this essay is taken from Steven Hassan, *Combatting Cult Mind Control* (Rochester, VT: Part Street Press, 1988), 35ff.

2. The remaining portion of this essay is taken from Rachel Andres and James R. Lane, eds., *Cults and Consequences* (Los Angeles: Commission on Cults and Missionaries of the Jewish Federation Council of Greater Los Angeles, 1988).

Missionaries / STUART FEDEROW

1. Walter Jacob, *Contemporary American Reform Responsa* (Central Conference of American Rabbis, 1987), 108, 112.

Feminism and Judaism / DEBBIE FLIEGELMAN

1. Blu Greenberg, *On Women and Judaism* (Philadelphia: Jewish Publication Society, 1981), 175.
2. Elizbeth Schussler Fiorenza, "In Search of Women's Heritage," in *On Being a Jewish Feminist,* ed. Susannah Heschel (New York: Schocken, 1983), 34.
3. Philip Birnbaum, *Daily Prayer Book: Ha-Siddur Ha-Shalem* (New York: Hebrew Publishing Company, 1949), 17–18.
4. Nessa Rapoport, *Preparing for Sabbath* (Sunnyside, NY: Biblio Press, 1981).
5. Alice Bloch, "Scenes from the Life of a Jewish Lesbian," in *On Being a Jewish Feminist*, ed. Susannah Heschel, 174.
6. Gail Shulman, "A Feminist Path to Judaism," in *On Being a Jewish Feminist,* ed. Susannah Heschel, 109.
7. Batya Bauman, "Women-Identified Women in Male-Identified Judaism," in *On Being a Jewish Feminist*, ed. Susannah Heschel, 94.

Suicide / RAMIE ARIAN

1. This statement is the "official" position of Reform Judaism as adopted by the UAHC Task Force on Youth Suicide Prevention. It was prepared by Rabbis Sanford Seltzer, Ramie Arian, and Bernard Zlotowitz.
2. The material presented in this brief paper is drawn substantially from Sydney Goldstein, *Suicide in Rabbinic Literature* (Hoboken, NJ: Ktav, 1989).
3. The principal textual source for this position is *Semachot* (2:1), a minor or apocryphal tractate appended to the

Babylonian Talmud. It is thought to date from the third or eighth century C.E.:

> For a suicide, no rites whatsoever should be observed. Rabbi Ishmael said, "He may be lamented: 'Alas, misguided fool! Alas, misguided fool!'"
>
> Whereupon Rabbi Akiva said to him, 'Leave him to his oblivion: Neither bless him nor curse him!" There should be no rending of clothes, no baring of shoulders, and no eulogizing for him. But people should line up for him, and the mourner's blessing should be recited over him, out of respect for the living. The general rule is: The public should participate in whatsoever is done out of respect for the living; it should not participate in whatsoever is done out of respect for the dead.

4. The text of *Semachot* (2:2–3) continues as follows:

> Who is to be accounted a suicide? Not one who climbs to the top of a tree or to the top of a roof and falls to his death. Rather it is one who says, 'Behold, I am going to climb to the top of the tree [or...to the top of the roof] and throw myself down to my death,' and thereupon others see him climb to the top of the tree or to the top of the roof and fall to his death. Such a person is presumed to be a suicide and for him no rite whatsoever should be observed.
>
> If a person is found strangled hanging from a tree or slain impaled upon a sword, he is presumed to have taken his own life unwittingly; to such a person no rites whatsoever may be denied.

5. The laws cited above from *Semachot* are derived indirectly from a statement in Genesis 9:5: "And surely your blood of your lives will I require; at the hand of every beast will I require it; and at the hand of man, even at the hand of every man's brother, will I require the life of man." Many interpret this passage to mean that God will consider guilty ("require") those who shed "the blood of your lives," including those who shed their own blood ("at the hand of man").

6. The following story is told in I Samuel 31:2–5:

> The Philistines pursued Saul and his sons, and the Philistines struck down Jonathan, Avinadav, and Malchishua, the sons of Saul. The battle raged around Saul and some of the archers hit him, and he was severely wounded by the archers. Saul said to his arms-bearer, "Draw your sword and run me through, so that the uncircumcised may not run me through and make sport of me." But his arms-bearer, in his great awe, refused; whereupon Saul grasped the sword and fell upon it. When his arms-bearer saw that Saul was dead, he, too, fell on his sword and died with him.

7. The logic and text background for each of the following is given in Goldstein, *Suicide*, 27–39.

8. Probably before the age of bar mitzvah.

9. With regard to mental illness, Jewish tradition engages in an interesting bit of circular reasoning, which goes roughly as follows: If you are mentally sound and commit suicide, you are guilty of certain penalties. No one in his or her right mind would commit suicide. Therefore, if a person commits suicide, that person must not be mentally sound (i.e., legally competent). Therefore, the evidence of having committed suicide is enough in itself to prevent the penalties from being applied.

10. In many instances, martyrdom by suicide is accounted not only blameless but even praiseworthy. Certain historical instances of this (including some mass suicides) are accorded the status of a *mitzvah*.

11. The following is from *Pe'at ha-Sadeh*, a commentary published in 1962, on a halachic treatise called *Sedeh Hemed:*

> If we should halachically accept the argument [extending further leniency in the definition of who is legally competent to be penalized for suicide] the law of [illegal] suicide would disappear...and because of this, in my humble opinion, it seems that it is now imperative to establish halachic parameters in favor of preserving life. We should let those [who consider committing suicide] feel guilty. We should not, moreover, favor them [by exempting them from the penalties for suicide].

Substance Abuse in the Jewish Community: *A Historical Perspective* / KERRY M. OLITZKY

1. See, for example, Allan Blaine, *Alcoholism and the Jewish Community* (New York: Commission on Synagogue Relations, Federation of Jewish Philanthropies of New York, 1980) and Charles Snyder, *Alcohol and the Jews* (Glencoe, IL: Free Press, 1958).
2. See, for example, C. R. Snyder, "Culture and Jewish Sobriety: The Ingroup-Outgroup Factor," in *The Jews: Social Patterns of the American Group*, ed. Marshall Sklare (Glencoe, IL, 1958), 160–194.
3. J. I. Shalhoo, "Some Cultural Factors in the Etiology of Alcohol," *Quarterly Journal of Studies of Alcohol* 2 (1941): 164–178.
4. See, for example, M. M. Glatt, "Drug Dependence amongst Jewry," *British Journal of Addictions* 64 (January 1970): 297–304; R. Greenberg, "Denial and Outreach: Jews Face the Facts of Drug Abuse," *Washington Jewish Week*, 11 September 1986, 12–14.
5. See, for example, Sheila Blume, "Current Trends Explored in Compulsive Gambling," *The Psychiatric Times*, December 1988, 28–29.

Abortion / GLYNIS CONYER REISS

1. *Words of Choice* (Washington DC: Religious Coalition for Abortion Rights, 1991).
2. Blu Greenberg, *On Women and Judaism: A View from Tradition* (Philadelphia: Jewish Publication Society, 1981), 150.
3. Ibid.
4. R. A. Zwerin and R. J. Shapiro, *Judaism and Abortion* (Washington, DC: Religious Coalition for Abortion Rights).
5. Ibid.

Homosexuality:
A Reform Jewish Perspective / JOHN E. HIRSCH

1. Bradley Shavit Artson, "Gay and Lesbian Jews: An Innovative Jewish Legal Position," *Jewish Spectator*, Winter 1990, 6.
2. Ibid.

Rape and Jewish Law / MELINDA PANKEN

1. This translation is taken from Rachel Biale, *Women and Jewish Law* (New York: Schocken Books, 1984), 247. See Biale's chapter on rape for a comprehensive study of how Jewish law understands rape.
2. Ibid., 255.

Racism / JOEL SOFFIN

1. Studs Terkel, *Race* (New York: The New York Press, 1992), v.
2. Ibid., 6.
3. Tim Giago, "I Hope the Redskins Lose," *Newsweek*, 27 January 1992, 8.
4. Rick Reilly, "Let's Bust Those Chops," *Sports Illustrated*, 28 October 1991, 110.
5. Ibid.
6. *The New York Times*, 5 March 1991, Al.
7. William B. Silverman, *Rabbinic Wisdom and Jewish Values* (New York: UAHC Press, 1971), 41.
8. Ibid.
9. *Where We Stand*, rev. ed. (New York: Union of American Hebrew Congregations, 1992).
10. Terkel, 112.

Separation of Church and State / RELIGIOUS ACTION CENTER

1. On Wednesday, June 25, 1997, the United States Supreme Court in a 6-3 decision declared the 1993 RFRA unconstitutional.

Credits

"A Reform View of Jewish Law," by Aron Hirt-Manheimer, is taken from *Keeping Posted*, March 1979, pp. 18–19.

"The Reforming of Reform Judaism," by Malcolm H. Stern, is adapted from the *American Jewish Historical Quarterly*, December 1973, pp. 111–117. Used by permission.

"The Messianic Age" by Eugene B. Borowitz, is taken from *Liberal Judaism* by Eugene B. Borowitz, © 1984, chapter 4. New York: UAHC Press.

"How Does God Speak to People?" by Eugene B. Borowitz, is taken from *Liberal Judaism*, by Eugene B. Borowitz, © 1984, chapter 5. New York: UAHC Press.

"Elements of Prayer" is taken from *Hamakor: The NFTY Resource Book*, Section V.

"Wrestling with Ritual," by Margaret Holub, is taken from *Reform Judaism*, Spring 1995, pp. 29–32.

"How to Be a Truly Spiritual Jew and Avoid the Pitfalls of Quick-Fix Religious Consumerism," by Jeffrey K. Salkin, is taken from *Reform Judaism*, Fall 1995, pp. 20–26.

"How We Celebrate," by Simeon J. Maslin, is taken from *What We Believe ... What We Do*, © 1993, pp. 3–13. New York: UAHC Press.

"Origins of Our Symbols," by Bernard M. Zlotowitz, is taken from *Journey through Judaism: The Best of Keeping Posted*, ed. Alan D. Bennett, © 1991, pp. 24–27. New York: UAHC Press.

"The Roots of Shabbat," by Bernard M. Zlotowitz, is taken from *Journey through Judaism: The Best of Keeping Posted*, ed. Alan D. Bennett, © 1991, p. 163. New York: UAHC Press.

"Understanding Shabbat," by Steven Schnur, Bernard M. Zlotowitz, and Aron Hirt-Manheimer, is taken from *Journey through Judaism: The Best of Keeping Posted*, ed. Alan D. Bennett, © 1991, pp. 161–164. New York: UAHC Press.